WITHDRAWN

THE WOMAN WHO RANG THE BELL

OTHER BOOKS BY PHILLIPS RUSSELL

Benjamin Franklin: The First Civilized American

John Paul Jones: Man of Action

Ralph Waldo Emerson: The Wisest American

Red Tiger

Fumbler

William the Conqueror

The Glittering Century

CORNELIA PHILLIPS SPENCER

From a miniature painted in Dresden. This portrait is
believed to have been made in her late thirties

The Woman Who Rang the Bell

THE STORY OF

Cornelia Phillips Spencer

BY

PHILLIPS RUSSELL

※

Chapel Hill

THE UNIVERSITY OF NORTH CAROLINA PRESS

To

JAMES LEE LOVE

CORNELIA AND JAMES SPENCER LOVE

CONTENTS

ILLUSTRATIONS

THE WOMAN WHO RANG THE BELL

I will never forget the esteem and almost sacred reverence in which she was held by the student body. "There goes Mrs. Spencer!" a student would almost whisper, and the entire group would stop and gaze respectfully, spellbound. I felt distinctly, as the others did, that she was a person who for some reason must be exceedingly respected and esteemed. I remember her appearance most distinctly, and had a feeling that she ought to be addressed in Latin. Her personality was most extraordinary. I cannot describe it. She simply radiated something invisible and inspiring; a sort of magnetic field. She could furnish an empty room by simply sitting there.

—Bruce Cotten,
student at the University
of North Carolina, 1891-1892

1

The Convict Dinner

I

LATE IN September, 1880, the steel rails that were to link Chapel Hill, seat of the University of North Carolina, with the world, were being daily brought closer to the village by a gang of one hundred Negro convicts. The railroad's approach gave the inhabitants a welcome new subject for conversation, and on empty afternoons it was the delight of the village ladies to drive out in their phaetons and buggies to watch the convicts at work, raising picks or lifting a rail in unison while their leader chanted an order.

Among these occasional spectators was an imposing woman with piercing dark-brown eyes and firm features. She was not very tall, but gave one the impression of being so. She was not a woman who would ever have been called pretty, and yet there were times when she looked very handsome. The other women treated her with marked deference; it was Mrs. Spencer this, and Mrs. Spencer that; and so the stranger would have rightly guessed that this was Cornelia Phillips Spencer, daughter of the late Dr. James Phillips of the University faculty. She had once called this village in which she now stood "the remotest town of the quietest county of the most backward old state in the Union." And there was none to say her nay.

One day Cornelia, after watching the convicts sweating in the red dust under a warm September sun, suggested that in celebration of the completion of the line to the outskirts of the village, a dinner be given to the convicts by the women of Chapel Hill who had been getting thrills from watching them work. The assembled

1

ladies clapped their hands in approval. Colonel Holt, superintendent of the convict gang, was asked if there would be any official
objection. "None," said Colonel Holt. The ladies climbed into their
thin-wheeled vehicles and went home to await word from Cornelia.

Mrs. Spencer was a woman of many interests. She was a historian, essayist, newspaper correspondent, editor, painter, botanist,
mother, and housekeeper; and she might have forgotten her proposal about the convict dinner had not her friends kept reminding
her of it. Chapel Hill had its charms, but life in the village sometimes went along too placidly to be exciting, and the convict dinner
promised to be a diversion at least. Hence friends dropped by
Cornelia's to ask not "Are we to have the convict dinner?" but
"When are we to have it?"

Thus prompted, she put on her bonnet one afternoon and made
the rounds of the village to discover who would give what for the
dinner and how much. All the chief inhabitants said certainly they
would give something, and they all favored having the dinner right
away. So Cornelia, Mrs. Watson, and Mrs. Long drove out to see
Colonel Holt again, and with his approval they decided to hold the
dinner at noon on October 8 under the trees in front of Sam Barbee's
house at the edge of the village. There Colonel Holt promised to
build a row of tables out of pine planks.

II

It was agreed that the management of the whole affair should
be left to Mrs. Spencer. She was not averse. She was living alone;
she had no exacting domestic ties; and she loved to manage things.
Hitherto, her projects had been of limited size. They had been confined to church and domestic circles. Never before had she been
made responsible for an affair of such magnitude. At first all went
well. Then she met the first opposition. It shocked her. It came
from a well-known matron. She stood in the door of her house and
told Mrs. Spencer she would do nothing for "such wretches." She
was surprised, she said, at Mrs. Spencer's interest in "wicked
criminals," who had only got their just deserts in being sentenced

to serve terms at hard labor. Mrs. Spencer, once she had recovered from the sudden attack, came back strongly. Jesus, she proclaimed, had not refused to talk with the thief on the cross and had often shown His preference for sinners and publicans rather than stiff-necked and self-righteous people.

For a moment the two women squared off as if for battle, and then Mrs. Spencer turned abruptly and went away. Her opponent gave in. She followed Mrs. Spencer to the front gate begging her not to go and promising to send something for the dinner after all. If after this encounter Mrs. Spencer felt a sense of triumph, it was short-lived, for on the street she met her coadjutor, Mrs. Long, who reported a refusal from another village inhabitant, a man. He had flatly declared that anything Mrs. Spencer had a hand in would get no help from him, and that Mrs. Spencer and her kin, the Phillipses and Battles, were "trying to run the town anyhow." Other people had supported Wilson, and then Postmaster Mickle told Mrs. Spencer herself that a dinner for one hundred convicts was out of the question, that the village did not have enough provisions to feed so many men.

III

Cornelia crept homeward, hurt. Never before had she encountered any rudeness in the village of Chapel Hill. And then on the street she ran up with Mrs. Jane Guthrie, a redoubtable figure in village life. Mrs. Guthrie was sympathetic and guided her to Mrs. John Carr's, where the two ladies talked soothingly to Mrs. Spencer, and calmed her. Mrs. Guthrie urged her not to pay any attention to doubters and fault-finders; she said there were some of the meanest, "the *dog-meanest,*" people in Chapel Hill to be found anywhere.

Whenever Mrs. Spencer felt deeply about anything, she always sat down and wrote a long letter to some one—usually to her daughter June, who at the time was studying art in New York. She now went home and wrote to June:

"I hate the presence of such an evil spirit in a community. Much as one may despise it, it has an effect to poison one's comfort. Dr.

and Mrs. Simonds came in the house just after I got home. . . . I said
I hoped they came to be friendly, for I felt quite broken down. . . .
Oh dear, dear, dear—how unhappy the whole situation makes
me. . . . I felt as if we ought to give the dinner up. And came home
and spent a sleepless night. I thought my hair w^d^ be white in the
morning. However, when I got up this morning and had a good cup
of coffee, I felt better. . . ."

IV

There was one person in Chapel Hill to whom Cornelia always
went when in trouble. This was Mrs. Martha (Patty) Battle, wife
of Dr. Kemp P. Battle, who was president of the University. He
was a nephew of Mrs. Charles Phillips, Mrs. Spencer's sister-in-
law. Mrs. Battle was a personage in the village. She was tall,
gracious, and fearless. She carried herself very erect and with a
cool dignity. There were persons who thought these two women
were born to be natural enemies, and pictured a conflict between
them as equal to the collision of two locomotives. But no such clash
ever occurred.

To Mrs. Battle Cornelia now told her worry. Mrs. Battle was
emphatic. Not for a moment, she said, must the dinner be given
up. She would if necessary help feed the convicts herself. Gentle
Dr. Battle came in and heard the story of persecution. "Go ahead
with the dinner," he counselled. So Mrs. Spencer took the Battle
phaeton and went out to do the necessary errands, for the village
in those days had no telephones or cars.

Not only were there gifts of food to collect, there was a power
of going and coming to be done and lots of messages to be sent and
received—a whirl of duties and activities of which Mrs. Spencer
was the center. For instance, she had wished Professor A. W.
Mangum to be the chaplain of the dinner. He had consented, but
at the last moment he sent word he could not come. She prevailed
on Jim Taylor, a young man of the village, to hunt up the Reverend Joseph B. Cheshire, the Episcopal minister (later bishop
of North Carolina), and produce him at the dinner.

The village gradually woke up to the occasion and food poured in—chicken, beef, ham, potatoes, biscuits, pickles, pies, custard, turnovers, cake, fruit. All the townspeople gave liberally—the Wards, Tenneys, Newtons, Partins, and Woodses. Mrs. Spencer got a spring wagon to load the contributions on. It was soon filled to overflowing. When it passed the postoffice, Andrew Mickle, the postmaster, halted it long enough to pour in two bushels of fine red apples, his face beaming.

Cornelia had sent all the assisting ladies ahead, so that when the time came for her to start for the dinner, no conveyance was at hand and she had to kiss her old mother and set out for the grounds, two miles distant, alone and on foot. The day and the unpaved streets were dusty. Nevertheless she was buoyed up by the feeling that the arrangements, so far, were going well, and by the knowledge that in her black dress, grey shawl, and bonnet she was looking "quite genteel," as she subsequently confessed in a letter to June. Before she had passed beyond the line of shops, she was joined by a firm friend, Mrs. Taylor, and together they trudged beyond the edge of the village to the field where the convicts had knocked together a long plank table. Here the ladies of the dinner committee, Mrs. Carr, Mrs. George T. Winston, Mrs. Tankersley, Mrs. Norwood, Mrs. Guthrie, Mrs. Ruff Cheek, Mrs. Algy Barbee, Miss Katie Pell, and Mrs. Thompson—were already busy unpacking baskets of food, assisted by Negro trusties from the convict camp.

The plank table had been set with ninety-six tin plates, spoons, and cups. A separate table had been prepared for Colonel Holt and the guards. On each table the food was heaped up until the wood could no longer be seen. The convicts were marched up to their places. Behind them stood the guards armed with rifles. A silence fell as the Reverend Joseph B. Cheshire asked the blessing. Then the convicts ate. The mountains of victuals melted away. They ate until their hands came up only languidly to their mouths. They ate till their eyes bulged. They were allowed to fill their pockets with whatever was left. Then they sat down in rows on the grass and watched the guards eat. Last the convicts' women-folk were fed. When the guards had finished, they made the prisoners stand up, pull off their hats, and cheer the ladies of Chapel Hill. Colonel Holt came around and spoke affably. He said that ever since the convicts had learned that a dinner was really going to be given to them, they had worked better than they ever had before. He invited the assembled ladies to meet him at the spot in six or seven weeks' time when the first train of cars would come in; then he would take them on an excursion to Niagara Falls, or any place they might be pleased to go to.

Mrs. Spencer was the last to go home. She rode back into town in the spring wagon and though she ached with tiredness, she took back to the owners every pot and pan she had borrowed. Then she made a round of visits to give a report on the dinner. She made the first report to her mother, Mrs. James Phillips, who had been invalided by a fall. Then she described the dinner to Dr. and Mrs. Kemp P. Battle and to her sister-in-law, Mrs. Charles Phillips, and to her nephew William B. Phillips and his wife Minnie. At last she crept home. But not to rest. After dinner she read stories to her mother's maid, Betty, and to Anne Brockwell, Betty's friend who had come to spend the night with her. At last she went to bed, worn out but triumphant.

v

It would never have occurred to any sane inhabitant of Chapel Hill to question Cornelia's leadership in such matters. She had always been regarded as the village arbiter. Nor would it have occurred to anyone to question her authority as judge and umpire in village affairs. It was assumed that if anyone ever was to the manor born, if any inhabitant unquestionably belonged, it was she. And yet she was by birth not a Chapel Hillian but a New Yorker. Much of her prestige was reflected from her father, a beloved and respected professor; however, he was not a native but an Englishman; and much came from her mother, known for her good works, but she was not a native, either, but a New Jersey woman, a daughter of the Vermeules, an old Dutch family long resident in New York and New Jersey.

Harlem before it was a part of New York City—in that village Cornelia was born on March 20, 1825. She was christened Cornelia Ann Phillips. The "Ann" in her name she never liked and she later dropped it. The name Phillips is supposed to be in origin Welsh—a contraction of "Philip's son." The records trace the Phillips family back to the village of Nevenden in the county of Essex, about twenty miles to the east of London. Here the Reverend Richard Phillips was rector in 1792. On April 22 of that year a son was born to him and his wife, whose name had been Susan Meade. He was named James. There were two older sons, Samuel and John. John died when a young man. When James was still a child, his mother died. Soon afterward the Reverend Richard Phillips moved from Essex to Staffordshire and then to Cornwall, where he became the rector at Roche. James Phillips used to tell his daughter Cornelia how he loved to play around the great rock of Roche. Here his father married again.

This was a determining circumstance in the lives of James and Samuel Phillips, for their father's second marriage caused a breach between him and his sons. Whether because of a stepmother's harshness or some other family estrangement, James and Samuel Phillips left their father's house. They never saw him again and, so far as is known, never communicated with him again, although he survived for many years and remained as rector at Roche until 1837.

VI

The brothers at once set about earning their own living. James found employment in the old town and seaport of Plymouth. Samuel enlisted in the British navy and remained there ten years. He took part in the battle of Corunna and used to tell how he once saw Napoleon Bonaparte at Plymouth Harbor as prisoner aboard the *Bellerophon*. Samuel's experiences at sea somehow were credited to James, who for years after he became a staid professor at the University of North Carolina was firmly believed by the students there to have been a pirate with a secret and bloodthirsty career.

The two brothers were ambitious and energetic. They saved a regular part of their earnings with a view to leaving England and finding a new life elsewhere. In 1818 they made a tour of France, not only to study the country but to test themselves. Could they bear to part with England? France proved to them that they could. Later that year they made a further venture—they sailed for America.

Samuel went into business and prospered. He moved to western New York and at Geneva married Ann King Hortsen, daughter of Dr. William Hortsen. For a time they lived in Detroit and then returned to New York City. Both lived to a great age, his wife surviving him many years. His grave is in the uptown cemetery of Trinity Church at 254th Street, New York City.

James's tastes were quite different and his career took him in another direction. He was a born teacher and he soon established a boys' classical school in Harlem and conducted it for several years. A fondness for mathematics developed which became a salient factor in his career, for mathematics took him into a circle of friends, brought him a university professorship, and earned him a bride. He became a contributor to *The Mathematical Repository* and *Nash's Diary*. The former was a journal edited by Dr. Robert Adrain, then a professor in and subsequently president of Rutgers College at New Brunswick, New Jersey.

"There were at that time in New York," wrote Cornelia, "a number of American and British mathematicians; among them were such men as McNulty, Ryan, Strong and Dr. Adrain. They had organized a Mathematical Club of which Mr. Phillips became a member and was soon recognized as an enthusiastic student and a regular contributor to its literary and scientific publications. . . . His friend Dr. Adrain, then professor in the college at New Brunswick, urged him in 1826 to apply for the chair of Mathematics and Natural Philosophy at Chapel Hill, just then become vacant."

One of the faculty members at Rutgers and a member of the Mathematical Club of New York was Cornelius C. Vermeule, a young man interested in religion, medicine, and mathematics. Common interests drew him and James Phillips together. Young Vermeule had an older brother, Richard, a doctor living on Grand Street, New York. Both brothers had received medical instruction from the celebrated Dr. Benjamin Rush of Philadelphia. Cornelius Vermeule at length deserted teaching for the ministry, and later quit the ministry in order to practice medicine with his brother.

An occasional visitor at the Grand Street house of Dr. Richard Vermeule was his younger sister, Judith, who lived at the old home in New Jersey. This was a big farm beyond the northern edge of Plainfield, New Jersey, just under the shadow of the Blue Hills and of the Washington Rock, so named because it was a favorite observation post of George Washington. The centre of this farm was a substantial two-story house that had been built by the father of Cornelius and Richard and Judith Vermeule, Captain Cornelius Vermeule, a leader of Jersey militia in the Revolutionary War and a friend of George Washington, who was more than once a guest in the Captain's house. This house still stands. But whereas it once stood alone among broad fields, it is now thickly surrounded by suburban houses in North Plainfield, New Jersey.

It may be surmised that James Phillips met Judith Vermeule at the home of one of her brothers in New York. She had many tastes that pleased him. She loved literature, wrote poetry, and revered the classics. She spoke French as became a descendant of a family that had originated in Burgundy, France. The original name was Dumoulin. This name, on removal of the family to Holland because of religious troubles, became van der Meulen, which is a literal translation of the French name meaning "of the mill." The Dutch name was contracted to Vermeule by the time the founder of the American family, Adrian Vermeule, came in 1670 from Flushing, Holland, to Harlem, New York, where in 1700 he was secretary of the Harlem Board of Overseers and where through marriage his descendants became related to many Dutch and English families living on both sides of the Hudson river.

VII

Three years after landing in America, James Phillips won Judith Vermeule as bride. Three children were born to them: Charles, Samuel Field, and Cornelia, who was named after her mother's father, the Jersey farmer and militia captain. Cornelia Phillips was thus the receiver of sundry heritages. And if there be anything in tradition, it might be said that from her Welsh ancestors she inherited the imaginativeness and love of poetry that were her salient traits; the English influence gave her a respect for integrity and truth; her Dutch blood gave her sturdiness and practicality; while the French strain imparted to her nature both vivacity and vitality. Of the Vermeules, Cornelia herself wrote that they were "religious, serious, thoughtful," while the Phillipses she deemed "more worldly and pleasure-loving, clever and good-natured."

When Cornelia was still a baby her father, who had continued to conduct his school for boys in Harlem, received a letter that must have been upsetting to educational routine. It was from Joseph Caldwell, president of the University of North Carolina at Chapel Hill, inviting him to make application for the post of professor of mathematics there. Dr. Caldwell, who was a graduate of Princeton College, added that Phillips's name had been given to him by Dr. Adrain of Rutgers College, who had highly recommended him.

To James Phillips there could have been but one answer. A professorship in a university would enable him to escape the details of school administration and give himself wholly to one love, mathematics. In due course, Ichabod Wetmore, secretary of the committee on appointments, notified Phillips that the chair was his. He at once accepted, disposed of his school, and prepared to leave New York for North Carolina. This was in the early summer of 1826. Cornelia was then barely more than one year old.

It is probable that James and Judith Phillips spent from eight to ten days transferring themselves, their books, and their children from the metropolis to the pine and hardwood forests of Orange County, North Carolina; for the journey south by way of Philadelphia, Baltimore, Petersburg, Virginia, and Raleigh required many changes from packet-boat to stage, and back again.

James Phillips was then thirty-four years old, broadly built and deep chested but with a scholar's refined face. His eyes were kindly and humorous, but the chin that rested deep between the points of his flaring stock collar was square and inflexible. Judith Vermeule Phillips was three years younger, tall and sprightly, with dark ringlets framing an oval face and moody eyes. James came to Chapel Hill with the resolute air of a man who had made up his mind, but Judith was a little like Lot's wife; she often looked back —to New Jersey.

As for their youngest child, Cornelia at once adopted the village and made it her own. As she grew up, she loved Chapel Hill and tended it with a brooding, hovering care that never relaxed. There was no whit, no inch, no item of the village that she did not watch over with a yearning affection. Its deep green campus, its great trees, its uneven sidewalks and graveled paths, its quiet professors and gentle professors' wives, its houses and lanes— all these she loved. The loafers and sinners avoided by the righteous —these she sought out and ministered to; Negroes, respectable or nondescript, she taught, fed, and scolded. Above all she loved the woods and fields that invaded and surrounded the village. For waters and wild flowers and streams, old mill sites, and springs, for all the village surroundings, she had an overflowing passion.

What we have to tell here will be called a biography. But really it will be a love story—Cornelia Phillips Spencer's love for a sleepy Southern village and the University it contained.

2

Villagers and Professors

I

THE Chapel Hill to which the Phillipses came in 1826 was hardly more than a wide place in the stage road that ran from Pittsboro, North Carolina, to the trading center of Petersburg, Virginia. The scattered hamlet of white and gray wooden houses rested on a ridge or hill which had once been topped by a chapel, called New Hope, of the Church of England, hence the name Chapel Hill.

"The early settlers in these backwoods," wrote Cornelia, "were not Episcopalians. The best of them were Scotch-Irish Presbyterians. . . . I do not believe this hill chapel was much frequented, though I like to fancy the Rev. Mr. Micklejohn, who is said to have been the rector, arriving on a Sunday morning more than one hundred years ago, entering the little building, adjusting his gown and bands, and calling on as many as were then and there present to accompany him in the prayers for his Majesty King George the third."

The University in 1826 had been open to students for thirty years, but consisted of little more than four brick buildings, a belfry, and a well. The railroad did not touch the village until fifty-four years later. Stretching away from the gaunt and severely plain buildings was the boundless forest of oak, hickory, and pines clinging thickly to a broken or rolling country cut by streams. Springs of cold fresh water ran from the edges of the campus, and the numerous slopes held large clumps of chinquapin bushes. The roads were little more than gashes in the orange-red clay which in rainy weather became all but impassable. Hillsboro, the county seat, was only fourteen miles away, but the barouches, in which the gentry travelled, often took half a day to make the journey; while Raleigh, the state capital, though only twenty-nine miles distant, could be reached only after a whole day's toilful travel.

Little wonder that upon first beholding the village James Phillips felt a sudden homesickness for the hum and stir of Harlem town, and that Mrs. Phillips was always going back in memory to the wide spaces, the plenteous comforts, of her father's home in New Jersey. They soon found, however, that Chapel Hill, though small, was a very complete little world in itself and had its interesting hierarchies and divisions. It even had its own race-track, out beyond what later became the railroad station, and its own set of eccentrics and ne'er-do-wells and rascally characters.

"He came to North Carolina in 1826," wrote Mrs. Spencer concerning her father afterwards, "and his first impressions of the University resulted rather in disappointment. I have heard him say that for several years he would have been glad to get away at any time, and nothing but his attachment to Dr. Caldwell, and the influence which the President exerted on him, kept him at the place. He was an ardent and enthusiastic Mathematician, and he wanted to introduce new methods of study and *more of it,* than young North Carolinians ... were willing to accept. He believed then and to the last of his life, in the discipline of the mind resulting from the study of the exact sciences, as the most important of all aids in its cultivation."

Finding no suitable textbook on conic sections, James Phillips wrote and published one, and later wrote another on differential and integral calculus which he never published.

II

Whatever society there was in the community had its "tone," and it was the testimony of Mrs. Spencer herself that this tone came from Mrs. Helen Caldwell, wife of the University's president. "She was a woman to take the lead and keep it," wrote Mrs.

Spencer in one of those portraits which she could sketch with such sure strokes. Mrs. Caldwell was the daughter of a learned and energetic Scotsman, James Hogg of Hillsboro, and, wrote Mrs. Spencer, "a good deal of the exclusiveness that characterized it [Chapel Hill] for years, even after she had ceased to preside there, were due to her old-world birth and breeding. . . ."

For this occasional haughtiness the President's wife was much criticized in some quarters, and even the President himself did not escape censure for his Federalist opinions among a plain people who were jealously maintaining their Republicanism. Dr. Caldwell was his wife's second husband. Her first was William Hooper, son of one of the North Carolina signers of the Declaration of Independence. Dr. Caldwell was a fit mate for a fastidious woman. "He looked," says Mrs. Spencer, "the president and thorough gentleman. . . . He had a high sense of the dignity of letters, and never forgot what was due to his position. Though not above a middle height, his appearance and manners were impressive. . . . His eyes were dark and penetrating, overhung by bushy eyebrows; his dress was always neat, precise and handsome. . . . He had very great administrative ability and power to inspire unlimited confidence in all who approached him." One more of Dr. Caldwell's traits has become a part of the Chapel Hill legend: he is said to have been the last man in the village who attended the University balls in knee breeches, silk stockings, and silver buckled shoes.

General Edward Mallett, a graduate of the University of North Carolina in 1818, has left this costume picture, which probably had not altered materially by the time the Phillips family arrived six years later except in one respect: in 1826 trousers, even in Chapel Hill, had definitely ousted breeches, which had just succeeded pantaloons.

"At a commencement ball (when I graduated)," said General Mallett, "my coat was broadcloth of sea green color, high velvet collar to match, swallow-tail, pockets outside, with lapels and large silver plated buttons; white satin damask vest, showing the edge of a blue undervest; a wide opening for bosom ruffles, and no shirt collar. The neck was dressed with a layer of four or five three cornered cravats, artistically laid and surmounted with a cambric stock, pleated, and buckled behind. My pantaloons were white Canton crape, lined with pink muslin, and showed a peach blossom tint. They were rather short, in order to display flesh colored silk stockings; and this exposure was increased by very low cut pumps, with shiny buckles. My hair was very black, very long, and *queued*. I would be taken for a lunatic or a harlequin in such a costume now."

There were other able and original figures in the village and University. Dr. Elisha Mitchell, who afterwards lost his life on the mountain that bears his name, gave an especial welcome to Professor Phillips because the latter took over the chair of mathematics, leaving him free to devote himself to his beloved chemistry and mineralogy. Dr. Mitchell was the University's bursar and, whenever Dr. Caldwell fell ill, its acting president. He was always furiously busy, yet he found time to walk the woods and fields in search of mineral and botanic specimens, to roam the state's trails on horseback, to read copiously, and occasionally to preach a sermon, for in his native Connecticut he had been ordained a Congregational minister.

"I have seen," wrote Mrs. Spencer in 1869, "a blank ledger among the many left behind him filled with his business accounts, which he devoted to notes of his studies—beginning September 19, 1818. The Preface was written in French and lays down a plan of study for each week. So many hours to Mathematics, so many to Latin and Greek, so many to History, so many to Hebrew, so much to the Spanish language and to botany. Till such an hour, '*I will not touch one book of belles lettres*'. . . .

"From his first arrival at Chapel Hill his pedestrian excursions into the surrounding country were constant. The above-mentioned ledger was full of notes of these excursions which extended, through years—gradually widening in their scope and aims, leading him all over the State from the marls of the seashore counties to the coal mines of Deep River, and, finally to fearful death in yonder wild gorge of the Black Mountain.

"Not a stream, or hill, or valley for miles around Chapel Hill that he was not familiar with; not a tree or shrub, or flower, or grass, or moss that he did not know and love. He chronicled his walks over Major Henderson's farm, over Kittrell's, over Merritt's, over Taylor's. Names that now awaken only faint echoes round Chapel Hill. By such a rock, in such a field is a plant that he must identify. By Scott's Hole, near the willows, is a *Carex* that he must watch. March 30, 1821, he finds yellow jessamine in bloom in Mrs. Hooper's garden, and 'in great abundance on the creek below Merritt's mill' (now Purefoy's)....He had the true scholar's disdain of taking anything at second-hand."

The energetic doctor and his good wife had three little girls, Mary, Ellen, and Margaret; and almost from the day the Phillipses landed in Chapel Hill they and Cornelia became ardent friends, studying lessons together under Cornelia's mother, and then joyfully out of doors running free.

"There was a good deal of simple happiness," wrote Mrs. Spencer concerning those times, "and much converse with the woods and hills and streams, the wild flowers and fruits of the country mixed with the books. The children grew up strong and healthy, ready for any work that might offer."

At the age of eight Mary Mitchell was studying Latin and reading Roman history, and when Cornelia was eleven she was reading Xenophon in Greek under Professor William Hooper, in a class that included her brothers and the two older Mitchell girls. When Cornelia was more than eighty years old, she was still writing letters to Margaret Mitchell about these happy, tranquil days of the eighteen-thirties.

III

If Dr. Mitchell was a bursar whose real love was plants and mountains and rocks, there was also another member of the faculty, a professor of modern languages whose real love was spiders. This was Nicholas Hentz, an Alsatian who was born in Versailles, France, and who had come to America to escape the political troubles consequent upon the rise of Napoleon. As soon as he had done his duty in the classroom, Professor Hentz would escape to the fields and engage in the glorious pursuit of insects. His book on spiders was for years the completest compendium of its kind in the New World.

"My earliest recollections," wrote Mrs. Spencer, "are of certain glass cases in his house filled with bugs and butterflies, impaled on pins." He had a dainty and graceful American wife whose maiden name had been Carolina Lee. "They both," wrote Mrs. Spencer in 1875, "drew in water colors, a very rare accomplishment in North Carolina back woods, fifty years ago." Mrs. Hentz had another distinction—she was Chapel Hill's first novelist. In one of her stories, *Lovel's Folly,* appeared such salient Chapel Hill characters as Dr. November, President Caldwell's Negro carriage driver, and Venus, his cook. By some residents the Hentzes were considered a little queer. Wrote Mrs. Spencer: "The first, and for many years, the only lightning rod in Chapel Hill was put up on their house in consequence of some extraordinary electrical display on their parlor floor during a severe thunder storm. They left Chapel Hill in 1830 and seem to have suffered from an attack of the same homesickness that all experience who have left the place."

Homesickness for Chapel Hill—that is a theme to which Mrs. Spencer's writings often recur. Her letters, her essays, her recollections, sound the note again and again.

IV

Although Mrs. James Phillips was often homesick in Chapel Hill, as a young professor's wife she found substantial friends among other professors' wives, and they in time helped her to reconcile herself to village life. One friend was Mrs. William Hooper, wife of the professor of rhetoric and logic. "She had," wrote Mrs. Spencer after Mrs. Hooper's death in 1863, "beauty and grace, and great amiability and kindness of heart. These gifts, with her gentle piety, her refined tastes, her love of flowers and the profusion of them she always cultivated around her, her love of painting and drawing, . . . these set her memory in a lovely and gracious light among the ladies of her day." In 1869 Mrs. Spencer added: "Mrs. Dr. Mitchell and Mrs. Dr. James Phillips are the only two left of that circle of lively and intellectual young women. They busied themselves with their flowers, with reading, with educating their children, with carrying on a union Sunday school in the village school house, which was built by subscriptions from all denominations. . . . Mrs. Hooper and Mrs. Mitchell and Mrs. Phillips organized the first Sunday School in that part of the country and carried it on successfully for many years. There are grey-haired citizens in Chapel Hill now who were among their first scholars. They had it first in Gerrard Hall where I happen to know that the Shorter Catechism *with proofs* was diligently required of us. If the youngsters of these degenerate days get the Shorter Catechism alone, it is regarded as a triumph."

v

When the Phillipses, James and Judith, had made up their minds to accept Chapel Hill with all its limitations, they established themselves five minutes from the campus in a queer boxlike house with steep roofs that had belonged to the Widow Puckett and been remodelled by Professor Denison Olmsted, who had resigned to go to Yale College just before the Phillipses arrived. His neighbors soon learned they could time their watches by Professor Phillips's departure for his classes, for, cane in hand, he always left his study at a quarter before the recitation hour.

"In his early years," wrote his daughter, "he was very active in person, gay and curt in his address, and fond of good society and of good cheer. But as his concentration upon the absorbing studies which he loved increased, and as years came on, he gradually gave up one by one his out door exercises and settled himself to his work and to his study. For many years the steady light in his library window was the last seen at night in the village. . . .

"A rigid taskmaster and disciplinarian in the recitation room, he unbent as soon as he came out of it. He tolerated young folks, and loved a joke. True Englishman as he was in his outspoken honesty and bluntness, and independence, yet he never made an enemy. Little children pulled at his gown, and claimed him for a playfellow. Our last recollections of this simple minded scholar and true gentleman, are, as he sat in his study chair, with a large old fashioned black leather bound Bible open before him, and one of his little grand-daughters asleep on his breast."

As soon as their children began to approach the 'teen age, James and Judith Phillips—who now preferred to sign herself Julia—tried to make up for the lack of a village school by tutoring Charles, Samuel, and Cornelia themselves. Other parents urged the Phillipses to set up a school to which they might send their children, particularly their girls, for whom there were no educational provisions whatever. This led to the opening of "the Phillips Female Academy" in the Phillips house. Advertisements announcing its courses were at first inserted over Professor Phillips's name, but subsequent advertisements in Raleigh and Wilmington papers were signed by Mrs. Phillips.

Regarding the schooling of children, including herself, in that day, Mrs. Spencer once wrote: "Any learning for them, outside certain established educational lines, was considered queer, i.e., revolutionary. Education was highly esteemed, carefully provided, but it must go the way the Fathers trod. Latin and Greek and French were the foundations, ancient history, ancient geography in preference to anything modern. The old was considered better than the new. Dead languages were considered preferable to the living.

"Dr. James Phillips and his wife, who did have some aspirations which might have been called altruistic, if the word had then been known, directed the education of their daughter very much along with that of her brothers, with this difference, that as they grew up theirs was expanded while hers remained stationary on the lines of its earliest direction."

Mrs. Phillips's School for Young Ladies was prepared to teach the "English, Latin, Greek, and French languages, Arithmetic, Algebra, Geometry, Natural History, Natural Philosophy, Music, Drawing and Needlework," but it laid special emphasis on its courses in the French language and literature. In January, 1838, the school prospectus announced that although all courses could be had for $65 per session, Landscape Painting and French as taught by "Mr. Marey (also spelled Maret and Maray), a French gentleman" cost only $3 per month. Another Frenchman named Bourgevin also gave language lessons in Chapel Hill. Cornelia learned enough French to be able to read French books with some ease and to copy chosen passages from them into her book of quotations. Whoever taught her Latin did it thoroughly. All her life she loved to quote from the Romans of statecraft and literature, while she knew the best of Horace by heart and often diverted herself by making newly rhymed translations of Horatian verse. "Dear old heathen," she called the Roman poet who no doubt had some part in sharpening the wit and enriching that humor of hers which made Zebulon B. Vance, North Carolina's Civil War governor, say to his secretary, R. H. Battle, "She is the smartest woman in the State, yes, and the smartest man too."

Mrs. Spencer was in the habit of speaking scornfully of her early schooling as lacking method and purpose, and of having got only the crumbs that accidentally dropped from the University's table; but actually her education, rambling and self-directed as it might have been, was both broad and sound. She had a never-satiated appetite for books, whether they were for instruction or entertainment, and she could roam at will in her father's library of 2,000 slowly collected volumes, all chosen with care; she could use the libraries of the two University literary societies; and she could borrow books from learned families like the Caldwells, the Mitchells, and the Hoopers. She had some taste for fiction, but better she loved essays, biography, history, and books on English politics.

For the rest she drew on that fount of folklore and earthly learning always provided for Southern children, the Negroes. Soon after arriving in Chapel Hill from New York, her father, following Southern custom, bought two Negro slaves as house servants, Ben and Dilsey. They belonged to the Craig family, which had been in Orange County since before the Revolutionary War, and were faithful and well-mannered. They had their own house in the rear of the Phillips home. Ben died early, but Aunt Dilsey lived to a great age, protected and watched over by Mrs. Spencer, as we shall see.

VI

In 1838, when Cornelia Phillips was thirteen years old, there came a man to Chapel Hill who was to have a substantial influence on her education. This was David Lowry Swain, former governor of the state. He had been chosen as president of the University to succeed Dr. Caldwell, who had died in 1835. Governor Swain, a mountain boy, had been in turn a legislator from Buncombe County, a superior court judge, and finally governor for three terms. "The Governor" was the title that stuck to him for the rest of his life.

Governor Swain was a very prince of ugliness. His person was long, his movements were ungainly, his features bony. The students called him "Old Warping Bars" or "Old Bunc." The faculty was at first prejudiced against him. Although he had been for eighteen months a student at the University over which he was now to preside, he was regarded as a politician rather than a scholar. "He was not a bookish man," wrote Cornelia. "He was eminently in all his beliefs and modes of action a man of the world. What power he had, and he had a great deal, was of his own acquisition among men more than among books. I think it very likely that he did undervalue the discipline of mere hard study and patient thought. He lacked sympathy with scholarship *per se* as a source of 'sweetness and light.' "

The Governor was a student of and a mixer with men. He loved to get people together under pleasant auspices. At Chapel Hill he introduced the custom of having cake, wine, and fruit served at faculty meetings.

"At this day," wrote Mrs. Spencer, "we can hardly realize how universal the practice of using stimulants was in the last generation. I have heard old inhabitants say that when Dr. Caldwell went out to oversee a clearing he would carry a jug of whiskey along for the hands." Governor Swain's mild and conciliatory methods won him friends and long before he had completed his thirty-three years' residence at Chapel Hill he was a venerated figure. "As to his scholarship," wrote Mrs. Spencer, "those who doubted it were soon silenced and obliged to confess that at any rate he knew how to use what he had. I have heard Dr. Phillips tell with great *gusto* the effect produced when on one occasion there being a considerable company assembled at Dr. Mitchell's, in the course of the conversation Gov. Swain picked up a small edition of the Iliad lying near, and turning to a certain page, translated fluently and elegantly a dozen or two lines having a very happy application to the matter under discussion. . . .

"He told me once that on his first coming to Chapel Hill he received many a hit from the college boys, many a fling from the walls of his recitation room in Person Hall. That he made it a rule never to notice these things, any further than to take a hint they might afford him. That he always revised himself and reformed, if needful, in whatever direction the jibe or the caricature pointed. *Fas est ab hoste doceri,* he added with a merry twinkle of the eye. . . .

"His boys loved him, revered him, and carried away from college a warm remembrance of that tall, ungainly figure, that sonorous voice, those nervous trembling hands, that look of infinite benignity and sympathy turned upon all who approached him."

VII

Governor Swain was living diagonally across the street from the Phillips house when Cornelia was entering her 'teens. She saw him often, and went to him for counsel when she could not reach her busy father. Gradually she came to idealize him as another father. From him the adoring girl learned what was to be learned from men and things as well as books. He showed her that she need not fear to swim out into the broad currents of the world. In return she defended him against his critics and took a discount off the detractions aimed at him. In 1865 she wrote in her journal: "I never have a long chat with Gov. Swain without wishing to put down much that he has said. I heartily wish now that I had begun to do it years ago." She was unshakable in her support even to the last of the series of tragedies that in the Governor's old age broke him down and slew him. At the first Commencement after the Governor's death, she wrote to Mrs. Swain:

"I think of the Governor with swelling tears. I long so to speak with him, to tell him of all these things, and to hear once more his words of moderation and wisdom and charity." She and Mrs. Swain kept up a correspondence long after his death. Of the Governor's lady she left this sharply etched portrait:

"Mrs. Swain possessed her husband's entire love and confidence to the last hour of his life, and in many respects deserved it. But on some she did not. She had many peculiarities; but her great weakness through life was her children, and her failure in their training was signal. She spoiled them all systematically, being unable to see any faults in them or to allow the least criticism of them from others. As they grew up, she made it her business to conceal all their shortcomings from their father; to stand between him and them in every attempt on his part to bring them to account. In this course she was ably assisted by a set of worthless, pampered Negroes, whom she indulged and petted on the same ground that she spoiled her children—because they were hers. The result of all this was that Governor Swain's family servants were a by-word for wickedness, and his children grew up to bring him infinite anxiety and sorrow...."

"The eldest, Anne Swain, is still remembered round Chapel Hill, and especially by the poor, with affection and pity.... Sometimes partially, sometimes wholly deranged, and sometimes brighter than the best of us, yet suffering the agony of knowing that she was smitten; always affectionate, generous, charitable, humble.... Dying, she asked that the colored people should sing a certain hymn at her grave, and this they did, many of them in tears as their simple melody rose in the air. She was buried temporarily in the garden under the cedar trees ... and there her father was placed beside her sixteen months after. He had made it his daily practice in all those months to go at or just before day dawn to pray at her grave."

The only surviving son, Richard Caswell Swain, known as "Bunk," "was in no respect," says Mrs. Spencer, "a source of comfort to his father." He was killed in a railroad collision. As for Ellie Hope Swain, the youngest child, she was later the artless cause of a sensation which split the Civil War society of Chapel Hill in two, and was an unwitting actor in the tragedy that closed the University after the war was over; for she, the President's daughter, smiled on, and then married, the chief Yankee invader. This romance, and the manner of it, will be told later, in Mrs. Spencer's own words.

VIII

The 1830's saw the child Cornelia Phillips graduate into girlhood. It was a decade in which the village and the University likewise began to cast off their provincial jackets and feel the stir of the nineteenth century's interest in science and the practical arts. In 1833 there was an attempt to found at Chapel Hill a periodical which would reflect the faculty's intellectual interests. It was called *The Harbinger*. Dr. Caldwell had a hand in it, and Drs. Mitchell, Hooper, and Phillips were among its contributors. Its editor was Isaac Partridge. It received thin financial support and died in a few months. In 1836 another literary effort brought forth a monthly, *The Columbian Repository*. Its editor was Hugh McQueen. It was also short-lived. Eight more years passed before the University had a permanent literary periodical. Although these early efforts were feeble, they sufficed to show that the village was harboring strong literary ambitions, and these influences could scarcely have failed to touch the intellectually eager girl living in the village's very center.

"I hate myself as a child," exclaimed Cornelia once in a survey of the past. "I must have been uncommonly wayward.... My years seem waste-baskets full of trash fit only to be burned." Compare this self-depreciation with an encomium from one of her admirers, W. H. Bailey, written to her from Charlotte, North Carolina, September 17, 1889: "You have one and have had another brother, very, very able, learned and worthy, but they will be entirely forgotten when you will be as well known—I mean two or three hundred years hence—as now. Your books will endure better than [those] of Mesdames Savigny [Sévigné?], Sand, Blessington, Eliot, Brontë, and will last as long as literature shall be cultivated."

This prediction by an enthusiast is a little extravagant; Mrs. Spencer's books were intended only to meet an immediate need; but her letters, especially those to her daughter June, were indeed as ardent and witty as Mme. de Sévigné's to her own daughter. Many moving passages from those eloquent letters to June will be given among these pages.

3

The Happy Forties

IN 1841 Cornelia Phillips was sixteen years old. "I can see you at this moment in mental vision—16 years old," wrote an old beau, Horace M. Polk,[1] to her from Bolivar, Tennessee, in 1881. "I am afraid to give the pen picture for fear you might possibly deem it insincere and therefore impertinent, and the coloring that might be given to that picture by an honest heart might not be taken for a grateful remembrance of one at least of the bright visions of my long since past youth. . . . No flattery from an old married man to say, without going further, [than] that the brightness of your eyes have never changed to memory since Lillington, Branch, and I used to disturb the slumbers of the fair maids of Chapel Hill with our annoying serenades."

At sixteen, if not before, most Southern girls are having beaux; but probably most of Cornelia's admirers were like Horace M. Polk—respectful and likely to keep their distance. Her eyes retained their brightness all her life, and she loved merriment and good conversation; but her early letters show no trace of any more than ordinary interest in the young men who passed her father's house. She was content to make firm friends with other girls, to read ravenously, and to write long, long letters, with lots of under-

1. Horace M. Polk was graduated from the University of North Carolina in 1841 as a classmate of Mrs. Spencer's brothers, Charles and Samuel Field Phillips. He went to Louisiana where he became a member of the General Assembly and later to Tennessee, where he was also an assemblyman.

scored words, to whoever would keep up a correspondence. Of those tranquil days she afterwards wrote:

"A merry laughing time it was, but I suppose utterly fruitless and unprofitable. . . . I seem to smell the jasmine and see the orange asclepias and yellow evening primrose in the fence corners, to hear Bob White calling from the wheat stubble. Summer vacation times in Chapel Hill in the Forties! All of us sweetly doing nothing through the long hot days—going to the University library and bringing home lots of books, novels, histories, biographies, etc., lying down after dinner to read. Going out later to find our Aunt Dilsey sitting at her cabin door smoking her pipe— perhaps patching for Uncle Ben. The very cats and dogs languidly stretched out under the shade of some pleasant bush. Lotos eaters we were in those Forties and Fifties."

Here again is the detracting Calvinistic note. It came from the dark suspicion with which, in that day, all pleasure, however harmless, was viewed; for the union of Puritanism and Calvinism in America produced ideas as narrowing in the warm and verdant South as in bleakest New England. We shall see in Cornelia Phillips this introspective spirit lying in ambush for her Latin gayety; we will see Pan rising from the reeds along the Greek rivers to do battle with the Dutch Reformed church.

II

The year 1841 was memorable to Cornelia for another reason. It was the year when her brothers, Charles and Samuel Field Phillips, were graduated from the University; and when she was compelled to realize that for her, as well as other Chapel Hill girls, there would be no further organized education except such "crumbs," as she called them, that might fall from the University's table. It was possibly at this time that she made the resolve that manifested itself later in her persistent demand for the education of North Carolina girls. The existence of two college buildings named for her, one on the University campus at Chapel Hill, the other at the Woman's College at Greensboro, North Carolina, is evidence that her efforts were not fruitless.

Both brothers were named among the five men graduated with special distinction, and both remained temporarily in Chapel Hill for further studies. Charles became the first secretary of the University of North Carolina Alumni Association and a professor of mathematics. Samuel prepared himself for the practice of law, later becoming speaker of the North Carolina House of Commons, auditor in Governor Vance's Civil War cabinet, and solicitor-general of the United States under President Grant. Charles first began the study of medicine under Dr. Johnston B. Jones, the Chapel Hill physician, but becoming interested in religion, he went in 1843 to Princeton to study theology. From there he returned to assist his father in teaching mathematics. In 1853 he was made professor of civil engineering. In 1856 he was licensed to preach by Orange Presbytery. In 1860 he became professor of pure mathematics at the University while his father retained the chair of mixed mathematics. Both father and son finished their lives as professors and Presbyterian preachers.

To her brothers Cornelia was deeply attached by ties of taste as well as sentiment. Both were men of massive build, ruddy-faced and deep-chested. If she looked up to Charles a little, she felt herself closest to Samuel. As he aged, Samuel became a very handsome man, with a great domed head and powerful face. He was reserved, dignified, and serene-natured. For half a century he and Cornelia regularly wrote each other long and affectionate letters, mostly about their childhood in Chapel Hill. Samuel entered the University at the age of thirteen and was graduated when only seventeen years old. He studied law under President Swain and then under Judge W. H. Battle, when the latter opened a law school at Chapel Hill in 1843. In 1844 "Mr. Sam" was named Master of Arts by his University, and in the same year, when the University students founded a literary magazine, he wrote for it copiously, surprising his friends with his humor and easy, graceful style. As a lawyer he earned large fees, but he could never keep any money, which he spent freely on his family and on books. He gave substantial sums to almost anyone who asked him. His sister always called him "dear old fellow." She loved to write biographical sketches of the people she admired, but she was never able to bring herself to write one about her brother Samuel.

When a boy, Charles Phillips, as his sister wrote in her gallery of portraits, "was distinguished among his mates by his activity of mind and body, easily foremost in all games, running eagerly into all dangers, first in all scrapes, and not a little inclined to be over-bearing."

In her mature years his sister was never seen in public without a cap on her head, usually triangular and touched with white ruching or lace. The story told among her intimates was that this cap covered a scar that had been made in childhood when a stone thrown by Charles grazed the top of her head.

Mrs. Spencer lets us see herself and brothers together in a childhood Greek class: "We recited in the brick office in Dr. Caldwell's yard. . . . Some words went down the line and came to me. 'Now Cornelia,' cried Dr. Hooper eagerly; 'beat them all, and you shall go to my garden and pull as many jonquils and hyacinths as you can carry home.' I opened my mouth and was going to give the translation, for I happened to know it—when my brother Charles snatched it from me, and saved himself—and I went mourning home without my jonquils."

Charles, wrote Mrs. Spencer, was not at first a good teacher. "He lacked deference, amiability, insight. But being all his life a keen student, necessarily he learned; and he learned patience as he went on, learned how to impart what he knew; how to recognize and respect, how to aid another's efforts. . . . When not on a sick bed he was always found cheerful, conversational, keenly interested in all matters public and private. . . . He was confined to a rolling chair for the last few years, and that chair was the center of attraction for many friends, the scene of many gracious, helpful, invigorating interviews. . . . He had the genial, generous, manly nature which belongs with a great heart."

III

"I was once as full of silly jokes as any one," wrote Cornelia of the happy Forties. "Some of them I remember and am ashamed of them! . . . The truth is that few very young people are good at jokes. Let them beware of attempts to be comic."

But this was written after she had become older and self-conscious. Those letters, verses, and other bits of composition by Cornelia that have survived show that when in her later 'teens she was full of what she called a "superabundance of laughing spirit," and that among her girlhood occupations were "walking and talking and no slight amount of laughing." All her writings exhibit the exuberance and gayety of a healthy American girl who has an established place in her world. She even made a little fun of her revered father in a rhyme which began:

> Refraction and reflection, Pa,
>   Canvassed with so much learning here,
> Lights beautiful phenomena,
>   Are all but lost on me, I fear.

About this time she began to write those letters, made up of gossip and trivia mixed with comment and philosophy, which were so eagerly received by her friends. These are passages from a letter written February 27, 1845, to Ellen Summerell, daughter of Dr. Elisha Mitchell, at Salisbury, North Carolina:

"You know that Mary Shaw is here—well! what with—walking and talking—and no slight degree of laughing—she and I bid fair to be pretty intimate—She looks very well and *seems* very gay—though that may be only a reflection from me—for I feel a little afraid that, for the last few weeks I have been what the Highlanders call "fey"—my spirits are so *topsy turvy.* . . .

"Mary Hall–Anne–Anne Swain—and I—having picked each other up at intervals along the way—all fell in at Mrs. Fetter's the other day—and while there conducted a most edifying conversation—with trying to recollect instances of when *most children* came at *one time*—! Mary knew a lady who had three—somebody else told of one who had four once upon a time—and I *thought*—though I wasn't *quite sure*—that I had seen somewhere—that once, somebody or other had *nine!*

"Don't get melancholy—or we shall have to send for you—one walk with Mary Shaw and me—could put you in a fair way of recovery.

"I suppose you have heard of the grand row in college—last week—well! the trustees who were sent for—don't seem to have been as hard upon the delinquents as the faculty wanted, instead of expelling—they only dismissed!"

This closing paragraph referred to an outbreak of students on the campus one night in February, 1845, supposed to have been due to the importation of whiskey. Considerable property was damaged. Expulsion, dismissals, and suspensions followed the episode. Mrs. Spencer's letters contain frequent references to the misbehavior of students and their occasional fights with tutors and professors.

IV

Obstreperous students were not the only serpents to invade this ante-bellum Eden. In only a little while Mary Shaw, with whom Cornelia so loved to walk and talk and laugh, was married; and then very soon Mary Shaw was dead. She was the first of Cornelia's circle of girlish friends to go; and in her memory Cornelia wrote one of those threnodies for which her pen became famous. In this essay Cornelia revealed one of her salient traits. She could admire and enjoy a pretty and charming woman with a connoisseurship almost masculine in its appreciation. Point by point she described Mary Shaw's beauties: the bright, dark blue eyes, the pencilled eyebrows, the soft brown hair, the brilliant complexion varying with every emotion—"all so irradiated with the light of goodness and gaiety," and then she added:

"There was a freshness and simplicity about her ways of talking and doing, inexpressibly charming to me, while her will and judgement, unsuspected by the majority of her intimate friends, were constantly referred to, and employed by herself; her manners were so gentle, so yielding, she was so ready to ask and defer to the opinion of others, that her friends made the natural mistake of supposing a want of will and self reliance among her faults. I think she was misjudged. Where principle was at stake I have seen her unpersuadable, and where her own will was concerned she could be even *imperious*. . . . Nor did her dignity and delicacy sit stiffly upon her, offending rather than influencing by any implied consciousness of superiority and self appreciation. She was ever free from the slightest appearance of self conceit, and readiest with a laugh at her own expense. Her self respect, though I think she had a full share of it, was too gracefully and easily worn to be even generally detected, much less resented."

V

Socially the most interesting event of the happy forties, in the eyes of Cornelia's circle of young women, must have been the decision of the young Dr. Johnston Blakely Jones to practice in Chapel Hill. Mrs. Spencer's writings describe him eloquently. He was fresh from Paris, he looked like Lord Byron, and, says Mrs. Spencer, "there was rather a negligent air about him, as of a man profoundly indifferent to popularity, to gossip, to current reports." What blending of male attractions could have been more impressive to ante-bellum femininity? Even after the lapse of forty-eight years, Mrs. Spencer could recall "the noble beauty of his features."

Dr. Jones was the son of Edward Jones, solicitor-general of the state, whose home was at "Rock Rest" in Chatham County, not many miles south of Chapel Hill. He was a graduate of the University in 1835, and after studying medicine in Charleston, South Carolina, and France, came to Chapel Hill as successor to Dr. Charles Yancey, who had been quietly drinking himself to death. His appearance was stunning to girls who had never before seen

Parisian sophistication united to American masculine beauty. Wrote Mrs. Spencer:

"In estimating the extraordinary magnetic influence that Dr. Jones appeared to exert unconsciously on all who came within his sphere, perhaps it should be stated that he was one of the handsomest men in the State. Unstudied and negligent as he was in air, dress and manner, the noble beauty of his features was remarkable and impressive. The profile of his head and face strikingly resembled Lord Byron's. He brought from Europe a fine cameo head of Byron set in a pin, and it was characteristic of him that when the growing likeness attracted more and more attention and remark, he threw the pin aside, not choosing to have it observed."

VI

Towards the close of the forties both of Cornelia's brothers married and took their brides to homes on either side of their father's dwelling. Charles married in 1847 Laura Battle, youngest and smallest sister of Judge William Horn Battle, who had come to the University to head its law school. Samuel in 1848 married Frances Lucas, granddaughter of Governor David Stone. Soon the babies came, and to them Cornelia became an aunt beyond compare. "Aunty" nursed them, read to them, walked with them, taught them, and tended them unwearyingly. Only Susie Phillips, youngest child of her brother Charles, did sometimes tax Cornelia's patience. She thus records a lesson:

"Susie has come and gone since I have been writing this. She cannot say a grammar lesson to save her life. 'The predicate is that which is affirmed of the subject.' She *can't* repeat it—predicate, subject, affirmed—the words convey no meaning to her ear whatever—& she makes awful nonsense of every attempt to repeat them. . . . '*Idleness & ignorance* write something about them, Susie.' She writes: 'Idleness & ignorance are very disagreeable virtues.' " (The lesson was abruptly ended for the day.)

The forties saw changes in the faculty as well as in the village. Professor Manuel Fetter came from Pennsylvania to teach lan-

guages. The Reverend William Mercer Green came from nearby
Hillsboro, the old colonial capital, to teach *belles lettres*. "The
Greens," wrote Mrs. Spencer, "had that air of gentility which is
not dependent upon tailors or upholsterers." Dr. Green later left
the village and became Episcopal Bishop of Mississippi. Then
there was a young C. F. Deems, Methodist chaplain and faculty
secretary. There could have been no way of knowing how important
this energetic young preacher, who later founded the Church of
the Strangers in New York, was to become to her career. The University, which Cornelia watched over so jealously, was growing in
size and power. It was attracting young men from other states,
even distant ones. Cornelia had no idea what bearing this fact was
to have on her inmost life. Nothing is so depressing to the pos-
sessor of a life than the seeming lack of pattern in it. Yet he can
sometimes look back upon it and perceive how steadily the frame-
work has grown, piece by piece, and how inevitably one fact, in
its ancient meaning of *thing done*, has led to another, so that his
life, which he thought he himself was shaping, seems to have been
rigidly determined for him.

4

The Fateful Fifties

I

THE THIRTIES, the forties of the nineteenth century passed, and although in each one of these decades Cornelia recorded every event that could be of interest to an alert and lettered young woman, and although she lived in a college village, there is in her many letters no hint that any man, University student or no, had ever made her pulse lose a beat. She reached her twenty-sixth year, and still there was no man. And yet she took a hand in all the village diversions. She went on hayrides, country visits, and long walks, and took note of all the village love affairs.

And then on a frozen day in January, 1851, Cornelia went with a party of skaters down to Tenney's mill pond, half a mile from her home. And there stood *the man*. He was introduced to her as Magnus Spencer of Alabama. How came he there?

II

In Beulah cemetery, Greene County, Alabama, is a stone inscribed: "Sacred to the memory of Jesse Spencer, a native of North Carolina, who departed this life November 19, 1836, aged 77 years, 1 month, and 21 days." Jesse Spencer and his wife, Elizabeth Otts, had five children. One of them, William, married Candis Parham, whose people had come from North Carolina. They had ten children. One of them was named James Munroe Spencer. By 1849 the University of North Carolina had become known as a good institution for Southern students to attend, and as a result of the personal care of Governor Swain its law school had been

35

strongly built up and attracted students from distant states. Owing
to this fact, and to his family's connection with North Carolina,
James Munroe Spencer, then twenty-two years old, enrolled as a
student at Chapel Hill. He won his first honor as a freshman de-
claimer at commencement exercises. The next year he was again
a commencement speaker and began to appear in the University
magazine. In 1853 he won a place among the seven seniors mentioned for "first distinction." Among his classmates was Solomon
Pool of Elizabeth City, North Carolina, a young man unfortunate
enough to earn Mrs. Spencer's dislike and to be hotly pursued by
her pen, as will be recorded later.

III

Here then, standing on the lower side of Tenney's frozen mill
pond, is Cornelia Phillips, spinster, facing the third-year student
and embryo lawyer from Alabama, James Munroe Spencer. The
boys call him "Magnus." He is tall and has a powerful face. His
eyes are deep-set. His hair, when he sweeps off his hat, falls into
his eyes. His voice is clear and trained. He is amiable, and although
the expression of his face is grave, he speaks with a quiet humor.
He crosses the ice with her and walks with her home. He comes
to call, and they talk of books and authors. They find they have
like tastes, and the talk wells up from each and runs like a river.
She encourages him to come often, and when his attention seems
to lag or his interest wanders, she uses an old device and gives him
employment in her service, writing him on a very small note-paper,
scalloped and edged with paper lace, a note like this:

> "Please return these books to the Library for me Mr.
> Spencer, before the session opens—I quite forgot to ask you
> last night. And please send me Schiller's Poems (translation).
> I've had them before in one blue volume. Don't trouble your-
> self to get it this evening—any time shortly will do. I'd rather
> have the 'Journal.'
>
> "Yours truly, C. A. Phillips"

The courtship went on through the winter and spring until April came. Chapel Hill in April sees the azalea, wood iris, trillium, redbud, the scented plum tree, the white dogwood in bloom, the wistaria hanging down in lavender cascades, the bluets thick on hill and pasture, and the birds hurrying north through the pines and hardwoods. All but the most laggard trees come to leaf and a young greenness paints the hills. In the air hangs an occasional summer haze and often there is a summer warmth.

On the very last day of April in that year, 1853, Magnus called for Cornelia at her father's house, and they went for a long walk. When they returned, they were engaged to be married. April 30 was thereafter a rubricated day in the calendar of their lives, and they celebrated it as one of their chief anniversaries. To him it was gaily known as Courting Day; to her it was a day embroidered with thrilling remembrances, and on the morning of every 30th of April for the rest of her life she awoke and remembered every tone of his voice, every look of his eyes.

In the following June, Magnus Spencer was graduated. He returned to Alabama and in two years deemed his prospects good enough to support a wife. He came back to Chapel Hill in 1855, and on June 20 of that year he married Cornelia. June was a month—and a name—that ever thereafter was an important one to Magnus and Cornelia. For a wedding journey they went to Magnus's home in Clinton, Alabama, where some of the leading families, although well-to-do, still lived in the log houses of the pioneers. The largest single item of expense in this journey was the fare, $53.75, by sea and land from Wilmington, North Carolina, to Montgomery, Alabama, as inscribed by the bridegroom in a little black book in which he made neat entries. But the fare by stage from Montgomery to Clinton was almost as large—$50.00. The total cost of the journey as recorded in Magnus's little black book was $141.75.

Visits to relatives and Magnus's law practice caused a good deal of travel in the three states of Alabama, Georgia, and Tennessee, and when she could, Cornelia went with her husband on these trips, often on horseback. For a time they lived in Fayetteville, Tennessee. Always eager for travel and always taking an intense interest in new people, she wrote gaily and often to her homefolk. Looking back upon these days, she wrote a few years later:

"How dear he was—how uniformly kind and good to me. How happy we were in each other—*how happy!*"

Yet even on the sunniest days there fell a shadow, and even in Cornelia's most exhilarating letters home there were references to her young husband's feeble health and lack of strength. There were days when pain racked him, but outwardly he kept such a cheerful face that the young wife felt no acute alarm. His ailment was mentioned only as some obscure form of spinal lesion. Four years after his marriage he admitted in a letter to his wife's mother that he was "very feeble" and had been troubled with a tumor, but added: "Still I can scramble about."

IV

June, 1859, came 'round, and on its very first day a child was born to Cornelia and Magnus at Clinton, Alabama. To honor her grandparents the baby was christened Julia James Spencer. But Magnus called her his "little June bug," and for the rest of her life she was always called June, and this was the name that she herself always preferred. Her father announced her arrival in this letter to Mrs. James Phillips at Chapel Hill:

"Clinton, Alabama
June 3, 1859

"My dear Madam: At the instance of Cornelia I write to communicate a piece of news that is *new* if it has no other merit. It is this— on the 1st day of June at half-past 9 o'clock in the County of Green and State of Ala, Lat. and Lon. not known, another *Granddaughter* of you and Dr. Phillips made her appearance. For this I suppose C. and myself are responsible and we hope that all whom it may concern, in and about C. Hill, will be as well pleased in regard to the matter as we are. . . . C. is a little disappointed at the sex of the little stranger. She had so often imagined it a fine boy, and labelled it 'James Phillips,' that she thought it would be so, but the best laid schemes of mice and *women* 'gang aft agley'. As for myself, I feel no disappointment. True, it is a girl, but a baby is a baby for all that, and a girl is as good as a boy any day, for which there are many reasons . . .

"With your permission we purpose to give it your name,—Julia Vermeule. C. hints that she wants to hold the 'Phillips' in reserve, for what I don't know. I think it a bonny baby, strong, healthy, of ten pounds weight, big eyes and mouth, round cheeks and a full head of hair, of which see specimen. . . .

"C. knows you will be surprised at not hearing something of the matter before now, but she kept her counsel in order to keep you from anxiety. . . . She has been remarkably well thro' the whole of it—not sick a day, nor at all depressed."

In the spring of the next year, 1860, Magnus was no better but rather worse. He was too weak to hold his child or walk with her. Day after day he lay on a couch and lived chiefly on milk drinks prepared by Cornelia. Late in the summer he rallied enough to make the long trip to Chapel Hill with his wife and baby. His brother-in-law, Samuel F. Phillips, believed the water at Kittrell's Springs would benefit him and took him there. Cornelia never forgot his haggard return. "How well I remember," says her diary, "running downstairs at hearing Cal say she heard the hack stop, and finding him sitting on the end of the bench by the door unable to get any further. Oh, how my heart sank when the light shone full on his poor face. How I hastened to get him upstairs. No better! No better!"

In the fall Magnus craved to go home to Alabama, and Cornelia and her baby got ready to return with him. Before her departure she consulted Dr. Johnston B. Jones and asked him to be frank with her as to her husband's condition. The doctor's reply was that his recovery was "not probable." It was with this knowledge that she once more left her father's house to return to Alabama.

On reaching his home Magnus improved somewhat; but by the spring of the next year, 1861, he was visibly weaker. On the last day of May she cut his hair as he lay in bed. On June 1st he insisted that his little daughter's birthday be celebrated in his presence, though he was then too weak to raise his head. "I shall never see another birthday of hers," he said. On June 24th, on a day when the crape myrtle, the pomegranate, and the cotton were in bloom all around the house, he died.

v

The birth of her daughter and her young husband's slow decline had so preoccupied Cornelia Spencer's mind that she scarcely noticed the other events and more formidable shadows that had been gathering in the nation. In 1856, the very year in which Magnus Spencer's illness began to be noticeable, the North Carolina *Standard,* edited at Raleigh by W. W. Holden, contained these remarks on the candidacy of John C. Frémont for the United States presidency on the Republican ticket:

"If there be Frémont men among us, let them be silenced or required to leave. . . . *That man is neither a fit nor a safe instructor of our young men, who even inclines to Frémont and black Republicanism.*" It was known that these sentiments were aimed at Professor B. S. Hedrick, a professor in the University of North Carolina, who had let his support of Frémont be known and who, moreover, had proclaimed his opposition to slavery.

In 1857 Dr. Elisha Mitchell, long an intimate friend of the Phillips family, died from a fall when exploring in western North Carolina the mountain peak that was afterward to bear his name.

In 1859 James Buchanan, President of the United States, attended the commencement exercises at Chapel Hill.[1] On the way

1. Of President Buchanan's visit to Chapel Hill on this occasion, a correspondent, possibly Cornelia's brother Charles, wrote in the *North Carolina Presbyterian:* "The President is of a large frame and a portly person, with a high and massive forehead lightly covered with white hair. His voice is very pleasant and clear, and his manners very affable. He has a

there he made a speech which was thought to contain a pointed reference to certain current agitations. He said:

"Let us swear by the memory of our fathers that we will resist every attempt to tear from the constellation the States of which the Union is composed, any fragment of light; and let the man be execrated for all time who will attempt to break up this great Union."

In 1859 John Brown was hanged after attacking the United States arsenal at Harper's Ferry.

In 1861 Buchanan was succeeded by Abraham Lincoln as president of the United States. Late in that year South Carolina seceded from the Union.

In the spring of 1861 Fort Sumter was captured by the seceders, and a fortnight after Magnus Spencer's death, Union and Confederate forces met in battle at Bethel.

But by Cornelia Spencer these embroilments were heard only as faint echoes from some distant world. Her battle had been already fought and lost. On November 21, 1861, she made this entry in Magnus's little black book, which she was now using as a diary:

"Thursday night. Took my child & went today to see the place where they laid him. Went to *Pleasant Hill.* And now Magnus— I have stood by your grave! Your baby has left the print of her little foot on the soil that covers you!—

"I planted some of the shrubs & flowers that you admired and loved so well about your resting place—the last work I can do for you."

This must have been written during one of the paroxysms of

---

kind word for every one who approaches him, and a hearty kiss for every pretty girl who has one for him. (I noticed that it is not a bachelor that the maidens are loath to osculate; it is only a young bachelor). President Buchanan is a hale, hearty, active, lively, nice old gentleman, with his eyes wide open all the time, and a way that leaves on all who converse with him a delightful impression of his candor." The President had in his entourage a Negro attendant who in Washington was the White House doorman.

grief, sometimes lasting several days, that overwhelmed her at intervals for years after Magnus died. On November 24, 1861, she wrote:

"The time for my departure from Clinton, Ala.—where I have buried all the hope & love of my life, is drawing nearer and nearer. I have been taking down our books, many of which have not been touched since *his* hand placed them on the shelves. Every one of them eloquent of our happy life together—the entire sympathy and congeniality of our tastes. From them flutters now and then a scrap of paper—or some other little memento of him—something of his writing. Oh what a rich & full mind was his. What sweet *companionship* I have lost forever."

From her father came a comforting letter assuring her of a refuge back in her old home. "This morning Charles went down to the postoffice," he wrote, "and brought back two letters from you, heart-rending ones, my dear daughter. . . . I have wept till I could not see."

In February, 1862, she was again living in her father's house in Chapel Hill. "I have been away from Clinton now two months," she wrote. "I sit here in the room where my beloved sat so many long dark hours so uncomplainingly through the fall of 1860. This room! these windows—I sit here and think of him, and go to bed at night and lie awake and think of him—think of the last days of his life—of his love and patience and gentleness—of his sufferings—till my heart seems as if it must break."

A month later found her no more reconciled. "I do not *get used* to the loss of my husband in the least degree. . . . My mind is always postponing the time when I shall give him up. My tears for him lie as shallow as they did last summer. . . ."

"Walked with Anne Swain this afternoon, thro' the woods 'round Judge B[attle]'s, and so to the graveyard. We talked a good deal of my beloved husband. I love to dwell upon him. I am always thinking of him and it is very *natural* to talk of him. I should be always doing it if I could get anyone to show much interest in the subject. One's sorrows soon exhaust the sympathy of our *every-*

day friends, and there are very few friends of any other sort. My husband—I love your memory more than anything else left to me in this world. . . ."

But her cup was not yet full. In the following June came the annual University commencement, but though she sent little June, her daughter, to the exercises, she herself remained at home for a reason that she was compelled to record in her diary:

"My hearing is going, and with it my youth and hope and love. . . . God in His Providence has brought me back here to sit among the ruins of my happiness, to *sit here,* and *look on,* and *remember.*"

On the first anniversary of Magnus's death she confessed in her diary: "My anguish was not as *bitter* that day as it is this. I was filled with a sense of God's goodness to him and to me. I thought more of his release from suffering—of his perfect rest— of his abundant entrance. I could have praised God aloud. . . . God help me to retain this sense of His mercy at all times."

It was August, 1862, before her diary recorded any assuagement of her grief. Then for the first time suffering greater than any individual's began to make itself felt throughout the land, and she wrote:

"The great battles fought lately near Richmond—the death of so many friends in them and the universal mourning all over the land have seemed to make me think less of my grief. As if it were selfish in me to mourn for such a peaceful and hopeful translation from earth as my beloved's was—when there are thousands around me who have died horribly in battle or laid lingering and mutilated in hospitals. If my husband had been alive and well during this war he would certainly have been foremost in it—and I would in all probability have lost him so—suddenly and unpreparedly. How many of our former friends and associates have joined him in that world of spirits—how many preceded him there. White—Woods—Allen—Merritt—Andrews —*John Andrews.* My tears fall for him lately dead at Richmond. A generous, brave and good man."

In the back of her notebook she recorded the names of other

friends who were victims: Phil McLemore, her husband's old chum;[2] Maxwell, Harkness, Rice, Thompson, McMillan, and Gordon of Alabama; Husted, Meares, Jennings, Morrow, Lord, the Wheats—J. T. and Rob, and Junius Battle of North Carolina. The last-named was a nephew of Cornelia's sister-in-law, Mrs. Laura Battle Phillips. Some of these lads were killed or stricken in the seven days' battles before Richmond that included encounters between Lee's men and McClellan's or Pope's at Fair Oaks, Mechanicsville, Gaines's Mill, White Oak Swamp or Malvern Hill in the long summer of '62.

There was another circumstance that called her away from her own griefs. On October 7, 1862, she took her little daughter June to play with little Richard Grant, only child of her friend, Eliza Mitchell Grant, daughter of Dr. Elisha Mitchell. The boy had had fever and a sore throat; nevertheless he was full of life. Ten days later she wrote in her diary: "Walked up after dark with Laura to see Eliza, now a *childless widow*. There lay her blooming little Rich[d], a corpse. . . . Membranous croup finally came on and after a few days hard struggle for his young life, he is gone and his poor mother sits desolate. . . . Let me think how if the case were mine— Could I face the prospect of losing my baby—Have I been living so as to be ready for such a call upon me? *No, no. I have not.*"

Daily she prayed that June be spared the illnesses and infections that swept through Chapel Hill in the winter of 1862-3.

VI

Thereafter her notes, as often as they mentioned the war, were chronicles of mourning and death:

"Dr. Jones's son Ed, has suffered amputation of one leg in the late battles. . . . Dr. Jones has brought Ed's body home. . . . The whole town assembled today to the funeral of young Rich. Mallett,

2. "They lived together in Eutaw [Alabama] in [lawyer] Webb's office and were licensed at the same time," she wrote. "M[agnus] was much attached to him. '*Phil McLemore*'—how often I have heard that name—how many little anecdotes and allusions."

killed by a deserter in Virginia. . . . The suffering and want around us are enough to shroud one's very soul in gloom continually even were one's own outward circumstances prosperous. Mrs. F. sent today to beg me for money to buy something to eat. . . ."

On New Year's Day, 1863, her anguish and restlessness were but little abated, and she wrote in her diary: "What can I do? *What can I do?* I do pray God to show me." Seventeen days later she was able to jot down this more cheerful note:

"Undertook to-day to teach Baker Mallett, Hannis Taylor [3] and Stephen Skinner—boys whose parents are refugees from the eastern part of the State. I was so elated to find that I *could* teach them —*could hear* well enough to teach! I think the employment will be the *very best thing* for me."

3. Hannis Taylor (1851-1922) became a lawyer in Mobile, Alabama, minister to Spain, and author of several books on constitutional law. His best known work is *The Origin and Growth of the English Constitution.*

5 •

War Years

I

DURING THE early days of the Civil War, Cornelia Spencer's sense of loss in the death of her young husband and her anxieties about her small daughter were so overwhelming that she was only dimly aware that the war was entering upon its middle and bloodiest phases. References in her diary to the struggle were scant. But gradually the war began to take a larger place in her writings. On December 1, 1862, after relating how at noon the women of the Confederacy had prayed for peace, she mentions the shock the women of Chapel Hill had received from reading in the Richmond, Virginia, newspapers that the men of the 4th Texas Regiment fighting near Fredericksburg were mostly barefooted. She at once wrote in her diary:

"We are going to make up a box for them. Our own troops are suffering too, but these Texans are far from their homes, their wives and mothers. We must help them and hope for a blessing on them and on us and ours."

She herself was one of the leaders in this effort to collect a case filled not only with shoes but with knitted articles and other comforts. She called on or sent a message to every house in the village. In less than two weeks a big box was filled and packed. "A great pleasure," she wrote, "to be able to get up such a token to them of our love and sympathy. But we have heard the fighting is begun . . . and many a gallant boy for whom we have been preparing these things will be lying cold and stiff on the soil he sought to defend long before they reach the Reg^t."

New Year's Day, 1863, she recorded as bright and sunny and added: "I feel as if there were brighter days in store for our country this year than last. I hope for Peace this year. God grant it!" She noted one other thing that day. On going over to a neighbor's, Mrs. Fetter's, diagonally across the street, she found there "Ellie" Swain, the president's daughter. Ellie, she noted, was looking "very pretty." Ellie was not dreaming of the drama she was about to bring upon the village.

II

That winter the cold lasted long; even by April 1st there was but little new greenness visible; and all the news that seeped into the village dragged at the spirits of all.

"There is great trouble through the country for bread, which is hoarded by speculators," she wrote. "We hear of a dreadful riot in Richmond—news of it suppressed by order of government. Oh that God would hear the prayers of his people and interfere for this land.... All at ch[urch] and I here alone. I do feel so bowed down, *so crushed,* sometimes, that I wonder I can lift my head up or talk at all. Declension in religion is declension in comfort—hope—peace, or happiness, in every affair of life. I am more unhappy than I was eighteen months ago in some respects, and it is no doubt because I am further from God. I seem to see less of His goodness than I did. I neglect my religion and it leaves me."

May 6 would have been her husband's birthday, but that was overshadowed by the news of the critical condition of Stonewall Jackson in Virginia, and then on May 14, 1863, she wrote of Jackson:

"He is dead. A dearly bought victory for us is this last one. Jackson has been the *hero* of the war so far, but great as the loss to our country, the loss to his poor wife is still greater. God help her."

On July 4 of that year she met Governor Swain, who told her he doubted if three-quarters of the people in Chapel Hill remembered the date. "It will never again be the day it has been to this country. Our children will not be brought up to reverence it. We have *no day* for them. . . . We are not attached to our *present* government and perhaps never will be.[1] The people of N. C. at any rate, will never celebrate secession day. *Never.*"

In this passage Mrs. Spencer revealed a little of the sentiment that was gradually crystallizing in her mind—opposition to secession and its fruits. In this feeling she was supported steadily by her father and brothers, who were willing to fight invasion but who could never reconcile themselves to secession.

III

In a few days she was compelled to record yet blacker news for the Southern armies. "C. Hill is in mourning now," she wrote, "for the results of the great battle at Gettysburg, Pa. A number of the best boys of the place were killed there. Vicksburg gone and Charleston will soon follow. Prospects look dark for the Confederacy. God help us!" And a month later she added: "The whole town of Chapel Hill assembled to-day to the funeral of young Richard Mallett, killed by a deserter in Va. . . . N. C. is seriously threatened with convulsion and Revolution in her own borders. One party clamorous for peace—on, it would seem, *almost any terms,* and led by the Raleigh Standard; the other party as bitterly opposed to all such views."

Meantime deaths multiplied. Judge and Mrs. William H. Battle had already lost one son, Junius, in the war. On the morning of September 11, 1863, they were informed that their youngest son, Lewis, was dead in the hospital at Gettysburg. He was the nephew of Laura, Mrs. Charles Phillips, Cornelia's sister-in-law and firm friend.

But the black year 1863 had not done its worst. In its closing weeks Cornelia's father, Dr. James Phillips, sank very low with

1. Zebulon B. Vance, the young war governor of North Carolina, whose friendship with Mrs. Spencer was lifelong, carried on a long feud with the Confederate government at Richmond and was often at odds with the Confederate secretary of war, James A. Seddon.

pneumonia and not even his daughter believed he could live; but he rallied and on New Year's day, 1864, was well enough to hear his small granddaughter, June Spencer, recite the 23rd Psalm, for which he gave her a silver quarter. This was a gift sensational enough to be recorded in Cornelia's journal, for it was worth at least $3.00 in Confederate money. Her journal for December 31, 1863, adds that wheat was then $20.00 and potatoes $8.00 a bushel, butter was $3.00 a pound, cotton cloth was $5.00 a yard, and shoes for women cost $50.00 a pair. In another month shoes had advanced to $65.00, with half soles costing $15.00.

There have been preserved some figures made by Dr. Charles Phillips, Cornelia's brother, which shed light on the question as to how the small-salaried people of Chapel Hill managed to live at this period. These figures show that thirty families contributed to a corn fund with which Andrew Mickle, subsequently the postmaster, was sent out to buy corn and bring it in. He bought a little over 383 barrels which cost the sum, including all expenses, of $2,460.61. This was in 1862. On this the thirty families chiefly lived all that winter.

IV

Cornelia's diary entries continued through 1864. May 25 she wrote: "I went on Sunday evening to see Melinda Brockwell, her husband having been slain in one of the late great battles above Richmond. There she sat with her four little fatherless children weeping, weeping. There seems to be less and less hope for our poor. Flour is $1.00 per lb., corn is $150. per bbl. . . . Oh our God, look upon the poor and destitute, upon the widows and orphans, upon the maimed, the dying, the broken-hearted, and come and help us."

"July 4. Our unhappy country stands just as it did 1-2-3 years ago. No nearer peace, and with rivers of her best blood flowing. The interest is all centered around Petersburg now. Cannonading there is heard here distinctly! Clouds and darkness rest upon our future."

She was happy in this summer weather to be very busy with tutoring. "It keeps my mind occupied," she wrote. "When left alone it swings back at once into melancholy." She had one pupil from six to seven before breakfast, and two just after prayers. Three mornings a week from eight to nine she gave a lecture to a class of girls on ancient history. Then until one o'clock she taught her brothers' children and her own daughter June. After dinner (the mid-day meal in the South was always "dinner," never lunch) she tutored in Latin and Greek until four in the afternoon. In the autumn she made this entry:

"October 1, 1864. [She was then thirty-nine years old.] A dark, raw, rainy day which I spent in making sorghum candy ... and putting to rights some of my trunks. Came across a package of old letters, notes, etc., relating to my life previous to my marriage and looked over them. Mary Shaw and Mary Green—how utterly they are passed away from the earth! These letters recall in some degree the period of my life from 19 to 22, but many of the allusions I have lost all trace of. ... A merry laughing time it was, but I suppose utterly fruitless and unprofitable. ... Will my married life also seem, after some time is passed over, like a dream?" (In 1886 she inserted here the word *"yes."*)

Near the end of that month she wrote: "The grief of my husband's death is healed over; that is there is no visible wound—bleeding at every touch. ... I have the feeling of being drifted on a mighty current."

"Nov. 16. A fast day appointed by Pres't Davis. I sat in church this morning with my mind wandering as usual and got to thinking how it would be if Magnus had lived or had been in this war."

"Jan. 13, 1865. I was telling her [June] the other night of some giant or fairy or king 'very rich—oh, had ever so much money.' She stopped me with a grave face—'was it Confederate money?' ... Since Sherman's march across Ga. and the fall of Savannah all faces seem to gather blackness. ... Flour is $250.00 to $300.00, $450.00 to $500.00. ... Cotton socks $5.00."

"Jan. 28. Since the fall of the Wilmington forts there are many rumors of peace negotiations—armistice—of intended 'recognition' by France and England."

"March 10. *Fast-day*, and truly there is need for the people to humble themselves. The 'Confederacy' to all human judgment w⁴ seem to be a failure. God help us."

Despite her most determined efforts to keep her mind and energies occupied, she could not keep the war and her grief separate. On March 13, 1865, she recorded the fact that her mother's servants, Tom, Charlotte, and Rose, had departed for their former home in Elizabeth City. A week later she wrote:

"Have had Ala. and my dear husband more in my mind even than usual by the coming through C.H. of a company of Alabamans in a detachment of Wheeler's cavalry—hurrying to Raleigh. Great numbers of soldiers have been passing thro' this past week, supply trains, artillery, etc.—everybody on the streets feeding them. . . . Very little appearance of spring—a few peach trees here and there in bloom. Some tree buds are swollen, but only a few. A sad and woeful spring for the South."

v

In 1854, when Cornelia Phillips was still single, she had started a commonplace book in which she made entries consisting of extracts and quotations from books read, chiefly biographies. Before her marriage this book lay for some years unused; she now took it up again to record her feelings about the latter days of the war. This entry, bitter and prophetic, but probably faithfully mirroring the feelings of many people living below the Potomac at the war's end, was made March 10, 1865:

"I write now in the very crisis and turning point of our great Southern *States Rights struggle*. The quiet and peace of our daily life in this secluded place afford strong confirmative evidence of Macaulay's saying that in great wars, after all but a small portion of a nation are actually engaged or affected. The plough-boy sings in the field, the wedding supper is provided, and the daily course of domestic life in general flows as smoothly as ever except immediately in the track of armies. This winter, Sherman has marched from one end of Georgia to the other without opposition and has this month calmly walked with 40,000 men through S. Carolina, has taken Columbia, and is now on the borders of our state apparently about to march thro' it in the same way. Charleston and Wilmington have been given up by us without a fight. The Southern Confederacy appears to be suffering under a stroke of paralysis. The end of the war w^d seem to be near at hand, its result our entire subjugation, and all the accompanying wretchedness. This state is filling with S[outh] C[arolina] refugees. What is to become of them or of us? The last mad proposition of our government, to arm the slaves, will only hasten the general dissolution and ruin of the framework of society. I do not know but that the strong hand of the United States law and authority would be preferable to the miserable prospect in store for us under Jefferson Davis and his bankrupt and reckless crew. I have no confidence in them. In fact, I believe Gen. Lee is the only man in authority in whom I do place much confidence.

"But I do love the South. I did hope she would in some way compel a recognition of her rights from the North in this struggle —tho' I never foresaw such a glowing future for her as our leaders and secessionists predicted. The spirit in which the Northern people began and have carried the war on, has alienated my feelings entirely from them, and this last refusal on Lincoln's part to enter into any negotiations for Peace has confirmed and rooted my aversion to them as a people. I look at the prospect of Reconstruction, either by our subjugation or by negotiation with extreme aversion. And if the stars and stripes again wave over this unhappy land I, for one, shall want to leave it forever.

"I suppose that all the anguish caused by the losses and bloodshed of this four years war will be as nothing to the profound bitterness of soul which will come upon unhappy Southerners in case of reconstruction. I have no doubt that to many of them

Death would be far preferable. I cannot bear to contemplate the picture—I dare not—

"God in his infinite mercy prevent it!"

VI

Ten days later her fears were in no way soothed by the news that General Sherman had marched into North Carolina from further south.

"Sherman has Fayetteville and we have heartrending accounts of the destruction of private and public property in that town. . . . All this we could endure if the end might be *independence of the South,* but to endure all this and yet be compelled to reunion! The thought is almost maddening.

"Troops have been hurrying down towards Raleigh all the past week. Those that have passed thro' this place are chiefly Wheeler's cavalry. Our whole town turned out to see and feed them. The streets were lined with girls offering smiles, food and flowers. It gives one a cheering sensation to see so many gallant fellows eager to fight and hopeful. But we fear they will be greatly outnumbered. In a few weeks they may be all retrograding in despair. I feel, the nearer the crisis approaches, more than ever determined to *hope* for the South. I must believe in her ultimate success. I *cannot* give it up."

Five days later she made this brief entry:

"Today we have buried the remains of our gallant friend, Col. Ed Mallett. May God help his widow and his orphan children. Killed at Bentonsville below Raleigh in a desperate fight between Johnson and Sherman. We retained the field, but Sherman moved off to Goldsboro where he is joined by Schofield and will refit his army. It is not known certainly whether he will come on to Raleigh or go on to join Grant at Richmond."

The detachments of Confederate cavalry which were coming through Chapel Hill at this period were not all popular with the North Carolina people—Governor Vance once wrote President Jefferson Davis threatening to have them arrested as marauders;

but Cornelia was delighted when her brother Charles invited two passing members of Wheeler's cavalry to stay overnight, because they proved to be from Alabama, her husband's state, and were "quiet respectable nice men." They were named Baker and Saunders of Dover P.O., Russell County, Alabama. They were veterans of three years' service. They said this was the first house where they had been kindly entertained.

"Poor fellows! they seemed so thankful," wrote Cornelia in her diary. "Great numbers of soldiers have been passing thro' this past week—supply trains, artillery, etc. Everybody on the streets feeding them."

VII

And then came the collapse of the Confederacy in April, 1865. Soon afterward Cornelia made these notes in her diary, recording for the first time a name that was soon to split the community.

"To-day—being Easter Monday the Federal troops under Genl. Atkins, part of Kilpatrick's command, entered C. H. and took quiet possession! A memorable day! Every house has a guard! . . ."

"April 30. It is all over! Johnson has surrendered. Peace is come—but what a peace! How different from what our hopes have so fondly pictured. The South lies prostrate—exhausted—helpless! . . . We seem to be aghast and stunned. . . . Every now and then squads of Lee's men come walking sadly and slowly along —paroled—going home. Home! Many of them have no home left to go to. Houses are burned, families dispersed."

In a notebook in which she was accustomed to record reflections arising from her avid reading, she thus reviewed on May 4, 1865, the last three weeks of the dying Confederacy as sensed from and in Chapel Hill:

"On Sunday morning, April 9th, Gov. Swain left for Hillsboro to see and confer with [Governor] Graham, leaving us all in a pitiable state of conjecture and uncertainty. Next day we heard he had gone to Raleigh, and next we heard that Johnson's army was retreating before Sherman, now advancing upon Raleigh from

Goldsboro. Soon this last was confirmed by our *retreating* army. On the 13th the soldiers and the supply trains began to pour thro'. What a spectacle for us it was. Still, they were all cheerful and yet confident. Next came a whisper of Lee's surrender, of the fall of Petersburg and Richmond.

"Wheeler's men and Hoke's brigade, who were passing thro', rejected it all however as a Yankee lie, and so we kept on trying to hope. On Friday 14—the renowned guerilla leader *Wheeler* himself came in—and Gov. Swain arrived at home, having been below R[aleigh] and had an interview with Sherman himself— and negotiated for the preservation of Raleigh and of Chapel Hill.[1]

"Wheeler and his men laid here till Sunday, having pickets out on every road and really seemed disposed to fortify the hill and have a fight here. The whole town was busy day and night cooking and feeding the men. My heart yearned toward every one of them, tho' they carried off many horses and mules from the country round.

"Easter Sunday. Wheeler called in his pickets and moved off by two o'c. And that evening after an hour or two's silence and quiet

1. Elsewhere Mrs. Spencer wrote: "The Governor liked to think himself important, liked to be summoned to a council of wise men, liked to tell of his exploits when he returned.

"We were a simple folk in Chapel Hill in those days. I think it likely that we a trifle over-estimated his influence and importance, and that he did too. . . . Governor Swain's visit to Sherman's camp below Raleigh just before his advance upon that city . . . . was to him the most interesting event of his life. He regarded it as a State negotiation of the greatest significance and of infinite value to Raleigh and to the University.

"It is likely that he did save Chapel Hill and the University from pillage and ruin by his personal intercession with Sherman.

"As to Raleigh, I do not imagine that he or Graham, or any other private citizen, could have modified Sherman's plans in the slightest degree. The State government had collapsed: the State Executive was in retreat; Raleigh people closed their window blinds and locked their front doors. The dogs crept under shelter; not a human being was visible that bright April morning when Sherman's advance guard rode up Fayetteville Street.

"Gov. Swain stood alone in front of the State House and surrendered the keys, and therewith the whole city, to the officer in command. It was the most exciting moment of his life."

in the place, a dozen Yankee bluejackets dashed in from the Raleigh road and we were captured."

VIII

"Monday [April] 17. Kilpatrick's cavalry, 4000, marched in. Guards were set at every house and we in town were treated with the utmost civility, thanks to Gov. Swain's interference. They remained 2½ weeks, and in that time the surrounding country was completely stripped bare of everything, houses were ransacked and plundered—corn, oats, fodder, flour, meat, everything eatable carried off. My soul sickened to see the marauders coming in day after day from every road, loaded with spoils. Much of what was so ruthlessly taken was wantonly wasted. The Negroes and prostitutes round the town were enriched with clothing of every sort and food.

"Genl. Atkins, commanding this brigade, and many of his officers seemed to be gentlemen, and deplored all this as one of the inevitable accompaniments of war. They visited some of our families and were extremely courteous and were treated with courtesy. The brigade was composed chiefly of western men— Ohio and Michigan—and they talked moderately and generously. I saw none but privates, who all spoke well and behaved well. Our guard was Oliver Fox (shoemaker) from Jackson, Mich. But all this civility to us could not keep my mind from the country round us where our friends were being robbed and insulted, *women outraged*, negroes carried off, property destroyed. I think I never spent a more wretched fortnight in all my life.

"Meanwhile each day brought fresh rumors. Johnson had surrendered—he had not—President Davis was a prisoner, or he had escaped. Hampton and Wheeler and Johnson were all at daggers drawing. Every wild and absurd story was afloat—Davis seen sitting crying in the streets of Greensboro, etc., etc. Lincoln's death was classed among these canards, and when his murder was ascertained beyond a doubt it only added to the horror of the time.

"At last on the 3rd of May Atkins received orders to leave for

Greensboro, and the cloud of locusts removed, except a guard of 35 men left for the University.

"On the 5th came thro' Couch's Brigade of infantry, and we were all supplied with guards until they had passed. What a most imposing and affecting spectacle is a moving army. What sights have we not seen in this quiet and remote village. . . .

"While the bluejackets were stationed here, riding to and fro, triumphant, marauding, secure, every now and then came walking wearily by squads of Lee's army, paroled, straggling homewards, foot-sore, penniless, despondent. Many of them had no homes to go to, their houses having been burned and their families houseless. . . . I went out to speak to them in every instance, to shake hands and say a kind word, and offer them something to eat. We fed a number of them. Our Michigan guard seemed struck by our feeling for them and said it was not so at the North—that soldiers were treated there with very little consideration.

"Some of Wheeler's men while here, and when the final news of Lee's surrender came as certain, said they had absolutely nowhere on earth to go, and knew not what to do. One of them said he had a 25 ct. Confederate note and that was all he possessed in the world. Lee's men told us that for five days before the end they had lived on parched corn, and Major Steadman of Fayette[ville?] said he and his men were so weak for want of food they could hardly sit in their saddles at the last charge. They all looked wasted.

"Oh our God! What sins we must have been guilty of, that we should be so humbled by Thee now.

"I feel a good deal as I did when my beloved M[agnus] died— as if something I had watched and loved and hoped and prayed for so long—was dead, was dead, and I had lost an incentive to prayer, or to exertion of any kind.

"May 7, '65, Sunday. I walked this evening alone, all over the hill back of our house where a reg^t was lately encamped. Not a blade of grass, a shrub, or leaf of any kind is to be found there. The ground is stamped as smooth and bare as a floor. A profound depression has seized upon me. I see before us only humiliation, privation, and a life of continued toil. This Southern land is ruined for this and the coming generation. I feel the overthrow of the Confederacy as keenly as if I had embarked in Secession with all my heart at the first, which was not so.

"The whole frame-work of our social system is dissolved. The Negroes are free, leaving their homes with very few exceptions, and these exceptions are only for a time. No one has any money. Not many have enough to live on till harvest. No one knows what is to be our condition—how we are to be treated by our conquerors. What arrears of taxes, what new ones, are to be demanded. We lie apparently quite at their mercy. The whole of this so lately flushed, defiant, hopeful, scornful South lies prostrate, cowed, submissive. ..."

IX

Commencement week had been for years Chapel Hill's eagerly anticipated festal occasion, but in this year of 1865 it was scant and gloomy. The graduates numbered only four. The total enrollment was scarcely a dozen students. Cornelia attended the exercises, and although the campus trees and lawn were as green as ever, she came away in low spirits, her mind filled with foreboding. "I can easily imagine," she wrote, "that insanity is lying in wait for those who brood over the condition of our country. *South.*"

Her next entry was made on June 8. In it she drew this picture of the inertia and slackness that were paralyzing the rural South: "I walked with Miss Nancy, Jane Cave and June down to Revd. Mr. Masons to spend the day. Very little pleasure properly so-called, but some amusement and food for curious speculation. Here are people who have had an independent and handsome property for years, living without anything but the barest comforts of life. '*Comforts!*' I don't call 6 or 8 or 10 great feather beds in such weather as this *comforts.* Homespun pillow-cases, sheets and counterpanes, not a chair but a split bottom in the house, not a fork but a two-pronged iron, not six tumblers nor a single set of table ware of any sort, not a carpet or a curtain or a napkin, not a castor, not a single article of luxury in the house—not even a common rocking chair. There is always something that chokes me about such places—a want of *civilization* apparent. You walk out on the piazzas. There are good shade trees and good grass; generally a prettily situated yard. But weeds in every fence corner, fence high. You climb over a low place—left purposely and the rails worn white and smooth with climbing, to the garden—where you find an ocean of *cabbages* and very little else. A great quantity of sage bushes, some balm, mint and lavender, a straggling lark-spur, a hollyhock or two, a few rows of onions, a potato bed, and a cucumber vine or two. *Weeds* every-where out of doors, *flies* everywhere indoors. You sit about uneasily, walk round, go to the water-bucket every half-hour, pick up an old fly-specked news-paper, pick up a copy of Spurgeon or an odd volume of Rollin, or the great Iron Wheel or The History of the World, or Josephus, or some equally sprightly reading for a blazing summer's day. You watch the clock. You watch the chickens in the yard with a feverish interest. Or your eyes stray away to the hot fields, over which wheeling turkey-buzzards cast momentary spots of shadow, to the distant woods, to the wheat fields ripe for the harvest. You specu-late on the chance of there being any ripe red-plums in yonder thicket. You wonder if anybody ever does ride along that hot lane. You ask yourself why people build their barns and stables within 20 yards of their houses. You watch the half-naked black wench churning in the shade of the old locust or catalpa near the well. You are suspicious of the cookery going on in that black kitchen, where you see even more flies than in the house. And finally the wonder grows till it crushes your mental faculties how people *can* live there and live *so*.

"You are summoned to dinner by $12\frac{1}{2}$, and are hungry. You sit down in a room with two feather beds, an enormous chest, a loom, a red-painted cupboard, and an immense and exceedingly dirty fireplace, in it—to a small square pine table which does duty sometimes to sit on, sometimes to iron on, sometimes to cut out on. You have a square of bacon in a wilderness of collard leaves at one end, an immense dish of hard boil'd irish potatoes on the other, and a tin pie plate full of corn bread. A great negro with sweat pouring down her face, sleeves rolled up, bare-foot and with her dress only partly pinned together in front and not overly clean, waves away the flies with a peach-switch. Another hands water. The guests have cloudy blown glass tumblers, the mistress of the house, with her youngest child on her lap, with a greasy mouth and what Swift or Sterne would call a sn—ty nose, is accommodated with a white tea-cup. For dessert we have a cherry-pie, crust as thick as a board and as heavy, sweetened with sorghum and plenty of milk. Thus we dine in barbaric state. . . .

"And in this very way live thousands of our Southern people whom Northern people envy because they have niggers to wait on them. People who are or have been worth from 10 to 50 thousand dollars. How many such a meal I have eaten. Its only good side is that you are generally—always I may say—heartily welcomed. Stranger or not, there are no apologies, no embarrassment, you are made at home. Everything about the house is at your service. Your visit is taken as a compliment and you leave, pleased with the simplicity and hospitality of your entertainers and a longing to show them a better way."

x

This long and acid description of an Orange County farm was symptomatic of a reaction that Cornelia Spencer was passing through. Defeat had shaken her faith in hallowed Southern institutions. At the moment she was disillusioned and disposed to be critical of all things wearing a Southern label. For example, this was her review of a volume called *Leisure Hours* by Martha Haines Butt:

"I saw this book at Mr. Mason's, and was glad to have a look at it, having seen it much puffed by some Richmond paper a year or two ago. I was utterly disappointed, tho' I ought not to have been. I ought to know by this time that a *Southern* book is in 99 cases out of 100 the merest trash as to thought, the merest pretence as to originality, the merest batch of blunders as to grammar and style, the merest farrago of superficiality and conceit. . . . A bigger book of stale trash I have never met with, and the dedication to *Narcissa Saunders,* whom I remember here at Commencement just 11 years ago, is as flat and fulsome as it well can be. . . . Oh, beloved and sunny South-land that I love, and love more now in thy day of humiliation and woe and ruin than ever before, thy day of regeneration and renovation will never dawn till thou hast learned to dig deep and lay thy foundations broad and firm, learned to educate thy children thoroughly, learned to distinguish gold from gilding, silver from tinsel. Why, we are 50 years behind the Northern people in our standards of taste, 50 years behind them as writers, thinkers or workers."

But she was too ardent a Southerner long to maintain this vein of condemnation, and she felt compelled to add this consoling Calvinistic footnote as an offset to her momentary bitterness:

"We are a *better* people, however, thank God. With all our faults, sins, weaknesses, we have this day a purer church, and a higher morality than the Yankees, and if with their intellectual superiority must come such infidelities—such moral and religious heresies—I pray that the South may stay where she is, be still satisfied to cry up Martha Butt and Marion Harland and Augusta Evans as the best novelists and essayists of the day, still accept such a phrase as 'Thine eyes doth make' as good grammar—, but withal bring up their children to fear God and keep His Commandments."

6

A Girl, a Uniform, and a Horse

I

IN STORY-BOOK wars the invader is often smitten by the bright eyes of a daughter of the conquered people, and at last marries her. This very story-book story was enacted before the astonished eyes of the inhabitants of Chapel Hill just as the Civil War ended. Scene by scene the drama was witnessed by Cornelia Spencer, who not only encouraged the romance but to a degree took part in it.

As already related in excerpts from Mrs. Spencer's diary, the 4,000 men belonging to Kilpatrick's Federal cavalry who swarmed into the village just as the Confederate horsemen under General Wheeler rode out of it on Easter Sunday, 1865, were led by a polite and dignified young officer, Brigadier General Smith D. Atkins, of Freeport, Illinois, editor of a newspaper there. One of General Atkins' first acts after taking possession of the village was to call formally at the house of the University's president, Governor David L. Swain. Most of the inhabitants of Chapel Hill had, on hearing of the approach of Sherman's army, hidden their most valuable possessions. But somehow neither President Swain nor any member of his family had the forethought to hide his comely young daughter, Eleanor. Hence when President Swain advanced to receive the Yankee officer, Ellie, as she was called, managed to be present, having no intention of perishing in a slow death of curiosity as to what the invader might look like.

President Swain had for years been collecting documents which he one day intended to use in writing a history of the Revolutionary War as it affected North Carolina. One of these documents was the order book that had belonged to Lord Cornwallis in his march through North Carolina. When in the course of a friendly conversation General Atkins showed interest in this relic, President Swain offered to show it to him and called his daughter Eleanor to fetch it.

"The young lady did so, perhaps not unwilling to have a look at the Yankee general," wrote Mrs. Spencer afterwards. "She threw up her head and marched in with great display of hauteur. An introduction was unavoidable, which was more than the Governor had intended. They 'changed' eyes at first sight, and a wooing followed on that first meeting which greatly incensed all who looked on, including the Federal army, and gave Governor Swain and his wife as much uneasiness as anything short of a death in the family could have done." [1]

The wooing was short, lasting scarcely three weeks, and it was anything but furtive. Every evening General Atkins sent the regimental band to play in President Swain's front yard. Ostensibly this was in compliment to a citizen who had been coöperative in every particular, but no one was misled. The whole village, occupying brigade and inhabitants alike, knew that whenever the band played, it was General Atkins serenading not the University President but the fair Eleanor, his daughter.

This music was played daily just across the street from Cornelia Spencer's home. The guard stationed at her father's house there (first a private named Fry, then another named Hendrix—both from Michigan) was distressed when he discovered that Mrs. Spencer got no pleasure from these musical offerings played so close to her.

"Our military captors," she wrote, "were very civil to the townspeople. They were under strict orders and behaved well. The officers called, and chatted pleasantly, and petted the children; the privates lounged in and out of the yards, and appeared in all respects like human beings."

1. For a confirmatory picture of the events described by Mrs. Spencer, see the notes in the latter pages of this volume.

One evening during a concert the honest young guard at the Phillips house came up to the porch.

"Can't you hear that, Mrs. Spencer?"

"No, not a note."

"Well, I declare, I hate to think about it. I'd give $200 if you could have your hearing."

She so recorded his naïve remark in her diary.

II

But elsewhere the relations between the invaders and the invaded were not so friendly. Among the Federal forces of occupation were officers and men who believed that the South had been guilty of starting the war, had maintained it in a spirit of pride and arrogance, and should be punished for it by humiliation and ostracism; in Chapel Hill itself were residents and refugees who resented the occupation of the village by this brigade of Sherman's army as a seizure by barbarians, and who remained bitter and resentful. Both parties watched with hot eyes the courtship of President Swain's daughter by the brigade commander, and when General Atkins made the Governor a present of a fine horse, the community buzzed; when the General followed this with the gift of another fine horse to Ellie, the community rocked; and gossip, accompanied by the sound of hissing, ran through the village like fire along a powder fuse. For it was said and repeated that both horses had come from Sherman's Southern loot; in fact, that both horses had either been robbed or forcibly taken from Southern owners. Whether or not this whisper was a true charge, there was no way of disproving it, and none to deny it. And so resentment, finding no nourishment in the behavior of the occupying Yankee cavalry, fed on this rumor and nursed it until its implications had become monstrous.

For accepting these horses from the blue-coated Northerner, Ellie, being only a young girl, was excused as having been swept off her feet by a uniform and brass buttons; but for Governor Swain no excuse was found. And slowly a weight of anger accumulated against the Governor of which he, ungainly and bland, was at first but little aware. In Governor Swain's view the war was over. He had in his heart never favored secession; and now that the lately warring armies were streaming homewards, he was happy to help onward the movements of reconciliation and re-habilitation; and he no doubt fondly hoped that the gift of this beautiful horse was a symbol of the brotherhood that was once more to unite the two halves of the nation.

Tragic Governor Swain! How could he know that this horse was to wreck the latter end of his long career, was to fill his later years with defeat, and was at last to cause his death?

III

As for Mrs. Spencer, who at the age of forty was coming to be a power in the community, she was at first wholly on the side of the lovely Southern girl and her Yankee lover; for having been cheated of the fullness of wedded happiness, she drew a partial compensation from watching the bliss of others. On June 11, 1865, she wrote in her diary:

"Have just seen E. H. Swain dressed and waiting for Genl. Atkins, who drove into town a few minutes ago. Dressed in a lavender barege and pink ribbons, with an oleander blossom in her bosom. So bright, so happy. Are there any days more happy in life than such? Has life anything better? I mean as to this world's happiness. Soberly, I think not.

"There is a pleasure in yielding to God's will even in the fur-nace. There is a pleasure even when stripped of everything dear and pleasant and hopeful in life in entire self-renunciation—entire resignation to God, a deeper, holier, more fruitful pleasure than anything this world alone can give; and from that depth upwards—or rather, I should say, from that height downwards—range a thousand different scales and degrees of pleasure, all centering in duty and all reaching out and away from the world. I speak not now of these, but of such sinless happiness as this life, this world alone, gives. God has ordained many for us, but of

them all, among them all, the brightest sunniest picture is that of
a young woman, with love-lighted eye and throbbing heart, prettily
and tastefully adorned waiting to see her lover. I have really a
great respect for *true Love* and all its belongings. Amo amantes."

IV

General Atkins carried on his courtship of Ellie until May 3,
after having entered Chapel Hill on April 16. He was then ordered
to another post. As soon as he was gone, Ellie wrote her parents
a note announcing that the General had proposed marriage to her
and that she had become engaged to him. She added a reminder
that she was now twenty-one years old. In agitation her father
took this letter to Mrs. Spencer. He also showed her two tender
notes written to Ellie by the General. Ellie then indignantly wrote
Mrs. Spencer on May 12, 1865:

"I never was more surprised, provoked, or distressed than when
I found out this evening that Pa had been showing letters (to
me) of all things on earth the most sacred—letters written for me
alone, and only trusted to my father as an act of duty, without
the thought that any but himself should read them. It was enough
to have him expose the *first* letter, but past comprehension the
second. It takes from the letters their true value to have them reduced to matter-of-fact, as much as to expose to the world's eye
the hidden treasures of the heart.

"As to what people say, Pa's great failing is to care too much.
As for myself, but one voice can prevent this affair, and that is
higher than man. No indeed, I have all I desire—a most noble
heart and mind intrusted to my keeping. I hope you did not think
me so wanting in true refinement of feeling that I should have been
willing to allow this exhibition.

"This note was written last night under the act of provocation.
I think better of it this morning, and send his photograph for your
inspection—and a very poor one it is. The upper part of the face
bears some resemblance. It was a gradual affair. Ellie is caught

in her own net. I had nothing to hide when the Yankees came except myself. I had no fear of being stolen, but see the result!"

On the back of this note Mrs. Spencer wrote a rhyme celebrating "General Atkins' Surrender." This is one stanza:

> The best artillery is found to be the oldest
> And peace hath conquests, too, by no means narrow.
> The wisest soldier and perchance the boldest
> Yields to a pair of blue eyes and a bow-and-arrow.

It can thus be seen that Mrs. Spencer was not opposed to the match. Governor Swain, however, was disturbed.

"I have never seen any man so deeply concerned and agitated," wrote Mrs. Spencer years later, "as Gov. Swain at this unexpected denouement. His whole mind and thoughts had been concentrated for weeks upon public affairs and the fate of the University. Suddenly his tenderest affections were touched, and in his own household he was called upon to act in a matter requiring the most delicate and cautious management. . . . He did not calculate on the continuance of the exasperated state of feeling left by the war in those who had lost sons, husbands, brothers, houses and fortunes and who had been subjected to insult and degradation."

Governor Swain was prudent enough to have General Atkins' prospects and antecedents investigated, and he satisfied himself that his daughter's suitor was a proper and well-connected young man. The Governor had never been accustomed to oppose any of his children's desires. Hence he was not long in giving his consent.

"Governor Swain believed this marriage," wrote Mrs. Spencer, "was but the first of many others like it to take place all over the South; that our Peace was to flow like a river, and that North and South were coming together *at once,* to be more firmly united than ever. He was a sagacious man and accustomed to calculate possibilities very closely and accurately, but he did not once dream of the party issues that were to spring up and divide the country even more effectually than the war, nor of the bitterness that was to be engendered and revived."

v

August, 1865, came, and with it the definite announcement that
Ellie Swain and General Atkins would be married in the course
of the month. One day Ellie brought over to Mrs. Spencer *John
Brent*, a novel, just given to her by her fiancé. Mrs. Spencer dismissed it in her diary as "pure Yankee, pure infidel, and Uni-
versalist infidel at that." Then Ellie sent over for Mrs. Spencer's
inspection a box of wedding gifts received from the General's
friends at home. On the same day Mrs. Spencer noted in her
journal: "I went down to see Mrs. Woods, sitting propped with
pillows by the side of the cradle, with a peach branch in her hand
keeping the flies off her dying baby—poor little emaciated creature
—and she as wasted. A sad, sad sight."

A few days later her feelings boiled over in this entry: "I have
come to the uncomfortable conclusion that the great American
people is a failure. I see in these days so much meanness, in-
justice, servility, malignity, narrow-minded bigotry and selfishness, envy, hatred and malice both *North and South* that I cannot
help thinking we must be a radically mean people.

"I have just read a long letter from Kemp B. to Sue [Kemp P.
Battle, of Raleigh, subsequently president of the University of
North Carolina, to his sister at Chapel Hill] (from New York)
taking strong ground in favor of a hearty union with the Northern
people, inviting and assisting emigration South, calling in capital,
welcoming free labor, opening up every source of national prosperity, and turning over a new leaf generally.

"It is all true—good sense every word of it—but for my own
single self I desire to have as little as possible to do with the
Northern people! My mind has not cooled down from the ire and
agitation of such a war as ours. Business however must go on—
the world is turning round, and we must turn with it. But tho'
my reason consents, I feel sad, and sore, and bitter. I do not love
my country. I feel rather as if I had no country to love and ven-
erate. . . ."

This passage might be regarded now as the outburst of a temporarily indignant woman. Yet it unquestionably mirrored the feelings at that moment not only of a considerable part of the Chapel Hill population but of the Southern people. General Sherman's destroying march from Georgia through the Carolinas was no doubt a powerful stroke in a military sense; yet it left behind not only a trail of destruction but of fiery though choked animosity. Then when it became evident that the lately seceded states were going to be militarily occupied for some time by the victorious Federal army, and that though a military peace had come, it was not to be a healing peace, numbers of the Southern people believed they were being needlessly humiliated. All during the summer of 1865 this resentment mounted, so that at the moment Ellie Swain and her Northern suitor were married it was probably at its apex. Mrs. Spencer attended this wedding in the company of her brother, Samuel F. Phillips, who had been auditor in the war cabinet of Governor Vance, and this is her journal's description of it:

"We went to E. H. Swain's wedding Wednesday night, 23^d [August, 1865]. Married in the face—in the very teeth—of all this bitterness and woeful humiliation, to the Yankee general who entered C.H. at the head of 4000 cavalry April 17. They 'fell in love' at first sight on occasion of his first call upon the Gov., and now are married. Very, very few people went to the wedding, tho' very general invitations were issued and a grand supper prepared. A few *faculty families*—Gov. and Mrs. Graham from H[illsboro], and Betty Scott. It passed off very well, whatever we might think of it all. We enjoyed the supper and spent the evening pleasantly. Gen. Atkins is a handsome man, rather grave in expression, sedate and courteous in manner. Elly looked well— beautifully dressed." (In 1869 Mrs. Spencer added: "One of the *notabilia* at the supper table was a large and handsomely decorated cake, sent by the *Freedmen* as a bridal present to their deliverer and liberator. There were a number of gallant ex-Confederate soldiers among the guests.") On the 25th Mrs. F[etter] had a party for her; 28th, Mrs. H[ubbard] gave one. Same people invited to each. A good deal of bitter feeling expressed in town about it all. Invitations were *spit upon* in one or two houses!

"I went to see Mary Mallett the day after to amuse her with an acc^t of matters. . . . Ann Saunders and Caroline Mallett were there, very *hot* against Ellie.

"The only way we can find an apology for it all is in believing honestly in the *Love* which appears to have brought it about. Let us all think and speak respectfully of a genuine love-affair. Since the world began it has been a wonderful agent for good, sometimes for evil, but *true Love* has done more good than harm. If this couple truly love each other I have no fears for them. . . . [August] 30th: Elly came over to tell us goodbye—left for *Illinois* at 2."

In 1869 Mrs. Spencer added: "Of this marriage I must be permitted to say that so far it has proved a happy one, and productive of nothing but happiness to those immediately concerned." She corresponded with both Ellie and General Atkins for many years.

The happy pair rode away from Chapel Hill without a soul to gainsay them. But bitterness and frustration, post-war products in every age, had to find a victim upon whom to wreak themselves, and this victim was kindly old Governor Swain.

7

After the War

I

IT IS A FACT well recognized that although war may be, in the words attributed to General Sherman, hell, the peace that follows war may be even worse. Mrs. Spencer, then a widow living with her child in her father's house and shut off from the active currents of contemporary life not only by that circumstance but by her increasing deafness, was in a measure able to keep up with the events that immediately followed the Civil War through her nearness to and friendship with Governor Swain, who had continued as president of the University all during the racking years of the war. She heard detailed stories from him at the end of June, 1865, just after he had completed a stay of several weeks North. In New York he had dined with Horace Greeley, and had had a talk with Bancroft, the historian. At West Point he had associated with military notables "on the pleasantest terms." In Boston he had dined with Governor John A. Andrew, war governor of Massachusetts.

"I was treated," Governor Swain told her, "with marked courtesy and hospitality. Every attention was shown me by the best representatives of Northern society. Yet I found it galling, and was glad to get back South. In our present low estate down here, we hardly realize that the last four years, so ruinous to us, have to the North been years of progress and power, with a vast increase in wealth and luxury."

He said he had been impressed rather favorably with President Andrew Johnson, to whom he had readily gained admittance because the Negro doorman at the White House had been in Chapel Hill several years before with President Buchanan and recognized Governor Swain. "Johnson is a man of decided ability and great firmness and decision of character," said Governor Swain. "And little likely to be influenced by any man, *especially if of gentle breeding.*" This last phrase the Governor particularly emphasized. The Governor said to Mrs. Spencer that he had had to listen to "the most atrocious tales" circulated about the South and its people, "while nothing we can say of their behavior to us— ravages of their armies etc.—can get even a hearing."

In her journal Cornelia noted: "Prof. Hepburn writes to C[harles] from Carlisle [Pa.] in the same terms of the bitterness of feeling against us there, and adds that as usual the ministers and the women are the bitterest, and lead in the fierceness of accusation." These rumors and rancors so much ruffled her feathers that she put down this outburst: "Prof. H. tells of reunion of the churches as something to be desired. *I trust it will never be. Let our religions be as far asunder as the poles.*"(!)

II

As July, 1865, advanced and midsummer heat enveloped the village, she noted that many deaths were being reported, especially among the Negroes. "They are dying off rapidly, poor things," she wrote. "Freedom is not what they expected as yet. It means now unlimited liberty to run about day and night, to expose themselves to all manner of company, to disease, to demoralization in general." One day near the middle of the month she walked over the campus with her mother, and noted the air of desolation that hung around the buildings.

"A group of Negroes was sitting on the steps of the old South [building]," she wrote. "Every kind of trash, *débris* of the Yankee camp, was scattered over the grounds; an immense mudhole at the well, with a great sow wallowing in it. In the library there is the utmost disorder, as if a party of madmen had encamped there; the basement rooms covered with horse litter; the grounds so forlorn; shrubbery untrimmed, turf destroyed, walks washed up, grass grown, windows open—broken. We had a sad and thoughtful walk. The future of this place is so entirely dependent on the life of the University that we cannot look at these empty halls without deep concern." This was written the day before the University opened a half-year term, with just twenty-two students enrolled. Evidently there had arrived a crisis in its life.

Since the early days of the war Chapel Hill had been sought as a desirable haven by a number of families from the eastern half and coastal parts of the state. They were known as "refugees." On July 2, 1865, Mrs. Spencer wrote this note full of overtones, concerning one of them:

"Today I attended the funeral services at Miss Nancy's [Miss Nancy Hilliard kept the local tavern] of a Newbern refugee—a very aged gentleman, a Dr. Boyd. He had been here three years, and in that time has made no acquaintances, a most reserved, solitary and self-enclosed gentleman, one of the old school of stately politeness. He was one of the seconds in the famous duel of Henry and Stanley some 40 odd years ago. It was a sad funeral —an aged man alone in the world, quite among strangers, laid to his rest far from home and with no one to drop a tear on his grave."

Two weeks later the community became suddenly aware that under Reconstruction the life of the University was threatened, and that most of its faculty members might soon be without a salary or other means of livelihood. President Swain so confessed to her in a talk that for her had important consequences in more than one way. She told about it in her journal thus:

"Gov. Swain returned from R[aleigh] last night and I had the pleasure of hearing him talk this morning. It is one of my few pleasures. He tells me the University has lost all its endowment fund—has absolutely nothing to go upon but the tuition fees. What is to become of the faculty no one can tell. . . . Gov. showed me some letters of Gov. Vance which increase my opinion of his sense of ability. He urges me to write for him a history of the last 90 days of the war in N. C., giving the full material in letters, facts, etc. . . . . New York Tribune of 8th giving account of the hanging of Mrs. Surratt and 3 others—men—implicated in the murder of Lincoln. Gov. S. thinks she ought not to have been hung. I think it quite likely she was innocent to a degree that ought to have saved her from such a death. I can easily imagine how she fell into such condemnation, ardently loving the cause of Secession and bringing herself to think that Lincoln's death could be its salvation. Interest in Booth—led on step by step—oh our God! lead us *not* into temptation."

III

The depression that hung over the whole village was bound to have its effect on one having as much sensibility as Mrs. Spencer; and in the midst of notes about the externals of contemporary life she suddenly wrote down this confession:

"I feel sometimes such an impatience of my life and its lot as I can hardly describe. I want to go and see and do something 'better than I have known.' From my window I see a pretty little narrow vista of hills and woods, very narrow and no ways uncommon, but that often sets me to longing for wide rivers rolling among mountains, lakes, parks, and some of the beautiful scenery that is so lavishly scattered in some parts of the world, but of w^h *this* part presents so little. I want to go, to take wings and fly, and leave these poor and sordid occupations. . . . I believe in the purifying influences of honest steady work, especially for such a temperament as mine. I am better—*happier*—at work, I know; and, thank God, I can take comfort in a sunset, or the effect of light and shade on one tree, or in the slope of one hill. But I cannot help feeling as if there were some rooms vacant and closed, some faculties rusting, some feelings getting narrowed. My life is passing in a narrow circle of ideas, and some of its most pure and precious enjoyments are unknown to me."

Though Mrs. Spencer was rarely seen in public without a smiling face and though her conversation when in friendly company was always cheerful and humorous, her journal shows she often had hours, and even days, of deep depression. These descents into Avernus were sometimes due to reminders of her widowed state or of her deafness; at other times they seemed to be without a cause, or were rooted in a sensitive, overwrought temperament. For these attacks of melancholy she knew the cure, as she wrote in a vein of self-accusation:

"These feelings surge up now and then, and overflow a bitterness into my cup, but they are only at intervals and momentary. I believe I do generally go to my work deeply and humbly thankful that I have it—that I *can* do it."

At intervals during the summer of 1865 she had long conversations with President Swain, who remained optimistic even in the face of evidence that the federally appointed governor of the state, W. W. Holden, was hostile to the University and to the ex-leaders of the late Confederacy. At this stage of affairs President Swain could find little to do except to pay visits to Raleigh; and oftener than any other citizen of Chapel Hill he went to Washington and New York. On his return from such centers he liked to show Mrs. Spencer letters and appeals for advice from bewildered or ruined Southerners.

"I despise," she indignantly wrote, "that bringing of all our Southern gentlemen to the bar of the United States government to *beg for pardon* with all the powers of my mind and heart and soul. It emanates from a meanness and littleness of soul that is far below my comprehension and which is eminently characteristic of the universal Yankee nation—a people utterly incapable of a noble or generous emotion *as a nation*—though I believe there are many individuals among them more generous and liberal than many at the South."

With these indignant comments on the political situation she often mingled in her journal equally fiery blasts concerning literary likes and dislikes; at this period she was reading copiously in books found in her father's collection or in the libraries maintained by the two student societies of the University. For example, she could not abide the prevailing devotion of the intelligentsia to the poetical works of George Herbert.

"It is the fashion now," she wrote, "to quote and appear to love 'Holy Herbert.' No church novel comes out without some saintly lady who adores Herbert and Thomas à Kempis. Very much of all this is pretense, to my thinking. . . . Reading Smith's 'Lectures on Modern History' which I like very much. . . . One thing historians who write of Elizabeth of England insist upon as striking in her character—she knew how to give graciously when she found concession on her part was inevitable. She made a favor which was about to be extracted from her by the people, appear as if it was her own free bounty. I think Southerners might take a hint from this policy in their present position with regard to the Negroes. We ought to treat them graciously, kindly, and have the air of bestowing on them that which we know we will *have* to give them. Not free suffrage, I have no idea they will or ought to have that, but certain little rights and privileges which mark the free man. Let us cheer them on in their poor attempts to assert themselves, and keep them as *friends.*

"I have no sort of patience or sympathy with such squabbles as were gotten up here a fortnight since. The boys have not been punished and no ill effects have ensued, but I really despise such conflicts in which Southerners have everything to lose and nothing to gain."

The conflict referred to here was described elsewhere by Mrs. Spencer herself as a "muss" between the young white men of the town and college and the Negro freedmen who were assembled in council to elect delegates to their Raleigh convention to endeavor to obtain the right of free suffrage. "There was a general row on the occasion," wrote Mrs. Spencer. "Some heads and arms broken etc. Many fear the result will be that a Negro guard will be sent up here."

IV

On October 13, 1865, Governor Swain returned from the North where he had vainly sought loans to strengthen the steadily weakening financial position of the University. The next morning he walked across the street to give a report to Mrs. Spencer. He had to confess he had been able to raise no money in New York, where 12 per cent interest was demanded on loans made in the South. The Governor also confessed that the University was being hampered by ill-feeling shown toward it in certain parts of North Carolina itself. In her diary Mrs. Spencer made this comment:

"Elly Swain's marriage has helped this along, no doubt."

The Governor brought something to Mrs. Spencer which she prized—recent Northern newspapers, some of them church papers. These she compared with church papers coming from closer home, and was disturbed to notice that a marked post-war bitterness existed among the church members. This caused her to remark:

"While the politicians are trying to heal up matters and make friends, the churches are exhibiting the utmost intolerance and bitterness toward Southerners." She found it pleasanter to listen to Governor Swain's impressions of President Andrew Johnson as he had found him at Washington. "He [Swain] says he looks every inch *the President*. . . . The Gov. is the greatest man I know for coincidences. He is all the time meeting with something in some way connected with the past, and affording a fine peg to hang a story or narrative upon."

On the 19th Chapel Hill felt uneasy under a total eclipse of the sun. "There is more *uneasiness*," she noted, "and speculation about it than I have ever noticed before at a similar phenomenon. People's minds are in such a state of excitement—looking for something to happen continually."

On the 28th she noted that the State Reconstruction Convention at Raleigh had adjourned. It seemed to her that the Convention had been "servile in tone, and lacked both spirit and ability." [1]

And this gave her an opportunity to relieve herself of certain feelings about the state, over which she more than once felt called upon to mourn:

1. For a letter to Mrs. Spencer from Judge E. G. Reade, on the State Reconstruction Convention, see the notes in the latter pages of this volume.

"I feel ashamed of N. Carolina in some respects. She seems to lack some element of greatness. . . . She always is in the rear . . . and always contrives to get more kicks than half-pence. No state in the Confederacy did more for the cause than she, no state acted more handsomely—in her people or in her soldiers—and no state was more abused. N.C. was positively insulted by the general government of the Confederacy as unloyal, unreliable, and was generally suspected and accused of being secretly disposed toward reconstruction, and this in the face of her efforts and her sacrifices in the Southern cause. Lo!! the tide turns, the Confederacy is nowhere, the Union triumphant—now where is N.C. Favored in any respect? Ahead of anybody or anything? Found to have been worthy of praise or distinction in any quarter? Not she. She has the meanest man in the State set over her for a Provisional Governor, a man who seizes the opportunity to humiliate her still further, who retards her progress toward reconstruction in every way, irritates and oppresses her, and she is positively behind even South Carolina in her progress toward reconciliation and reunion.

"She appears neither one thing nor the other, appears great in no aspect. Her convention was servile. Her newspapers are feeble and spiteful, her people are cowed. I think she lacks *esprit,* that something without which a State or a man may be thoroughly good, honest, brave, *respectable,* but will yet lack the glance of fire, and the high and free and bold bearing that shows good blood and secures deference and a place above the salt, without having to ask for it."

v

On November 10, 1865, Mrs. Spencer wrote a significant line in her diary: "Wrote second letter to Gov. V[ance]."

This meant that she was going seriously to work collecting material for the book on the last ninety days of the war, which the Reverend Charles F. Deems proposed to publish. It also meant the launching of a long friendship and correspondence with North

Carolina's war governor, Zebulon B. Vance, who had been recently a prisoner in a Federal jail. As the year 1865 was about to die, Governor Swain brought her a book entitled *The Great March,* which apparently referred to General Sherman's recent exploit. In her journal she wrote:

"I cannot read the Yankee glorifications with any coolness. It is like enveloping oneself in a blister. How I do hate the whole Yankee nation as I lay such a book down—and feel the bitterness of death roll over me afresh as I contemplate the Southern failure, Southern errors and delusions, and Southern humiliation and ruin. . . . I hate a brutal, ignorant, hard-hearted and vulgar slave-driver, and I hate an intelligent, sprightly, eager, malicious and vicious abolitionist. I hardly know which I have the least charity for. Between them they have crushed the sunny South."

VI

Musing upon abolitionists and such made her think of New England and New England ways, and suddenly her journal darted, as it was sometimes wont to do, off at a tangent:

"The history of the religious movement in New England in the first part of the century must afford an interesting study to those who are curious in such matters. For myself it is all dust and chaff. Such themes of discussion . . . that raged furiously and split the churches into fragments, such topics as 'inability,' 'free will,' 'Election,' and the like may lie at the very roots and foundation of all orthodoxy of belief, but they do not possess any interest for my mind. . . . If God is perfect, there must be Pre-destination. Of that I am convinced and am equally convinced that Predestination does not interfere with our own free will. We exercise our will freely. How the two exist together I cannot under-take to decide. I simply believe, and am not able to argue upon it. *God is good,* whatever happens. He cannot do wrong, however it be ordered."

At the end of the year she put away the things of 1865 with this note: "Aunt Dilsey said this morning, 'Thank God we are all alive, and have got a little something to eat.' . . . We all have a new road to travel, and a pretty hard one it will be for a while. But that the South will be infinitely better off—richer, happier—ten years hence [2] than it has ever been, I do believe. God grant it, and take care of the widows and orphans."

2. In 1900 Mrs. Spencer inserted this note: "It took thirty years."

8

Days of Wrath

I

CORNELIA'S diary entry for the first Sunday of 1866 described a visit to the Dialectic library, maintained by one of the two student societies. "Walked alone up and down before the building, looking at every tree—and path and every building with the same interest we look into a friend's eyes who is talking to us. The natural objects are all there—the same great oaks, the steps, the turf. Things are so little changed, and yet so greatly. So much is gone, and so much remains. I never walk thro' those grounds without pangs of heart. There are some doors and windows in which I seem to see a familiar face and form. . . ."

In March, 1866, Governor Swain returned from a three weeks' stay in Washington and told Cornelia of his adventures, as a late rebel, in procuring admission to the presence of high officials, including Secretary Harlan. He told Cornelia he owed his interview with Harlan to the Secretary's mulatto doorkeeper and confidential servant. The Negro had recognized Governor Swain and had called him by name, explaining that he had accompanied President Buchanan to Chapel Hill in 1857 and had been kindly treated at the Swain home. Swain reported he had been able to see President Johnson three times and had been kindly received. He believed the President to be "in earnest to do the South justice and will give her her rights if man can do anything."

Swain mentioned that Governor W. A. Graham, then the actual chief executive of North Carolina, had been with him, but had not been allowed to visit any of the government departments. Swain had been permitted to enter and go through the United States Treasury building "on condition of not taking a lady along!"

On the first anniversary of the entrance of Federal troops into Chapel Hill occurred the funeral of Junius and Lewis Battle, sons of Judge William H. Battle. They had been killed in the war, the one in Maryland, the other in Pennsylvania. "The bodies," wrote Cornelia, "were brought in in plain wooden boxes on the shoulders of Confederate ex-soldiers. And truly it was a most touching sight."

II

Early in May Mrs. James Phillips, Cornelia's mother, was able to do what she had been yearning to do for several years—visit her kindred, the Vermeules and Middaghs, in New York and New Jersey. Mrs. Phillips's health had for some time been feeble and when she kissed her daughter goodby she said: "It may be a final parting, my dear, but if it is, it will not be for long." Cornelia ran back into the house to give way to tears. For several days she suffered, and confessed in her diary: "I have a dreadful sinking of the heart at times—when I am alone in this old house. I wander up and down and through it and the garden, and start at every sound. . . ."

These apprehensions, so far as they concerned her mother, were needless, for Mrs. Phillips soon recovered her health and tone. If these dim fears had been felt for Cornelia's father, Dr. James Phillips, then hale and active, they would have been more justified. But with the coming of the peaceful Chapel Hill summer these uneasy feelings passed away, and when June commencement came she was glad to see that the seniors at commencement were not giving up their usual ball. They outraged her, however, by inscribing the name of Jefferson Davis, lately the Confederate president and now an inmate of a Federal prison, among the ball-managers, and she wrote:

"President Davis! One year in close confinement as the representative of the Southern people—may God bless and support him. He was an honest president, tho' a very mistaken one. His severe imprisonment and his noble and dignified bearing and silence under it have done a great deal to warm the Southern people towards him. There is a kinder feeling for him today among those who execrated and derided his policy, than when he was in power. I am afraid we have not thought enough of him in his prison, or prayed enough for him and his family."

III

When Commencement Day came, the University's graduating seniors numbered just three. "A large crowd here," she wrote. "Many young ladies. Everything went off well. Vance's coming was a good thing. I hope it may be one of the helps to do away the prejudice existing at present against the University and the faculty." The Vance referred to here was the young ex-war governor, Zebulon B. Vance, who on this occasion spoke on "The Duties of Defeat." Vance was one of the few former Confederate officials who had survived the war with an enhanced reputation and a greater popularity. Though he and other former state leaders were trying to keep a cheerful face before the world, they were at heart worried by the outlook for the University. It had many critics and enemies. One faction, led by the Federal governor and Raleigh editor, W. W. Holden, was denouncing the University as a center of aristocracy and rebellion. Another faction was accusing it of undue sympathy with Yankees and atheists. President Swain had failed to raise needed funds at both Washington and New York. Students were not coming back in the numbers expected. Cornelia's diary at this period often contained forebodings, for she was sensitive to every influence that in any way affected the University or the village.

But in the midst of her anxieties she did not forget the young husband she had lost in Alabama. "Today, 5 years ago," said her journal, "my most dear, most beloved and mourned-for M[agnus] entered upon the rest for which he longed. I desire never to lose the memories and reflections which this anniversary and indeed this whole season of the year brings me. I do trust I shall *always* meet it with thoughtful tender dispositions, never forgetting, never repining, blessing God that I had such a husband, blessing Him for my hope in his death, blessing Him for my hope to meet him again, putting my whole trust and confidence in Him who is the husband of the widow and the father of the fatherless."

To Dr. Alexander Wilson, her father's good friend, she wrote: "And I do get horribly bemired in the Slough of Despond sometimes. To look forward and see only a life of toil, or worse, perhaps of dependence, and poorly requited toil besides—for one's self and one's children—well, never mind—there's no use writing about it. I am not afraid of work, nobody works harder than I do these days, and oh how thankful I am to have it to do!"

To Eliza North of New London, Connecticut, sister of Mrs. Elisha Mitchell, she wrote these candid confessions: "I seem to be addressing you on the other side of a great gulf—a gulf at one time impassable, but which has been bridged over, and which I do humbly and heartily pray may be filled up sometime or other. Not yet, and not now, but some day in God's own good time. Meanwhile let us send kindly messages over our bridge and along our telegraph line.

"My dear friend, I see you feel very strongly upon the subject of the 'Rebellion,' but I don't think you feel any more strongly than I do, and I am a moderate compared with many of my friends here. I am often at issue with your folks, Mary, Margaret, and Ellen, but I yield to no one in love to the South, devotion to her cause, and anguish over her humiliation. I never thought the South had any pretense of right to make war. I felt she had great provocations, but nothing that could justify an appeal to arms. . . .

"Dear Miss Eliza, can you not see how people who resisted secession, who foresaw in it nothing but ruin, yet when it became the law of the state, when our national honor was pledged to support it, sprang to arms and fought to the last gasp for the Confederacy? Yes, for North Carolinians fought for a government they did not love, and had little cause to respect, fought because their honor was involved, and because they were *Southerners*. . . .

"I believe the lying that was done by the newspaper press on both sides was enough to sink the whole continent to perdition.

"I believe that the South sinned. Sinned in her pride, her prosperity, her confidence. Sinned in the way she allowed a few fanatical demagogues to precipitate her into the war. God has humbled her. But as strongly as I feel all this, so strongly do I feel that, though we have fallen we shall rise again. God chastens whom He loves. He has a great mercy in store for us, low as we lie under His hand; and I declare to you now, that I would rather be the South in her humiliation than the North in her triumph. . . .

"We are all well, thank God, and have enough to eat, and have not been reduced to fig-leaves; though when calico was $50.00 a yard and factory cloth $25.00 there really was a danger of it. Dear Miss Eliza, let us shake hands across the gulf and say, God bless you! I do with all my heart."

IV

On July 4 of that year the Negroes of Chapel Hill were to have a grand emancipation celebration. At the head of the procession they wanted to have a great banner, and they came to Cornelia for help in making it. She worked out a design in pink and white cambric with a motto on each side. One side said, "Respect for former owners"; the other, "Our hope is in God." About a thousand freedmen were present at the postoffice, where Colonel W. S. Guthrie addressed them. After a reading of part of the Declaration of Independence, they marched out to the edge of town where lay a piece of ground bought from the Craig family for their schoolhouse. There they had dinner and further speeches from their own orators, "showing," said a note by Cornelia, "a good temper and good dispositions."

"Poor things!" she exclaimed in her diary. "I believe all decent white people are disposed kindlily towards them. I thought their procession a right affecting sight. At night Col. Guthrie let them have his large dining room to dance in."

The lack of any genuine feeling of unity pervading the nation was at this period often on her mind. "The great Union convention is now taking place at Phila[delphia]," she wrote. "S. Carolina and Mass. delegates walking in arm in arm. All such exhibitions appear to me to belong to a species of clap-trap—but if good can be effected these days by even clap-trap let us have it by all means. . . . But the elements of strife are yet abroad. . . ."

One of the books she read in the course of the warm summer of 1866 was one much discussed. Written by a Dr. Craven, it was a detailed account of the prison life of Jefferson Davis. "The surgeon," she wrote, "seems to have become captivated by his prisoner, and evidently writes from a kindly interest in him. But what shall we say of the sense of honor and decency that could induce a man to note down every day the confidential conversations held with a crushed, sick, prisoner of war, for the purpose of making a book out of them! . . . I am afraid that I am incapable of a dispassionate survey or a calm decision about anything bearing on *North and South.*"

All during this summer she wrote steadily on her book, *The Last Ninety Days of the War.* Such work was a solace to her when she was becoming so completely deaf she could not wholly follow the conversations between her old father and her little daughter June.

"Such a quiet summer!" she wrote. And then with the clairvoyant, prophetic gift that often distinguished her, she added: "How often I may look back to these days with Pa and June as halcyon times. He and she seem so fond of each other. They have long talks together on the piazza of evenings as we sit by him with his pipe. I cannot hear a word but now and then Pa laughs out and tells me some queer remark of hers."

v

In October Bishop William Mercer Green came up from Mississippi to revisit Chapel Hill. Cornelia thought he looked "thin and shrunken—hair very white," but he was actually very hale, for he lived for twenty-one more years. After looking over the

University, the Bishop said aloud what other persons had been only thinking: *There must be a change in the head of the University.* He even said that certain parties were favoring Joseph E. Johnston, ex-Confederate general, as the new president.

Governor Swain had been for some time outwardly cheerful, and as long as there were prospects of his getting funds from some source, he retained his post as president of the University without challenge. But when a year had gone by and when it became evident that the University and its equipment were daily growing shabbier, there was a murmur that the new conditions demanded a new sort of man to meet them. Governor Swain was bound to feel the pressure, and the uneasiness that engraved itself in his face could no longer be hidden from his friends, especially from so close an observer as Cornelia. Knowing that he was already distressed by the behavior of his erratic children, she deeply sympathized with him. "Let no man be called happy or prosperous till the day of his death ..." she exclaimed. "Heaven help the Republic. I think it in more danger than during the war."

VI

Her nights became haunted by unpleasant dreams. One night in October, 1866, she dreamed that her father was dead. "My distress was as great as if it had been a reality," she wrote. "In the middle of it I woke up and could sleep no more till day began to dawn. I tried to reason myself out of my fright and anguish in vain. I wanted to get up and go to him."

There was another saddening influence; neighbors were beginning to move away from the village in search of more stirring life or a better livelihood. One of them was Professor Kimberley.

"I passed thro' Mr. Kimberley's yard—deserted and forlorn," she wrote the day after his departure. "I knew very little of the family, yet there is something touching in looking at a place from which late neighbors have departed forever. Their place shall know them no more. ... The trees are putting on all their October glory. I never saw the Lagerstroemia [crape myrtle] look so brilliant.

All thro' the campus, the sun shining brightly on the trees dotted here and there made each one look as if on fire."

She tried to be outwardly cheerful for the sake of her observant small daughter, and one day in November, 1866, she sat with the children on the steps of the college library and watched the students play baseball. She noted the date in her diary with the comment that "one draws in a large stock of vitality in such an half hour." Then she went to call on some friends and the clouds returned. "I hear a great deal against Governor S. and the University these days. Everybody seems resolved the Gov. must resign. . . . How can they dismiss so old a public servant as the Gov., and yet what can be done otherwise? . . . The Governor has *at present* no thought of resigning. He thinks he will live it all down."

And then on December 7 she was able to record the event that launched her upon the sea of authorship—a sea she was to traverse often but always under the same colors.

"My book arrived today. I am much pleased with the way in wʰ it is gotten up. Very pretty and very neat. Gov. Swain unfortunately is not here to receive his copy and the surprise of the Dedication as I wanted. I had however the pleasure of giving my dear old father his copy. *Now if North Carolinians will only buy it.*"

VII

Toward the end of 1866 her anxieties about the health of her mother, who was still in New York, increased, but no amount of entreaty served to bring that lady home. Cornelia knew her mother had never been happy in Chapel Hill, so far from her kindred and the mode of life she had been accustomed to as a girl. "I feel very unhappy about her," said Cornelia's diary. Gloomy letters came from Dr. Deems in New York; his paper, *The Watchman,* was failing and the sales of *The Last Ninety Days of the War* were slow. Friends sent Cornelia books, but she could take little interest in them. Of one of them, a novel by Bayard Taylor, she wrote sarcastically:

"Some of these Yankee writers appear to be on the point of

bursting with self conceit. I wish they would. Then the world would be rid of them and so much the better off."

On Christmas eve she walked up the street to the shops and spent what little money she had for gifts. For the widows of Confederate soldiers she bought coffee and sugar, and for her daughter June she was able to afford nothing more sumptuous than a slate and five slate pencils. With these and a few other presents from friends June was the next day entirely happy. On the last day of the year Cornelia wrote in her journal this entry:

"I have spent the day mending an old nightgown and making a new flannel shirt for June and writing a letter to Ma. A year of constant hope deferred to those interested in this college. A year of much pleasurable, if not profitable, employment to me, thanks to Dr. Deems. I have much to be thankful for—much to be ashamed of—much to be encouraged by in looking back at 1866. . . . Our servants are a source of great worry to us all. They are inclined to do as little, and get as much as they possibly can. Sarah seems willing to remain with us. Aunt Dilsey and Ben seem to sit rather loose. Their *interest* however will be served by their staying and I have little doubt they will. But we are eaten up by our negroes. They and their kinfolks—they and their stealing. Many of our neighbors have lost heavily by theft. . . . I have just given Pa a glass of ale and a piece of toast. It is 11 o'c. The old year is passing. . . . God bless and keep us all. I desire to spend the coming year in *more active service*. 'Not slothful in business,' I have taken for my year's motto. *God help me this year also.*"

9

The Civil War as Seen by a Woman

I

The Last Ninety Days of the War, Cornelia's first published book, appeared in 1866 as issued by the Watchman Publishing Company of New York. This company had been formed to publish *The Watchman,* a journal of reconciliation edited by Charles F. Deems, a brisk and resourceful young preacher who at the age of twenty-two had been a University professor at Chapel Hill for five years beginning in 1843. Dr. Deems was the founder, with the financial help of "Commodore" Cornelius Vanderbilt, of the Church of the Strangers in New York City and later of the Deems fund at the University of North Carolina, which in the course of years has helped hundreds of students to procure a college education.

He was brought to Chapel Hill by Governor Swain as adjunct professor of logic and rhetoric. He had previously been North Carolina agent of the American Bible Society. He was born in Baltimore and educated at Dickinson College, Pennsylvania. From Chapel Hill he went to Randolph-Macon College, Virginia, as a professor for a year. He was then elected president of Greensboro, North Carolina, Female College for four years, after which he returned to pastoral connections. When the Civil War broke out, he accompanied Lee's Confederate army into Maryland. His oldest son, Theodore, was mortally wounded when fighting under Stonewall Jackson in Virginia.

After the war's end, Dr. Deems went to New York and founded *The Watchman* with the hope of reuniting the lately warring sections of the country. Cornelia was one of his first contributors. The enterprise took all his money. His next enterprise was to organize for the benefit of the wanderers and transients in New York the Church of the Strangers, which attracted the notice of Commodore Cornelius Vanderbilt through his second wife, who was an Alabama woman. Vanderbilt gave Dr. Deems $50,000 to buy an edifice in Mercer Street, New York. Dr. Deems was a busy pastor, lecturer, and writer all his life until at the age of seventy-three he was stricken with paralysis. His body lies in the Moravian cemetery at New Dorp, Staten Island, New York, not far from the cemetery where the Vanderbilts and other Dutch families are buried.

II

The Last Ninety Days was a Whig review of the war. It was dedicated to President Swain, having been begun at his suggestion and completed by aid of his "invaluable advice, encouragement, and assistance," in the words of Cornelia. She explained in a preface that the papers composing the book had been begun in the hope of doing "justice to North Carolina, and to place beyond cavil or reproach the attitude of her leaders at the close of the great Southern States Rights struggle—to present a faithful picture of the times, and a just judgment, whether writing of friend or foe." Her opening chapter declared that in entering the Civil War North Carolina had "accepted a destiny which she was unable to control"; that the State had never been allowed "her just weight of influence in the councils of the Southern Confederacy"; and that North Carolina's efforts in 1861 to "maintain peace and preserve the Union" had never been appreciated. Cornelia gave at some length quotations from a letter written in 1864 by Zebulon B. Vance, North Carolina's war governor, to "a gentleman of the highest consideration in the State" (probably ex-governor W. A. Graham) mirroring his growing despair and citing evidence of "the utter demoralization of the [Southern] people."

"It shows what I have always believed," wrote Vance, "that

the great popular heart is not now, and never has been in this war. It was a revolution of the *Politicians,* not the *People;* and was fought at first by the natural enthusiasm of our young men, and has been kept going by State and sectional pride, assisted by that bitterness of feeling produced by the cruelties and brutalities of the enemy."

III

In the same chapter Cornelia disclosed what was one of her ultimate purposes: to call attention to General Sherman's announced purpose in his march upward from Georgia—"to shorten the war by increasing its severity." She gave many pages to historical contrasts between the magnanimity shown by victors to rebels in the past and the behavior of Sherman's army and its followers in North Carolinia during the last days of the Confederacy. Sherman's attitude and conduct she thus summed up:

"In the civil policy he has always advocated toward the South, he has shown himself at once generous and politic. If he had pursued an equally far-sighted course as a soldier; if he had advocated a humane forbearance toward the defenceless people who were crushed beneath his march; if he had enforced a strict discipline in his army, and chosen to appear as a restorer rather than as a destroyer, there are few at the South who would not join to pronounce him the hero of the war on the Northern side."

A rereading of Cornelia's book at this distance from the war of 1861-65 makes it plain that although Sherman's famous march through Georgia to North Carolina may have been a military success, it was a psychological mistake. For although this march split the Confederacy, it also split a union that was about to recover itself, and sowed salt into the wound so that its festering alienated the South from the rest of the country for years after opposing generals and bellicose governments had become dust. Cornelia tried hard to tell her story fairly and without undue bias; yet as she recalled instances of shame and humiliation suffered—unnecessarily, as she saw it—by her neighbors and friends, one could almost see the tremor in her printed lines; and at moments she was not able to keep her resentment from bursting through.

"Peace we had longed and prayed for; but not *this peace*," she wrote. "The reunion was not *this* reunion."

IV

She did not gloss over what was bogus and pretentious about the Confederacy. "Looking back at our delusions, errors, and miscalculations for the four years of the war, the wonder is, that the Confederacy lasted as long as it did."

What was no doubt in the back of Cornelia's mind was a hope that through her papers in *The Watchman* and their appearance in book form, she could help to avert the military occupation and the punitive peace that seemed to impend under the name of Reconstruction. That hope fell low when news came of Lincoln's death. She had to admit that war's distortions had given her a twisted picture of the President:

"He was always presented to us in caricature. The Southern press never mentioned him but with some added *sobriquet* of contempt and hatred. . . . They judged him by the party which took possession of him after his inauguration, and by his advisers. But a sense of remorse fills my mind now as I write of him, realizing how much that was really good and guileless, and well-intentioned and generous, may have come to an untimely end in the atrocious tragedy at Ford's Theatre."

But that which now remains most memorable in the book are Cornelia's sketches and vignettes of the war scenes that took place under her own eyes in Chapel Hill. For example, this is a passage dealing with Confederate conscription:

"It was a severe shock to our high-strung theories of Southern chivalry and patriotism, to think of Southerners hiding in dens and caves of the earth, resolved with great constancy NOT to be martyrs, having to be unearthed in these burrows and dragged out to the fight. One warrior lived for weeks in a hollow tree, fed by his wife; another was conscripted from beneath his own hen-house, where he had dug out a sort of grave, into which, well supplied with blankets, he descended in peace every morning. One took possession of an old, deserted, and forgotten mine in his neighborhood, and by a skillful disposal of brush and rubbish at the entrance, kept house quite comfortably for months, plying his trade of shoemaker meanwhile, and supplied with food from home."

Writing of the occupancy of Chapel Hill by Wheeler's Confederate cavalry just before the arrival of detachments of Sherman's army, she said:

"There were mechanics from Georgia and planters from Alabama: one of the latter I especially remember, who had been a country physician in the northeast corner of the State; a frank and steady, gray-haired man, whose very address inspired confidence and whose eldest boy rode by his side: there were gay Frenchmen from Louisiana and lawyers from Tennessee, some of whom had graduated at this University in the happy days gone by. . . . Many of these men had not been paid one cent, even of Confederate currency, in more than a year. Few of them had more than the well-worn suit he had on, the inefficient arms he carried, and the poor and poorly equipped horse he rode. A lieutenant, not four years before a graduate of this University, who had not seen his home within a year, and who had not long before received intelligence that his house in Tennessee had been burned to the ground by the enemy, and that his wife and child were homeless, when the certain news was brought by Governor Swain of General Lee's surrender, covered his face with his hands to hide a brave man's tears. He told us that a twenty-five-cent Confederate note was all that he possessed in the world beside his horse. . . .

"These men rode up frankly to our gates. 'May I have my dinner here?' 'Can you give me a biscuit?' Well, it was not much we had, but we gave it joyfully—dried fruit, sorghum, dried peas, and early vegetables. . . . Their faces were weather-beaten but cheery; their uniforms were faded, stained, and worn; but they stepped lightly, and had a passing joke for the town gazers, and a kindly glance for the pretty girls who lined the sidewalks, standing in the checkered shade of the young elms. . . .

"On Sunday, at two p.m., General Wheeler called in his pickets; and once more, and for the last time, we saw the gallant sight of our gray-clad Confederate soldiers, and waved our last farewell to our army. A few hours of absolute and Sabbath stillness and silence ensued. The groves stood thick and solemn, the bright sun shining through the great boles and down the grassy slopes, while a pleasant fragrance was wafted from the purple panicles of the Paullonia. All that nature can do was still done with order and beauty, while men's hearts were failing them for fear, and for looking after those things which were coming on the earth.

"We sat in our pleasant piazzas and awaited events with quiet resignation. The silver had all been buried—some of it in springs, some of it under rocks in the streams, some of it in fence-corners, which, after the fences had been burned down, was pretty hard to find again; some of it in the woods, some of it in the cellars. There was not much provision to be carried off—that was one comfort. . . .

"So we talked and speculated, while the very peace and profound quiet of the place sustained and soothed our minds. Just at sunset a sedate and soldierly-looking man, at the head of a dozen men *dressed in blue,* rode quietly in by the Raleigh road. Governor Swain, accompanied by a few of the principal citizens, met them at the entrance, and stated that he had General Sherman's promise that the town and university should be saved from pillage. The soldier replied that such were his orders, and they should be observed. They then rode in, galloped up and down the streets inquiring for rebels; and being informed that *there were none* in town, they withdrew for the night to their camp; and the next morning, being Easter Monday, April seventeenth, General Atkins, at the head of a detachment of four thousand cavalry, entered about eight a.m., and we were captured.

"That was surely a day to be remembered by us all. For the first time in four years we saw the old flag—the 'Stars and Stripes,' in whose defense we would once have been willing to die, but which certainly excited very little enthusiasm now. Never before had we realized how entirely our hearts had been turned away from what was once our whole country, till we felt the bitterness aroused by the sight of that flag shaking out its red and white folds over us. The utmost quiet and good order prevailed. Guards were placed at every house immediately, and with a promptness that was needful; for one residence, standing a little apart, was entered by a squad of bummers in advance of the guard, and in less than ten minutes the lower rooms, store rooms, and bedrooms were overhauled and plundered with a swift and business-like thoroughness only attainable by long and extensive practice. A guard arriving, they left; but their plunder was not restored. The village guards, belonging to the ninth Michigan cavalry, deserve especial mention as being a decent set of men, who, while they were here, behaved with civility and propriety."

10

Upheavals and Descents

I

EARLY IN 1867 Cornelia began a new term for the pupils who came to her to be taught in her father's home, "although," she wrote, "not one of my scholars of last session had paid me one cent on their return!"

There were other signs of the disintegration of the village's life. Dr. Johnston B. Jones, long the village's only physician, moved away to Charlotte; and professors began to look for posts elsewhere. Cornelia could not shake off her recurring depressions, although in small ways the winter was a happy one. "Every night after supper," she wrote, "June and Pa and I have a good time. . . . June sits on Pa's lap while he smokes and they have great games with a scrap of paper. . . . I look back at each one of these quiet days we are spending with thankfulness. It may be 'the torrent's smoothness,' but I am deeply grateful that Pa and I and June are so happy and as Pa says 'so peaceful' together."

And yet she could not rid herself of a sense of approaching change. She could no longer go to her bedroom at night without looking into her father's study to see if he were sitting upright in his chair, and was often kept awake nights by undefined dreads; these she tried to explain to herself by attributing them to worry about her absent mother. "She, however, writes cheerfully, except when she is writing of us and our poverty. I pray for 'daily bread' these days with a sense of its uncertainty, except for the day."

On the evening of March 10, 1867, visitors dropped in to call on Dr. Phillips in his study. After they had gone Cornelia wrote in her diary: "I was looking at Pa across his table and thought he looked the handsomest old man I had ever seen. I cut his hair yesterday. He seems very well and bright and cheerful. He and June went to church together this morning. Kate [Fetter] and I watched them going down street hand in hand. She said 'June's grandpa is so fond and proud of her he can hardly walk at all.'"

II

The next morning, Mrs. Spencer's father took off the new dressing gown she had recently made for him and put on his cape of Confederate grey. A few minutes before 9 o'clock, under a lowering sky and a drizzling rain, he started for the University chapel. There he took his usual seat behind the reading desk to wait for the sound of the bell which would open the day's exercises. In one hand was the key of his recitation room, in the other was Peirce's *Plane and Solid Geometry.* As the bell rang, the students began to file in. One of them had reached the front row and was about to be seated when he saw Dr. Phillips fall forward from his chair. The student sprang up and caught the venerable professor just as his body sagged to the floor. This student was Alexander Graham, whose son, Frank Porter Graham, became president of the University in 1930. Dr. Mallett, the new village physician, was summoned. But Dr. Phillips was dead.

He was in his seventy-fifth year. He had been a professor in the University for forty-one years. The students carried his body home and laid him in his library where the manuscript of the sermon he was preparing for the following Sunday lay open on his desk. His younger son, Samuel, was absent at the county seat of Hillsboro. His older son, Charles, was ill in bed. His wife, Julia Vermeule, was in New Jersey. Cornelia, alone of his family, was present to receive his body. He was buried while snow lay on the ground. "A better, braver, nobler man I have never known," wrote Governor Swain. Cornelia went to her journal and wrote:

"Here I thank God solemnly that I had such a father as mine was. I am thankful for his example of honesty and integrity of purpose, for the simplicity of his character, for his ardent faith, and for his zealous upholding of the standards of his belief. He was a manly man."

III

Before the spring was far advanced Cornelia went to New York to bring home her ailing mother. But Mrs. James Phillips showed small interest in returning to Chapel Hill, and Cornelia stayed on till she should change her mind. It was a comfort to Cornelia to visit at the New York home of her English-born uncle, Samuel Phillips, and to talk with him of her father. "They are very unlike," she wrote, "and yet there was resemblance enough to make me cling to him." In New York and Plainfield, New Jersey, she also had an opportunity to renew ties with her kindred, the descendants of Adrian Vermeule, the one-time secretary of the Haarlem, New York, Board of Overseers, and the families with which they had intermarried, the Clarksons, Fieldses, and Cadmuses. But the postwar prosperity in evidence on every hand in the North depressed her.

"New York I found immensely grown," she wrote, "since I was familiar with its streets fourteen years before. It seemed to me twice as large, twice as imposing in its appearance of power and wealth and greatness. Such prosperity everywhere there, such smiling prosperity over the fields of New Jersey—such growth—and I was all the time comparing it with the poor broken-down unhappy poverty stricken South."

Cornelia was hoping to induce her mother soon to return to Chapel Hill when the latter suffered at her father's old home in Plainfield, New Jersey, a fall that kept her in bed several weeks. Then she and Cornelia started South by sea. "A sad and bitter coming home," wrote Cornelia. "There seems to me nothing before me now but change and sadness—only memories of past happiness to cheer. Yet God is good. Everybody in Chapel Hill, black and white, came to see us on our return." It was two months before she went again into her father's study. Everything was just as he had left it—even to the dressing-gown with a fresh handkerchief in the pocket.

IV

By the autumn of 1867 affairs seemingly had not improved either for Cornelia or the University. "The fall is wearing away in sadness," she wrote in her journal. "Only about 50 students in college. Everything goes on gloomily and hopelessly and in a depression that seems to be only a looking forward to more trouble."

In those fall months occurred certain events that were of major importance to Cornelia Spencer. Her brother Charles succeeded his father as professor of pure mathematics in the University. Almost at the same time the other brother, Samuel, who had been in Governor Vance's war cabinet, made it known that he was about to leave Chapel Hill and establish himself and family in Raleigh, the state capital, where he had been made Supreme Court reporter. To a woman so devoted to her clan and family as Cornelia Spencer this was desolating news; it meant that family ties were being sundered at the very time that other relations were being broken up.

Samuel was the brother on whom she most leaned, with whom she had most in common. Within a few years she had lost her husband and her father; now she was to part with her most loved brother. But she made no complaint. "I am best under the rod," she used to say. Even when Samuel, always a strong upholder of the union of states, attended the Reconstruction Convention and began to accept more and more those principles that eventually carried him into the Republican party—which to all the loyal Southerners of the period was the party of Satan—she had no word of criticism for him. She was a woman who by nature craved a father, and when she was no longer able to find consolation in the presence of her husband, or her natural father, or Governor Swain, she relied more and more on the counsel of her brother Sam; to him she was utterly loyal, and the fact that he had the courage to follow his convictions out of the old Whig party increased her admiration for him, although his eventual acceptance of an appointment by President Grant as solicitor general of the United States probably caused her many secret sighs.

V

At the end of the year her brother Sam persuaded Cornelia to leave her old home and move next door into the house he was just vacating in order to remove to Raleigh. Here she took several young men, students at the University, as boarders at $15.00 a month each. She had small liking for this employment, but later she could look back on this period with tenderness, for it was the means of cementing friendships that endured the rest of her life. A number of these students subsequently became distinguished, and none failed to take pride in the fact that he had once been one of Mrs. Spencer's boarders. Among them were George and Will Maverick, of a name subsequently famous in Texas, and the ex-Confederate captain, W. H. S. Burgwyn. Among other boarders at this time were Hoke Smith, later of President Cleveland's cabinet, and Fabius H. Busbee of Raleigh. Mr. Busbee later wrote her concerning those days: "Upon no portion of my college life can I look back with more pleasure than that spent around your table. I think it ought to compensate you for the ill-paid trouble of taking boarders to fix your position so strongly in the hearts of not a few of those who met around your board."

Scarcely had she settled down into the new house when her father's two former slaves, Aunt Dilsey and Uncle Ben Craig, decided to have a taste of freedom and left her. "Dear old soul," Cornelia wrote in her diary concerning Dilsey. "I trust she and I will live together again." They did, as later chapters will show. Cornelia tried to be cheerful. "I seem to drag my life along. What I read does me no good. Where is my religion?" It was plain to all concerned that the University, whose life governed the whole community's life, was stumbling down the road toward some dark fate. The election to the governor's seat of W. W. Holden, who regarded the University as the citadel of an outworn aristocracy, meant that the state government at Raleigh would be aloof or hostile. Cornelia felt that the commencement of 1868 would be the last under the old regime, although President Swain was sure something would turn up.

"I am so worried and tormented as it were out of my very life!" she wrote. "I have many blessings, but oh, for a vanished hand—a hand full of kindness and love—warm—generous—tender."

VI

The last entry but one in her diary for 1868 was this abrupt one: "Holden's Gov^t has announced that the University shall *not* be reopened on the 17th July as Governor Swain had advertised. All is at an end."

These terse words scarcely give a hint of the tragedy that was overwhelming the University which Cornelia Spencer so loved— a tragedy which also was overtaking its president, good old Governor Swain. In 1867 just after President of the United States Andrew Johnson, accompanied by Secretary of State William H. Seward, Postmaster General A. W. Randall, and General Daniel E. Sickles, had attended the University commencement, it was plain that the institution was so impoverished, because of loss of revenue, that it could scarcely last another year. At that time Kemp P. Battle, state treasurer, and Professor Charles Phillips, brother of Cornelia and secretary of the faculty, procured the resignations of President Swain and of all members of the faculty, including Professor Phillips' own. Battle then obtained the appointment by Governor Worth of a committee of five which was to study the University's situation and before the year's end suggest how it could be bettered. Named on this committee were William A. Graham, Thomas Settle, Thomas S. Ashe, Kemp P. Battle, and Samuel F. Phillips. These five submitted a report recommending greater attention to the sciences and mathematics, higher standards of admission, and more stringent examinations. The new scheme was to take effect in the fall of 1868. In March of that year a new state constitution was adopted. It placed the University under a new board of trustees to be elected by the state board of education instead of the General Assembly. At a meeting of the trustees in July, 1868, President Swain's resignation and those of the faculty were accepted as final.

VII

To President Swain the news of this summary action was stunning. He could not believe it, even when Negro soldiers had forcibly closed the doors of the University. His unlucky month, August, came. He sat down and wrote an eloquent protest to the new state governor, W. W. Holden, who had once been a fiery secessionist but who had now gone over to the other side. Swain got no reply. And then came a sudden end to the whole question. On August 11 Swain had the horse that had been given to him by General Atkins hitched to a buggy, and he invited Professor Manuel Fetter to take a ride with him. They drove out six miles to a plantation called Babylon owned by President Swain. On the return trip the horse— which gossip insisted had been stolen by Sherman's troopers from a Southern stable—suddenly shied. Professor Fetter was driving, but instead of leaving matters to him, Swain tried to help control the animal by grasping at the reins. A wheel of the buggy struck a stump, and both men were thrown heavily to the ground. Fetter was only lightly bruised, but President Swain was so weakened by shock that he had to be taken home on a stretcher.

In a few days Swain was able to receive his friends in his bedroom, but he did not improve. He read much in his Bible and often rested with closed eyes, his lips moving. "I believe in the communion of saints," he was heard to murmur. On mornings before daylight he often chanted familiar hymns. On August 27 he sat up in bed and seemed to be stronger, but suddenly he collapsed. Cornelia was sent for, and she stood by his bedside. "I saw him pass," she said, "gently and without a sigh." His funeral was preached by Cornelia's brother, Charles. He was buried in the garden in the rear of his house beside his gentle, deranged daughter, Anne, and his son David.

"With him died the University," wrote Cornelia. "And with the University perished the prosperity of the town. Within two years of his death thirty of the best families in the place had removed to other homes. . . . One by one they disappeared to California, to Tennessee, to Ohio, to New York, to Texas, and to other towns and villages in North Carolina. The gentlemen of the faculty within a few weeks met once more together; knelt in prayer together once more, and parted."

11

Beelzebub as Governor

I

EARLY IN 1868 Cornelia recorded this note: "The spring elections have resulted in the election of Holden for Gov. . . . A terribly bitter thing for all the respectable people in the state. But it is done!" She was right in her surmise that neither the University nor the state had yet completed their travail. Humiliation had not ceased when the last of Sherman's bummers had marched away; for Reconstruction brought disfranchisement and poverty to many citizens who had formerly belonged to North Carolina's ruling class; established a military reign in important towns; and overthrew the long political dominance of the Whig party, to which belonged most members of the state's upper strata.

Symbol of this downfall of the old and the rise of new elements in political society was the former printer's apprentice, Governor W. W. Holden. To most of the Whig families of the periods just before and after the Civil War, Holden was Beelzebub himself; and Cornelia was only one of the numerous Whig-minded spokesmen who believed and taught that Holden was half scoundrel and half leper. Yet time softens and thins the harshest portraits, and it is now possible to see Holden as caught in a situation which he had not the character or strength to resolve, and as being demagogic rather than rascally, and more fearful than vicious.

Holden was born on a farm not many miles from Chapel Hill. He apprenticed himself in boyhood to Dennis Heartt, printer and editor of the Hillsboro, North Carolina, *Recorder*. Hillsboro, once the colonial capital, was for a long time one of the centers of the

North Carolina intellectual, professional, and property-owning classes; and Holden, being able neither to mingle with the local aristocracy nor to get a University education, seems to have acquired a hampering sense of inferiority, while at the same time resolving to rise to the top so that no man could look down on him. When about twenty years old he moved to Raleigh, the state capital, and got a job on the *Star*, a Whig paper. Holden said afterwards he had left behind him a debt for $150, mainly for a gold watch he had bought on credit, and for a broadcloth coat the material of which had cost him $3.00 a yard. In the light of his subsequent career, these are significant items.

II

Holden proved himself to be a facile and ingenious writer, and in 1843 he was made editor of the Raleigh *Standard*, organ of the rising Democratic party which had for its slogan, "The many instead of the few." Holden at once proclaimed he had been at heart a Democrat all the time. In a few years he was able to buy control of the *Standard* largely through a loan procured from Judge Duncan Cameron, president of the state bank. Holden had been meantime reading law, and Judge Cameron said to him, "My advice is, as you have chosen the press, to abandon all idea of the law."

Holden acted accordingly and, having a gift for political humor and satire, he raised his paper's circulation, aided by the state printing, until he was enjoying an income of $8,000 a year. He had begun work in Raleigh at $8.00 a week.

For the decade before the Civil War the Democrats were in control of North Carolina's government; among them Holden became a powerful figure. When the shadow of the war drew nigh, Holden was one of the state's most virulent secessionists and roared loudly at any critic of slavery. He declared in 1854 that "the worst spirit now out of perdition is the spirit of abolition." When it became known that Professor B. F. Hedrick of the University at Chapel Hill had publicly declared he intended to vote for John C. Frémont as president and was privately opposed to slavery, Holden frightened the University administration into asking for Hedrick's resignation. Cornelia was not sure Hedrick had acted judiciously, but she remained his friend and in later years visited him in Washington when he was a government employee.

III

In the middle of the war Holden turned his coat again. He suddenly became a spokesman of the peace parties that sprang up in North Carolina largely because of impatience with the centralization of the Confederate government, but also because, as Governor Vance wrote to ex-Governor W. A. Graham in 1864, "The great popular heart is not now, and never has been, in this war." Late in 1863 Confederate troops passing through Raleigh sacked Holden's office and destroyed his presses.

Holden, having once deserted the war party, swung further and further over to the Federal side, with the result that he attracted the attention of the Washington authorities; and it was no surprise when after the war he was appointed provisional governor of North Carolina by President Andrew Johnson. For his acceptance of this office Holden was bitterly condemned by those who preserved their Confederate sentiments. But what drew upon him storms of wrath was his declaration, when he was the Republican governor in 1870, that because certain counties were in a state of insurrection, the civil laws were suspended, whereupon he sent armed detachments of militia there. This was about the time that the Ku-Klux Klan was becoming active in certain areas. In 1871 Holden was impeached by the State Senate and voted out of office, but Presidents Grant and Hayes kept him as postmaster at Raleigh for eight more years. Holden thenceforth lived quietly to a good old age. In his later years he became very religious, but even in religion he could not maintain a steady course; he was first a Baptist, then a Methodist. He never seemed to bear any resentment against his old enemies, and before he died he was a respected figure among those persons who esteemed his personal honesty and his kindness as a family man and as an employer.

IV

So far as known, Cornelia never met Holden, or talked with him. She took her opinion from the harsh partisan views of that day; and she was of course influenced by the sayings attributed to Holden in regard to the University—"it's time to clean out the rickety old concern," and the like.

In one respect Holden was right: the pre-war University was well suited to the ante-bellum plantation system, and it did well enough for the sons of landowners and of the professional men who served the leading planters. But now that slavery was gone, the plantation system was gone with it. Nationally speaking, the war had broken the old agrarian rule and set up a new financial and industrial power under which banks and business men would be foremost. Governor Swain had been unable to recognize that this basic change had taken place; consequently he saw no reason to alter the status quo. But the younger men were able to see that both state and University were dealing with new conditions. One of them was Kemp P. Battle, then in his thirties. He was a Raleigh lawyer who was a graduate of and a former tutor at the University. Cornelia well stated his views when after the war's end she wrote:

"I have just read a long letter from Kemp Battle from New York, taking strong ground in favor of a hearty union with the Northern people, inviting and assisting immigration South, calling in capital, welcoming workers, opening up every source of national prosperity and turning over a new leaf generally. . . . Business . . . must go on. The world is turning round, and though my reason consents, I feel sad."

Battle became the leader of those forces laboring for a modernization of the University. He was joined by Professor Charles Phillips. Together they cleared the way for the appointment by the trustees of the committee of five which investigated and reported on the merits of a new system. They found that the old Graeco-Latin curriculum was so predominant as to keep the nascent sciences strangled. For example, in a four-year course the student had to take 740 hours of ancient languages while in chemistry, mineralogy, and geology he took only 81 hours combined. Zoology, botany, physiology, and other sciences were not taught at all. The committee recommended the creation of ten independent academic departments, each to have its head professor, so as to give more attention to the physical and political sciences and to modern languages.

v

Cornelia was, when guided by her head, in favor of all this; but her heart was with the handsome and stately ex-Governor Graham, who uniformly opposed these innovations. She perceived that commerce, growing in power, was demanding new ways and weapons; but she feared that when the old hedges were broken down, a loud and cheap vulgarization would rush in. She was now in the middle forties, that time when the human mind, disillusioned by the present and no longer expecting miracles from the future, turns its thought to the past as something safe and not to be changed by whim, and as having an imperishable glamor. She had the handicap of a hardening deafness that cut her off from the flow of the life around her and made her too often dependent for her information on partisan journalism and the gossip of those fearful of the future.

Of one thing, however, she was never guilty: she never, even during the worst days of this apprehensive period, gave way to fears of or prejudice against the freed Negroes of the community. She knew that behind white attitudes lay a fear of what the suddenly unshackled slaves might do under the protection of alien military men and politicians. Her course was already determined upon; it was to be humanly friendly with all the Negroes around her, to teach them and visit them, and occasionally to scold them; but never to be afraid of them or to stand in their light. About this time she wrote to Mrs. Swain this sketch of attentions to an old ante-bellum Negro woman:

"I hurried right down to poor Louisa with your bounty. . . .

I found her sitting up before the fire, while Dicy and Nicy were changing her clothes. Poor creature, she was the merest skeleton. She seized my hand and put it to her withered lips and said: 'Tell Mis' I kissed your hand for her, tell her the Lord reward her for thinkin' about me in my misery, and may the Lord bless her when she comes to lie down and die.'...I never saw anyone show more feeling and gratitude than she did. And I felt like thanking and blessing you too, for giving a poor dying creature so much pleasure and adding some comforts to her last days. ...I read to her Luke's account of the crucifixion. I used to go and sing for her, which she appeared to enjoy. Mr. Brent, the Methodist minister, was there yesterday and prayed with her. She told him she was *ready and willing*, and broke out praising God as she talked." And then after mentioning the struggles of the University to keep alive, Cornelia closed the letter by saying: "I seem to myself sometimes to be living alone among the ruins of all that made life pleasant and dear." Again she wrote to Mrs. Swain: "It seems to me that as time flies by and the possibility of renewing the scenes at Chapel Hill is just more and more clearly out of sight, those scenes become more dear to us. Chapel Hill and its life was a growth—it was not a creation. . . . Sometimes the Governor would say to me 'I think that the wagon has run back down to the bottom of the hill at last. We may now hope that it will begin to go up for good.' "

Cornelia's greatest fear was of what Governor Holden, with his control of the state board of education and of the trustees, might do to the University. One of the trustees was John Pool, a United States senator, a graduate of the University in 1847, and a lawyer. In 1860 Pool had been the Whig candidate for governor. During the war he remained a union and peace advocate. It was rumored that Pool favored "cleaning out" the University and reorganizing it, and that he was acting as a sort of educational counsellor to Governor Holden. Meantime the University continued to decline. The people of the state, apprehensive of its treatment by the Holden government, feared to send their sons to Chapel Hill. They knew not what to expect there. But Holden soon showed them. One day in 1868 he sent a detachment of Negro militia to Chapel Hill, closed the University, and put it under guard.

"Oh, how I sorrow for Chapel Hill!" wrote ex-Governor Vance to Cornelia from his law office in Charlotte. "How worse than desolate it must look under the oaks! I don't know how you can live on there, thinking always of the past. How I miss my dear friend, Governor Swain! Alas, alas, our pleasant village is broken up and destroyed indeed!"

12

Post-Bellum War

I

GOVERNOR HOLDEN caused the University to be reopened at the beginning of the year 1869 with a new president and new faculty. The new president was Solomon Pool, a brother of Senator John Pool; and almost at once Cornelia opened on him a blistering attack. The fact that President Pool had been a classmate of her husband's, a pupil of her father's, and a tutor in the University, did not save him; he had charged the University with being under the undue influence of aristocracy and family connections, and had counselled, "Better close it than have it a nursery of treason." This was enough to bring down on him the scorching heat of Cornelia's pen.

By now she had taken the enfeebled University under her maternal mantle. It was a strange spectacle. In a state weakened and impoverished by four years of war, the men, with a few exceptions, were too busy trying to save themselves and families from the wreck of a civilization to give more than passing help to the weakened University. It was a woman who mounted guard over the bed of sickness, warning off all intruders, with nothing more formidable than a steel pen dipped into ink, and saying to all marauders: "Touch not a hair of yon grey head!"

"A bogus president, and faculty men unfit for their office and unworthy of public confidence." This was among the mildest opinions she voiced about the new regime. But here again Cornelia was drawing conclusions from a suspicious press and from biassed gossip. There have been worse college presidents than Solomon

Pool and professors more unfit than the men he brought with him to Chapel Hill; but the community was then in no mood to give a just appraisal either to him or to his faculty.

II

The Reverend Solomon Pool, like his brothers, Senator John and Dr. William G. Pool, was born on a farm near Elizabeth City in the Albemarle section of northeastern North Carolina. He was a second-honor graduate and a tutor of the University in 1853. Three years later he was licensed to preach. In 1861 he was raised to the post of adjunct professor of mathematics under Dr. James Phillips; this argues that he could not have been the numskull that his Whig critics made him out to be. In 1866 he left Chapel Hill to become a deputy revenue appraiser at Raleigh. Here he became friendly with Governor Holden, and when the Reconstruction agitation about the position of the University became acute, he joined in the demand for a reorganization, saying, "Let the present board of trustees be superseded by a loyal board, and the University will be a blessing instead of a curse." He could have written no words more damning in the eyes of Cornelia, and during his six years of office he was never free from her galling rifle fire. When he left Chapel Hill in 1875, he taught a school at Cary, near Raleigh, and filled various ministerial vacancies in Methodist churches at Raleigh, Winston, and Greensboro. He was an able writer and speaker, but he was handicapped by a lack of magnetism, while his sense of humor was meagre. Cornelia's father criticized him for inability to "grow," owing to his defects of temperament, and he never succeeded in winning over any part of the people of Chapel Hill. But when he died in 1901, he was a respected figure and his pastor said of him: "I profoundly believe that, take him all in all, he was the purest and best man I ever knew."

III

The new professor of the Greek language and literature, Fisk P. Brewer, came to Chapel Hill under a handicap because he had been principal of a school at Raleigh for Negroes supported chiefly by Northern money. He had been a tutor at Yale College and was a brother of a justice of the United States Supreme Court. His ability was never questioned, but when it was reported that he had entertained Negroes as his equals at his home in Raleigh, the white people drew around him a ring that was never crossed.

The new Latin professor and bursar, David Settle Patrick, was a University graduate of 1856. He came up from Arkansas where he had been principal of a school. He was a native of Rockingham county, North Carolina, and a nephew of Judge Thomas Settle, an old opponent of Governor Vance. He took his family to live in Governor Swain's old home, almost opposite Cornelia's, where he kept three servants. The curious Cornelia asked Aunt Dicey Lane, a privileged colored personage of the village, what she thought of the newcomers. The reply was: "As common-looking white folks as I ever saw."

It was not denied that the new head of the English school, James A. Martling, was a political professor. He was a brother-in-law of the State Superintendent of Public Instruction and had been recommended by him. He came from Missouri and had been a school-teacher. Nothing was known about his competency.

George Dixon, an English Quaker, somehow wandered in from his native Yorkshire to be professor of agriculture. He was in Chapel Hill only a few months. He went home to England on leave and never came back.

IV

The one member of the new faculty who to the village appeared to be civilized was Professor Alexander McIver, a native Tar Heel, an honor graduate of the University in 1853, of the same class as Pool, and subsequently a tutor. He had just been let out at Davidson College because he purposed to vote for President Grant, his case being remarkably parallel to that of Professor Hedrick at Chapel Hill. McIver was sagacious enough to do what Pool, if he had been well advised, would have done: he went at once and presented himself before Cornelia, asking to be spared if found in doubtful company. She was at first dignified and aloof, compelling the professor to make a flanking attack. He reminded her he had been a classmate of her husband, Magnus Spencer. This was a masterly stroke, weakening the other side in a vital spot. He pursued his advantage by fondly recalling Dr. Phillips, Cornelia's father, Governor Swain, and other members of the old faculty. Cornelia had no defense against these memories. She melted and was almost won over in one sitting, so much so that she wrote to Mrs. Swain in Raleigh: "He talked like a good man as well as a sensible one. He would have been much the best choice for president."

All these professors were Republicans of the same shade as Governor Holden. They soon became known as the "radical faculty." Miss Nancy Hilliard called it a "stump-tail" faculty. It quickly became evident that not only the village but the state was going to boycott the whole Pool regime. Classrooms were opened for instruction on January 3, 1869. But not a student was in evidence. One appeared for a day, but finding that he would be the entire student body, and not welcoming this status, he disappeared. Battle lines were at once drawn up for what might prove to be a war of extinction over the body of the University. The general on the one side was President Pool, who had the additional title of Professor of Intellectual and Moral Philosophy. On the other was Cornelia, widowed and alone.

13

Dispersal

I

WHILE THESE THINGS were going on, other events were occurring of even greater import to Cornelia. Foreseeing the break-up and possible death of the University, faculty members and townspeople, fearing their inability even to gain a livelihood, began to pack their furniture and move to other fields. It was a diaspora that robbed the community of most of its leaders and laid a blight on the village's life. If "rookery" it was, in Governor Holden's words, there was no doubt about its being "cleaned out." Judge W. H. Battle, Miss Nancy Hilliard,[1] and Dr. Mallett, the village physician, moved to Raleigh, and Professors Fetter, Hubbard, Hepburn, Martin, Kimberley, and Smith, and Professor Mitchell's four daughters, all went to other fields. The families that joined the hegira left so great a gap as to force other families having business or professional connections to move also. Most of them came to Cornelia to say goodby. At parting Mrs. Hubbard gave her a half dozen sperm candles, and the night of his departure the widowed Professor Fetter came over from the big house across the street, where his three daughters

---

1. Cornelia wrote at this very time [June 8, 1869] of Miss Hilliard: "She was for many years one of the *institutions* of Chapel Hill ... having the largest number of boarders and keeping the best table of any woman in the State. . . . She was a trifle too indulgent to 'her boys,' her kind heart too often interfering with her interests, in their behalf, so that she was often, and is to this day, largely a loser by them. . . . When any of her especial pets got into trouble, she would put on her bonnet and walk over to Governor Swain, and 'beg' for them. . . ."

sat among their boxes, and left at Cornelia's home the front door key and a brass candlestick. She kept these things for thirty-seven years, never being able to see them without aching recollections of these neighbors, some of whom she never saw again.

"Such poignant melancholy seizes me when I recall them," she afterwards wrote. "Why should I feel so sad? I have other dead friends whose memory is not distressing nor depressing. . . . I am simply broken hearted when I recall these friends so linked together, 'the eyes that shone, now dimmed and gone.'"

Cornelia sometimes condemned herself for these fits of melancholy and ascribed them to her "English blood." But the wonder is that in the apocalyptic break-up of the whole manner of life to which she had been accustomed, she kept so firmly her sanity and alertness. She lived in a manless house with her enfeebled mother and small daughter; and them and herself she was trying to support by any means that offered. At various times she taught school and tutored private pupils, she kept boarders and sewed garments, she wrote for the papers, painted china, and did odd jobs for the University; but her annual income seldom rose above $1,000, while for many years it was less than half that. In fact, in 1882 she told her daughter June, in explaining some enforced economy, that her basic income had been for several years only $275 a year. Of this she paid $180 a year for room, board, and fuel and $20 for laundry. Out of the $75 remaining, she gave her church $25, leaving $50 a year for her own needs, including "dress, charity, books, papers, magazines, groundpeas, postage, paints, presents, and other delights!" At another time she wrote: "I remember one time during the war when I had just $70 in Confederate money. When grandpa died, what had I? How have I lived since? I do not know."

II

But among these post-war wrenches the worst was yet to happen. It came when her brother Charles joined the exodus from the village and took his wife, Laura, and lively family to Davidson

College, where he was professor of mathematics and where he became the teacher of "Tommy" Woodrow Wilson, subsequently president of the United States. Dr. Charles Phillips took the chair just vacated by Professor McIver, who had moved to Chapel Hill and taken Dr. Phillips's post.

"I can hardly express to anyone," Cornelia wrote, "the sense of loss and desolation which has seized upon me since Charles and Laura left—they were the last. Poor Charles went through all his packing and parting with apparent equanimity, but when he said farewell to us he broke completely down. He got into the hack, sobbing like a child. There was a great crowd of Negroes around the gate, his Sunday school scholars whom he had taught so long, who wept with him. Poor Ma was quite overcome. As the hack drove off she turned to me and thanked God, crying aloud that she had one child left."

So empty after these losses did the village appear that Cornelia felt she too must leave Chapel Hill; at one time she considered returning to Alabama, where she was assured her husband's relatives and friends would give her a welcome. Letters of protest came. One was from Zeb Vance, the war governor who was now practicing law in Charlotte, North Carolina:

"Somehow I want you, and all those who have labored to serve the dear old State, to feel toward North Carolina as I do—that we should not desert her in the day of her humiliation. I love her the more because of her sorrows and degradation. I should be greatly pleased to hear that the way has been opened for you to remain here and abet us in watching for the better day whose dawning we do not doubt."

And from W. H. S. Burgwyn, the Confederate captain who had been one of the boarders at Samuel F. Phillips's former home when Cornelia was keeping house there and who was now studying law at Harvard, came this plea and prophecy:

"If you will only remain in Chapel Hill it will be one more link to connect our thoughts with the past. You may see the old faculty yet come back to reoccupy their homes, and add dignity and reputation to the institution. Something may turn up, the trustees may inaugurate a better system, another legislature may appropriate the necessary funds, the loved and venerated spot may become once more a flourishing, happy and not a deserted village."

III

Probably one deciding factor in this crisis was Mrs. James Phillips, Cornelia's mother, who having received an injury from a fall [2] could not be easily moved, and who was firmly opposed to being moved anyway. Another factor was an invitation from the *North Carolina Presbyterian* at Fayetteville, North Carolina, to contribute a weekly column on subjects of her own choosing. The pay was to be $400 a year. Her mother had a small income derived partly from the estate of her late father, Captain Cornelius Vermeule, in New Jersey, and partly from her own earnings as a teacher of young ladies. These two sums together would go far toward driving the wolf from the door. Cornelia, who was no stranger to the columns of the *Presbyterian*, began the work with zest. She had earned small sums from *The Watchman* and other journals to which she had occasionally contributed; but this was the first time she had enjoyed a fixed salary and a sense of security in her writing. She made her column in the *Presbyterian* famous. Readers of religious papers were not used to sprightliness or humor, and Cornelia furnished both. This is a sample of her writings at this period, being part of an essay on old-fashioned North Carolina preachers and in particular on the Reverend Dr. Alexander Wilson, who was a teacher as well as preacher and who was an intimate of her father's:

2. "I happened to see her fall," wrote John W. Fries of Winston-Salem, N.C., to Mrs. Hope Chamberlain in 1926. "Capt. Melville Carter and I were walking out Franklin Street after supper at Miss Nancy Hilliard's, and saw Mrs. Phillips leave Governor Swain's and fall on those horrid steps from the sidewalk to the street. I do not know where they came from, but there were a number of other students on the ground immediately; someone brought a chair from Governor Swain's and we carried her to her home across the street."

"Dr. Wilson had been in this country many more years than he had lived in Ireland, yet he was very strikingly in many points *an Irishman;* and more and more of one as he grew older and his character mellowed and ripened. It was so with Dr. Phillips who, unmistakably an Englishman always, was never so distinctly one as in his later years. And they were both fair types of their races. There was some Scotch blood in Dr. Wilson (he came from Belfast) which tempered the Irish impetuosity and carelessness, and gave a toning down, so to speak, to his whole character. He was a most delightful companion—never boisterous, but with a peculiarly enjoyable smile and gleam of genuine humor in his bright blue eye that added a grace to his genial talk. He was in his element in a library. It was delicious to walk round his own with him and see him take down a rare edition and handle it as if he loved it."

IV

A little later Cornelia established another journalistic connection of equal value on the secular side. In April, 1869, she began a series of "Pen and Ink Sketches" in the Raleigh *Sentinel,* an organ of the conservatives, dealing with events and personalities associated with the University in its glorious ante-bellum days. She described her contributions as "a series of short spicy numbers giving a popular account of its [the University's] rise and progress, officering, managements, presidents, professors, etc., with, of course, poisoned arrows for the present incomparable incapables."

About this time, the spring of 1869, she and her mother moved from the house of brother Samuel to the just-vacated home of Charles, which in subsequent years was the Presbyterian manse. Mrs. Phillips was more content here, and being a notional old lady she insisted on letting pet pigs roam in the front yard, much to her daughter's annoyance. We can follow the events of the village as viewed by the eagle eye of Cornelia through a series of letters written to Mrs. Swain, widow of the late president, and to Mrs. Laura Battle Phillips, Cornelia's sister-in-law:

"The University opened on the 3rd. No students have appeared or can be detected with the aid of a magnifying glass. I am divided between exultation that it is so, and sorrow for the poor village, so utterly dependent on the college for its living. . . .

"Mrs. Baudry tells me that she hears that Mrs. Pool has laid great plans for society, and figuring therein. That Chapel Hill people always dropped her, and now she means to drop them. . . .

"I took the children and went to Purefoy's last Thurs. . . . The creek was very full, so there was no fishing done. . . . Coming back . . . we got over a break in the college wall, and walked up the grove back of the Old South. There was Will Barham [Negro janitor], burning leaves. He touched his hat and asked me if I cd recommend him to some place where he cd get work *and pay*. He had got little or nothing from Mr. Fetter for seven mos. work and was working now for nothing. . . .

"We came along behind the Kimberley lot, (I *won't* say Brewer) and there met a whole raft of little scalawags, McIvers, Patricks, Brewers, and Martlings. The Martling and B. children all *mince* dreadfully—the others are plain enough. I went to see Mrs. Patrick last week. . . . Singular that all four new Prof's are *Presbyterian*. Or at least count that way. . . .

"The hills and woods are beginning to look very very lovely now, White dogwood and pink judas-tree, and the tender and varied tints of green, and distant wheat fields. All is not gone from dear C.H. The glory of the grass, and the splendor of the flower—we still have these. . . .

"I hear the McIvers are both greatly depressed and low . . . but Pool says the college *shall go on*. I suppose that Purefoy's son is the only one of the *day scholars* who will pay. . . . Barham, John Ashe, and Wils Swain are the college serv^ts. They say they have rec^d nary cent as yet."

A new source of exasperation against the University regime this spring was the cutting down of many of the great trees in President Swain's old yard and on the campus, possibly as a part of the new clean-up campaign. "The oaks that remain in the old yard," she wrote, "are putting out their leaves as if unmindful of their old friends who have been out and down. I cannot tell you, Mrs. Swain, how I felt as those great trees went crashing down, trees which had sheltered the good and great who made Chapel Hill what it was. . . . What astonishes me about the tree-cutting is its *impudence,* as if they felt themselves owners and seated for life. . . .

"Our Sunday School superintendent has got Mrs. Brewer as one of the teachers. I did not like it, but said nothing, but when last Sunday in came Professor Brewer, affable, distributing papers, I said if he ever came there in any official capacity, I would withdraw. *I cannot help it! . . .*

"Pool told Mr. Carr in their talk . . . that if no white students wd come here, he wd have Negroes!! I think P. must say such things just to exasperate. Can you conceive of any amount of kicking as too severe for such a man? . . .

"What magnificent nights! I walked the front porch last night alone till late. How very very beautiful—the moonlight shining through the young foliage of your elms and ashes. So still—so peaceful. Everything quiet but this raging heart!"

14

Battle Joined

I

FOR THE WAR with President Pool which was now in its pre-liminary or skirmishing stage, Cornelia was well equipped. She had the use and support of two powerful organs of opinion, one religious and one secular; she had the sentiment of the educated classes on her side; and she knew where lay the enemy's chief weaknesses. Her objective was well defined: it was to keep students away from the University as then governed until the Pool administration should be brought down and banished.

The adversary was also well armed for the fray. He had the backing of the Governor and the use of the state's money; he had the blessing of a new class of business and professional men that had come into power since the war; and he had the support of the people who loved change for its own sake. But President Pool and his faculty suffered from three internal weaknesses: they had no local support, they lacked cohesiveness, and they had no defined program or goal. That the state's young men were boy-cotting them was soon evident. Before the spring of 1869 was old, Cornelia was able to report with glee that the University under Pool had only three regular students and that an appearance of activity was being kept up by the enrollment of preparatory students. When it was noised about the state that the preparatory department in order to make a showing had begun to enroll Negroes, the reaction was terrific; for the Negro, though free, was not yet a human being but an emotional symbol.

II

As spring advanced, Cornelia was made aware that her articles in the *Sentinel* were making an impression. They were reprinted in other journals and commented on by men of influence. W. C. Kerr, state geologist, was among those who cheered Cornelia on. He told her she had "done great good in awakening interest in the University" and that her "Pen and Ink Sketches" were "universally read and enjoyed." Thus encouraged, Cornelia began to barb her articles with hinted demands that the Pool faculty make room for men of more competence. She won to her side a strong ally in the person of Editor Engelhard of the Wilmington *Daily Journal,* who allowed Cornelia to say this in one of her contributed articles:

"When Gov. Swain could get a senior class of young men older than the average, he always said all college went on well. It was the senior class who gave tone to college, and it was a dozen or two seniors who led the class. The class of 1853 was such a one. [President Pool, Professor McIver, and Magnus Spencer, Cornelia's husband, were members.] It contained many young men who were over 20 years of age when they joined the college, and who were of more than average maturity of mind, and Prof. McIver was one of its best members. He, it may be said in passing, is the only man now in the present 'faculty' at all fit to be there, and he will best secure his reputation in North Carolina by being the first to get out of it. As an old friend said to him last week on first meeting with him after many years: 'Prof. McIver, I am sorry, sir, to see you *here*.' "

The *Journal* itself in its Raleigh correspondence singled out Professor Brewer as the target of a blast calculated to arouse many prejudices: "In person he is the embodiment of a New England Yankee: lank, cadaverous, and sharp-nosed. . . . His gait is as rapid as if a silver dollar lay at the end of his every journey. He is a Congregationalist in faith and an ardent nigger-worshipper in practice. . . . He is convinced that Homer was a Guinea nigger and Demosthenes a son of Ethiop." The *Journal* on June 6, 1869, followed this with a two-column editorial on the University's plight, which said:

"We are still ready to yield to that institution an earnest, honest, hearty, and zealous support at the first moment in which we can send our sons there without degradation. This time will not arrive, however, until such pismires as now infest the place shall be swept away. . . . We do demand the appointment of a president and professors upon other recommendations than those of partisan malice, partisan prejudice, and family ties."

III

Meantime the opposition was not silent. "The Democrats are endeavoring to destroy the University," said the Raleigh *Daily Standard*, organ of the Republican party and of Governor Holden. "Their strenuous, bitter and untruthful opposition is a confession that they thus injured the institution. They controlled the University once. You know what it was then. We have often heard it denounced as, when under that control, a hotbed of aristocracy and secession." And again: "When Gen. Atkins visited Chapel Hill, he was insulted by the students, because he had been a Federal officer. When Andrew Johnson visited the same University, a Confederate flag was found hanging in one of the society halls. The majority of the people of Chapel Hill did not denounce these exhibitions of rebellious sentiments as they should have done publicly; but rather seemed to uphold the students in their reckless course. These, with similar offences, demanded of loyal men in the State a reorganization of the University. This being done, the consequence is that the ultra Democrats of the State have ceased to patronize the college." This tended to bear out the *Sentinel*'s charge that there were only eight students then at the University—"John Pool's two little nephews and six village children."

IV

As June approached and preparations were made to celebrate
the completion of President Pool's first term of office, it was commonly agreed that the commencement exercises of that month would
be regarded as a test of the administration's standing in the eyes
of the community and state. It was announced from the president's
office that not only Governor Holden and a cluster of personages
from Raleigh would attend, but that President U. S. Grant was
coming down from Washington to be present at what was variously
called the "installation" or "inauguration" of President Pool and
his associates.

Cornelia was moved to write to Mrs. Swain concerning Governor
Swain: "It seems this afternoon as if I must see him once more—
must hear the drum and trumpets of the band—must see something
of the pageantry that for 74 years had made commencement day,
the first Thursday of June, the day of all the year to Chapel Hill."

In quite a different strain was a triumphant letter to Mrs. Charles
Phillips written after the commencement: *"Nobody* came. Thursday ten trustees, and seven others arrived. . . . Rodman [Justice of
the State Supreme Court] was very emphatic with the reminder
that these men [Pool and faculty] were here provisionally. . . .

"McIver told me, this Sat. morning, . . . Pool says . . . that Rodman did *not* use the word 'provisional,' and encourages himself
and his men to hold on. McIver . . . is pretty well satisfied that the
game is up, here. . . . Pool's speech (prepared for his inaugural)
. . . was all I have said of it in the papers. McIver said it was
'sophomoric, hifalutin, and *commonplace.'* Holden went up to him
and congratulated him. Rodman said not a word. By the way,
Judge R[odman] sent me a very polite message, wished to call,
but being here few hours he cd not get time, etc., and told McIver
the 'Sketches' were more beautifully written and had more good
clear sense in them than anything he had read in many a day!
Aha! Also, Mr. Kerr said they had done immense good, and been
greatly sought after, and read, and were 'delightful.' I have had

several letters to that effect—from one, an old student. . . . It was so well-done of C. H. people to stand aloof, and let the world see they would not sanction this crew."

Delightful to Cornelia were these evidences that her campaign for a boycott of the Pool regime was succeeding. She drew extra enjoyment from the fact that her authorship of certain newspaper correspondence from Chapel Hill was kept concealed. Her brothers were suspected, and so were former University professors, but it was not believed a woman could write so pungently. However, when various satiric paragraphs and sketches, aimed at the Pool regime, began to appear in the papers over the signature of "Billy Barlow," she was at once accused. She made no denials, but actually the author of these squibs was Thomas M. Argo, lawyer and son-in-law of Professor Hubbard. All during that summer the ambushing of President Pool and his faculty was kept up, and Cornelia made regular reports of developments to her intimates.

"You know Pool has resigned his revenue office. McI[ver] advised him if he resigned either of his offices to let go of the Presidency. Pool said that all N. Carolina cannot make him do that. . . .

"Sally Caudle lives with the Brewers. She reports them as *poor-folksy*.[1] Miss Brewer has come on to take the negro school I hear. She is Prof. B.'s sister. . . .

"Pool announces that there will be from 60 to 80 students in next session. We shall see!"

1. Cornelia often poured scorn on the niggardliness of faculty members at this time. But Battle's *History of the University*, II, 12, records that President Pool was paid only $1,500 the first year and some of the professors were paid only a fourth or fifth of that amount.

15

War after War

I

IN THE FALL OF 1869 the battle of the Conservatives against the
"Radicals" at Raleigh became rapidly more savage. In various
counties there were brawls, night-ridings, and whippings. At last
the Ku-Klux Klan began to ride openly in communities not far
from Chapel Hill. And then one midnight the hooded riders appeared in the University village "clad in their usual uniform of
disguise," as the Raleigh *Standard* had it.

"They passed through the streets upon horses, making *goosy
noises*," wrote a Chapel Hill correspondent of this organ of Governor Holden. "And after enquiring the whereabouts of the negroes
and white radicals 'that were going to shoot K. K.'s if they interfered with them,' and breaking into the house of Mr. Henry Jones,
colored (knowing that he was from home) and rocking the residence of the notable November, Esq., whom Billy Barlow
complimented and esteemed so highly in his correspondence, they
retired, as they would be pleased to have it, to parts unknown. It
was supposed by some that there were fifty in number—by others
approximating two hundred. This makes the fourth turnout for
the last few months they have made, and in each instance disturbing
the quiet repose of the citizens, and openly violating the civil
law. . . . Give us the proper civil officers and many of these
ghostly beings will be arrested and found to be persons in this
community. Many of them are now recognized, and some of them
are living in and about Chapel Hill; and without shrouds, goosy
quackings and pig-like squealings, they are, in the daytime, in

their everyday associations, as clerks, carpenters, loafers, etc., *tolerably* respectable citizens."

The "notable November" referred to here was President Swain's old Negro coachman, Dr. November. In a village rife with titles he was always called "Doctor." This midnight visit was thus chronicled by Cornelia:

"The Ku Klux paid C. H. a visit last week and by mistake stoned November's house—breaking it in, etc. Chapel Hill people had nothing to do with [it], in spite of the long and intemperate article in 'Standard' on the subject. A few of the C. H. boys went to follow the K. K.'s around to see what they were at and were ignominiously ordered off. It is said they all came from Chatham."

Whether these midnight riders were brought into the village for political purposes, or to annoy and intimidate the University faculty, which was supposed to contain "Negro-lovers," was not explained. But President Pool saw in the visitation another move against him; and he was frightened enough to go to the state capital and ask the governor for the protection of the state militia. But Holden, knowing what an outcry this would cause, advised Pool first to get the county magistrates to sign a petition requesting the militia to come. This Pool was never able to do. It is not clear whether it was Pool or some other person who gave Holden, at times a highly vain and suggestible man, the notion of using the militia to quell the Ku-Klux; at any rate a few months later the governor did begin to order the state's armed forces into communities politically hostile to him, and it was this use of the militia that formed one of the leading charges against him when he was impeached.

II

"It is hard to live here and be a Christian," Cornelia wrote Charles Phillips. "I went to the E[piscopal] ch[urch] last Sunday and joined them at communion, having asked permission and being assured of welcome. I sat there shedding many tears—recalling the friends who once filled those pews. I believe I was the

only person there who was there when that ch[urch] was con-
secrated. . . . About a dozen in all. What is to become of our
poor? Already they are beginning their piteous stories. Mr. Carr
says he never felt so gloomy as now."

In the same letter, September 8, 1869, she added: "I sent
Lossing the portrait of Gov. S[wain], carefully enveloped in a
stiff newspaper, the *Nouveau Monde*. He writes that it had been
opened, presumably in the C. Hill office, and the portrait badly
torn!"

Mr. Lossing, engraver and historical writer and author of *Field
Book of the Revolution*, was then at work on his *Field Book of the
Civil War*. He had asked Cornelia for help in finding material and
a considerable correspondence ensued.

III

Near the end of the year Cornelia wrote her sister-in-law describing a walk through the village's streets with her little daughter
June. They passed President Pool's house, newly painted and
fenced in.

"June squeezed my hand and pointed over at it derisively, and
then, to my surprise and indignation, though it was getting dusk,
spit towards the mansion and said '*Yonder's the dog-kennel!*' I
was dumbfounded, I assure you. She doesn't get such as that from
me. Does she?" Mrs. Phillips's opinion on this point is not recorded.

In the same letter Cornelia told Laura Phillips of the exhuma-
tion of the bodies of Governor and Anne Swain, at the order of
Mrs. Swain, for removal to Raleigh. "It rained hard all day
Wednesday," she said, "and strange to say, that was the day appointed to exhume them. And when done, towards night, it was
finished, where do you suppose the bodies were placed for the
night? *In the barn!* By [Prof.] Patrick's order I hear, though both
the offices are vacant. . . . Dear Gov. Swain. I should like to stop
now and have a good fit of crying, as I think of many things."

As 1869 waned, Cornelia had to record one more atrocity of

President Pool's. Miss Nancy Hilliard's house, where many a student had been warmed and fed, was sold at auction. Pool bought it for $150. "I cannot understand how such a sale can be legal," wrote Cornelia. "No honest man would keep it. Poor Miss Nancy! I do not know what she means to do."

As for Cornelia, she was in no doubt what she herself meant to do. For her, the inertness and passivity that had enfeebled North Carolina ever since Lee's surrender was at an end. The close of the year 1869 found her no longer among those waiting for something to turn up. Her energetic nature would not permit her to watch the University sink and decay. Her weapons were not numerous, but one of them was far mightier than the lately sheathed sword of the Confederacy—her pen.

16

She Wrote Letters

I am writing letters. It is the only thing I can do."

It was thus in a note to Mrs. Swain early in 1870 that Cornelia Phillips Spencer signalized the beginning of her campaign of rescue. It was a campaign designed not only to restore the University but to defeat defeatism, and revivify the state and its people. Her letters were addressed to the leading men of the state, Whigs, Democrats, and Republicans. She asked them whether they would permit the University to remain any longer in the poorhouse; what concrete steps they would propose for its redemption; and what they thought of a state-financed and free system of schools and colleges. This last question undoubtedly was provoked by Governor Holden's speech at the 1869 Commencement when he had declared that under the old ante-bellum system the children of the greater part of the state's people had been practically excluded from the University.

"Education," he said, "should know no color or condition. It must be free like air, and as pervading and universal."

In saying this Governor Holden undoubtedly gave voice to a sentiment that was becoming common. The old plantation aristocracy was no longer in the seats of power; a new class was pushing its way upward through the old upper crust. But matters were still formless. When Cornelia wrote to the elder statesmen to ask, "What shall we do?" they could answer only in generalities. Ex-Governor Vance was one who replied. Writing from his home in Charlotte, he referred to the forthcoming elections

132

in which a well organized effort was being made to defeat the Republican machine headed by Governor Holden, and said:

"I will proceed to answer your question, 'How can Chapel Hill be redeemed?' I believe the next legislature will represent the true people of North Carolina, and that *concern* you have with you will feel the first and fiercest of public indignation. I am more in heart about public matters now than I have been for years. I knew from the first that people would see some day that ignorance could not control. I can see the streaks of purple and gold in the east, thank God."

This was not very explicit, and she wrote to ex-Governor Graham in Hillsboro urging him to say whether he thought immediate action could be taken:

"Does the State really mean to let Chapel Hill die? Every month that it is let to languish in its present condition sinks it lower and farther from aid.

"That the State property here is undergoing constant deterioration is very true, and is at the same time the strongest argument in favor of speedy reformation. Those persons now in charge have but one motive of action—their own interests and how to make the most of their position.

"The last detachment of Holden's troops broke into the Phi library and defaced and carried off, I am told, valuable books. ('Picture books' it is to be presumed, as they had not the appearance of literary characters)....A few more years of Negro and white soldiery, and carpet-bag and scalawag faculty rule, and the property will indeed be past all necessity for oversight.... The 'Professors' say openly it makes no difference to them whether any students come here or not. There are now some 15 boys from abroad, all from the lower classes of society, all beneficiaries and most of them boarding with Negroes.

"Chapel Hill is in a peculiar sense the child of the State.... All this you know, dear Governor Graham, as well as I do. I know you love the place and have grieved over its fate as a son should do for his foster mother. But if you had lived here these past two years, and had your righteous soul vexed from day to day by the ungodly deeds of the men in power, you would kindle such a flame of indignation in North Carolina as would burn out the last vestige of its oppression and degradation. May I beg you to write to me and say if there is any chance of reform and relief for Chapel Hill this winter?"

To this Mr. Graham replied:

"In regard to the University, in which I am pleased to find your interest suffering no abatement, I have thought, considering the experience of the last two years, there is no hope of the revival of the University under the management of the present board of trustees, and that a convention to change the Constitution would be necessary to effect this. I conceive, with you, the necessity of re-establishing the institution as soon as practicable. I think I see already the want of the annual crop of impartially educated young men we sent forth from our Commencements.

"What will be the most effective means to this end when authority shall permit action, will require more information than I can command at present. I much incline to the system of educating downwards—and that more good may be accomplished with limited means by endowing the University and sustaining it, than by expending the like amount in common schools, if both are not possible.

"Whether or not this be so, I am clearly of opinion that the grounds, groves, buildings, libraries, etc., of our University should not be allowed to lie in disuse any longer than want of power for restoration shall paralyze our energies."

II

The commencement exercises of 1870, the second under President Pool, were falser, Cornelia thought, than the first. "Only fourteen strangers, children and all, came," she wrote her brother Charles at Davidson College. "James Taylor [a trustee from Raleigh] came to see me.... He said he never was in such hot water. He told me he found things better in some respects than he expected, worse in others. He said the faculty was incompetent, the college a disgrace, and declared that Holden was the head and front of it all. . . . O Charles, it is a most exasperating business to live here these days! I feel boiling at times with spite, rage and scorn. If I did not feel that anything so rotten *must* come to an end before long, I *could not* stay here." To Laura Battle Phillips she wrote concerning the removal of Professor Hubbard's family: "I went into his study and saw his books taken down from their accustomed shelves and boxed up for transportation. Mrs. Hubbard threw up her hands as we stood looking and said: 'It is all over. It is like death!' "

In August, 1870, she recorded the first entry into the village of Governor Holden's armed forces, recruited by him to suppress insurrection. They camped in the woods behind the University buildings. Their state commander, George W. Kirk, of Tennessee, who had been a Federal officer in the late war, later came to Hillsboro, fourteen miles from Chapel Hill, and arrested Josiah Turner, editor of the Raleigh *Sentinel,* Democratic party organ, to which Cornelia sometimes contributed. When Holden proclaimed that, in this use of state-paid militia, he had the approval of President Grant, many citizens fled from their homes and hid themselves in the woods or on remote farms. This was called "bushing up."

It was a time of fear and turbulence, and all during the summer of 1870 it appeared that North Carolina might be subjected to an even worse form of civil war than that which had just prostrated the state. Fortunately, both sides refrained from extremer measures until the results of the August political elections could be seen; but Governor Holden's organ, the Raleigh *Standard,* declared openly that "the local magistrates and civil tribunals having failed to bring the perpetrators of repeated crimes to justice . . . some extraordinary and violent exercise of authority has become necessary and absolutely obligatory upon the Executive of the State." The savage political skirmishes of the summer rose to a climax when Kirk, Governor Holden's military commander, refused to release prisoners even on habeas corpus writs signed by the state's chief justice, R. M. Pearson, and when companies of Negro militia were brought into Raleigh on the governor's order.

III

In making these maneuvers Governor Holden overreached himself and frightened the state's conservative people. The Republican list of candidates, headed by Samuel F. Phillips, Cornelia's own much-admired brother, who was put up for attorney-general, was a respectable one. But there was a revulsion against displays of a state-supported militarism, and when the August votes were counted it was found that the Conservatives had won a substantial victory over the Radicals. Holden had lost so much face that the Conservatives went on to destroy his political power, and at length they impeached and deposed him.

This August election was afterwards described as "a revolution." In a sense, it was; it put an end to the political hopes of a group of Republican politicians representing the lower half of the state's middle class and crushed what might have become one of the petty dictatorships which in later years got control of various state governments in the South. Thenceforward the control of North Carolina's state government and its institutions rested chiefly in the hands of business and professional men who had been faithful to the Confederacy as long as it lasted but who had never relinquished a hope that the old union of states would be restored. Some of these men had been slave-owners, but were now glad slavery was gone. They wanted to forget the scars of war and cause North Carolina to turn its face toward a new day, welcoming the advent of industry and foreign capital, of new men and new faces.

IV

"I suppose," wrote Cornelia to Mrs. Swain in Illinois, "you have felt, as we have, a great pleasure over the result of the election. It was indeed delightful to me to feel that the days of that party were numbered. Chapel Hillians especially were bound to rejoice, you may be sure. Poor Miss Nancy Hilliard talks as if she already saw all the old faculty reinstated, and three hundred students coming in. I doubt if any of the old faculty ever come back, and it will be long before prosperity is restored to an institution so degraded. I want the first step toward reform taken by the new legislature, by the reorganization of the University. I want this crew turned out."

From ex-Governor Vance came this letter: "I was much delighted to receive your letter yesterday, so full of your cheerful congratulations on the happy results of the election.... There is indeed matter for congratulation and rejoicing in the work which has been accomplished. It was the almost unaided work of the people, and blesses us with the thought that tho' slow to move, yet they *will* move with strength and power to preserve their liberties. I am quite sure now that my impatience with the people for not voting down the Constitution in 1868 was wrong; and that [it] is better we should have been taught the evils of Radicalism by suffering, as we have been taught. Had we rejected it without trial, our triumph might have been uncertain and temporary— now the popular feeling against that party is justified by experience, and the horror inspired by its conceptions and tyranny *will last.*

"In short, as my dear wife is always telling me, with that simple faith in God which is so much better and wiser than the statesman's wisdom, 'All things are overruled for the best.' I wish I had time to tell you half I feel on this subject. We are in a great crisis, and much wisdom and moderation will be required to enable us to make a proper use of our victory. We are singularly unfortunate in this, that we have so few men of experience in the Legislature. In the Senate, it is true, there will be a few old stagers and some young men of talent, but the House is as sorry a lot of boys as ever filled a legislative body. Still there seems to be a general desire for moderation and prudence.

"Of course I can indulge in no unseemly rejoicing over the defeat of your brother. I did feel, however, his defection more than that of any man in the State. You know the respect and kind regard in which I have always held him, and when he, with all his dignity and personal uprightness accepted the nomination and undertook the defense of the miserable band of thieves who lead that party, I almost thought he must be mad, I was positively *shocked*. Yet I refrained from any unkind expressions about him and am doubly glad I did so. I replied to him at Statesville and from the manner of my friends thought I was failing in my *stump* powers. We all make mistakes, this was the great one of his life. I hope to see him on the Supreme Court bench yet...."

From Kemp P. Battle, young Raleigh lawyer and nephew of Cornelia's sister-in-law, Laura Battle Phillips, came this letter also relating to Cornelia's brother:

"Mr. Sam was nominated by the honest element of the Republican Party led by Tod Caldwell. It was a bitter pill for Holden. I have not had such pain in years; but he is so truthful, honorable, and noble he will outlive the false impression of the present day."

In Cornelia's many letters of this period there is no criticism of her brother's lack of political orthodoxy, although his acceptance of a place on the Republican ticket must have been even more shocking to her than to Zeb Vance and far more painful to her than to Kemp Battle. It was many years, when she was living in another state and era, before she was able to voice her feelings in this way: "What a mistake it was, dear Sam's joining the Republican Party. When I recall those days of humiliation, exasperation, and despair it does not seem so very long ago."

What made "Mr. Sam's" desertion of his own class and party the more mystifying was his reputation for complete integrity. At no previous stage of his life had he ever been queer in his behavior or odd in his opinions. His acceptance of a place on the Holden ticket cost him many friendships and considerably reduced his possible law practice. He was at length the victim of something like a social as well as a political boycott, so much so that when an opportunity came to start a new career in Washington during the Grant administration, he eagerly seized it. Yet from his opinions, once adopted, he never retreated; nor did he ever offer any explanation for his change of political base, not even to the sister on whose affection he always relied. From what remains of his personal and political correspondence it can only be surmised that as a firm Unionist he believed his place was in the Republican party; and he was convinced that the South's tendency to put all its eggs in one political basket, and keep them there, was bad for its people and for the nation. He regarded orthodoxy of belief and uniformity of opinion as the props of mental stodginess and decay. And all such he despised.

v

In the midst of these tumults and stresses, Cornelia tried to keep herself tranquil. She consoled herself with the children whom she delighted to gather around her. That summer her nieces, Elinor and Lucy Phillips, came to visit her daughter June, and this is an account of one of their diversions written to Laura Phillips while elsewhere the politicans and rulers fought among themselves:

"The girls took Eliza [a little Negro nurse] and went wading Sunday afternoon. I promised to meet them at Aunt Dilsey's about 5:30, and sent down a basket of supper for us all—a batch of rolls just out of the oven (made by Jane), an apple pie, a pound of sugar, one-half pound of coffee, and a parcel of ginger cakes. So that Aunt Dilsey had nothing to do but make coffee. . . . She had some delicious fresh buttermilk for us and Uncle Ben brought in some peaches and melons. So we had a good time, Eliza and all, and got home after dark. The girls will look back to these little parties with pleasure maybe fifty years hence, when you and I and Aunt Dilsey are all gone."

[The author's mother was one of the little girls at this picnic. She clearly remembered it seventy-four years later.]

In the North Carolina *Presbyterian* Cornelia described a Fourth of July celebration as carried out in Chapel Hill in 1871 by the Negroes of the village:

"Jordan Swain was the orator of the day, and he took occasion to remind his audience that it was not properly the colored man's holiday. 'We are not to talk of our forefathers making this a glorious anniversary—it was rather our *foremasters*—and we as colored people have no particular interest in it. Our independence day is on Emancipation anniversary.' Nevertheless, Jordan read the old Declaration of Independence, and he and old Uncle Ben Craig gave their people some very good advice— to keep out of politics, to get an education, to be industrious and quiet, and attend to their own business and raise their children well. Jordan especially disclaimed politics and said expressly that no white men had been invited to join their celebration for fear of getting up political speeches. So Uncle Ben gave out a hymn and they all sang as only colored people can sing, with all their heart, and Green Caudle addressed a religious exhortation which was well received."

Cornelia was delighted to be able to get back to books and reading. The use of the libraries belonging to the two student literary and debating societies, "the Di and Phi," which had been denied her when the Pool regime took charge, was restored to her late in 1870; but she wrote a correspondent that those libraries had been "sadly pillaged since Holden's Negro troops first arrived and took charge."

And then came the crash. The University under President Pool could not and did not survive the year 1870, and the trustees suddenly ordered it closed. Faculty members were virtually abandoned. They could not pay their debts to storekeepers, and were reduced to cutting the groves of the campus for firewood. Cornelia herself sent food to some of the professors' homes for the benefit of their children.

VI

In the autumn of 1871 Cornelia was able to record a great triumph over the enemy. Secretary Lassiter of the despairing trustees came to Chapel Hill to see her. Had she a plan for restor-

ing the University? And would she write out her ideas? She told
him the Pool administration ought to resign unconditionally, and
that the only hope of restoration would be through the alumni,
who should be invited to take charge. Mr. Lassiter went away
sorrowful. But Cornelia's was the plan that was eventually adopted.
"I endeavored," she wrote ex-Governor Vance, "to feel not unduly
elated by the honor thus thrust upon me." Wherein is visible
the secret smile of those who must do good by stealth.

17

Politician in Skirts

I

AT THE VERY opening of 1872, Cornelia's long battle for the reorganization of the University began to bear fruit. Alexander McIver, who had been one of the professors under President Pool, was appointed state superintendent of public instruction; and one of his first acts was to call a meeting of the University alumni at Raleigh to consider means by which the institution might be revived. In this movement, his chief lieutenant and instigator was Cornelia. She wrote letters to influential men praying their attendance; and she induced the newspapers to give publicity to the cause, even contributing editorials to the Raleigh journals. In the midst of these activities she was employed by W. C. Kerr, the state geologist, to make for him a large map of North Carolina to be used on his lecturing trips, and this task took her down to Raleigh, where she could see what the alumni would do.

The first meeting was held in the Senate chamber of the capitol, February 2, 1872. About fifty old students attended. "It was a sight to me," she wrote her mother, "that made tears lie very near the surface. There were Graham and his boys, and Barringer, and Battle and his sons, and the Binghams and the Haywoods, and many another familiar name and face." A committee composed of Graham, Battle, and Barringer was appointed to confer with the trustees' executive committee. Disappointing to Cornelia was the late arrival of her brother Sam. When he did appear, he disappointed her again by saying nothing. "They all tell me," she wrote her mother, "I must be made an hon[orary] member. I

142

tell them if being mad for three years entitles one, I have a right
—and say many pretty things about my pen and pencil.... One
old student who graduated in '44 told me he had been in love
with me ever since he left college."

II

Before the month was gone, "Mr. Sam," Cornelia's dignified
but unpredictable brother, was appointed solicitor general of the
United States by President Grant. He at once went to Washington
to take up his new duties; he was no doubt glad to do so, for in
his native State his life was no longer comfortable. His law firm,
Phillips and Merrimon, at Raleigh, was doing well enough, but
because he was prominent in the Republican party he was subjected to social barriers to which he himself was more or less
indifferent but which to his womenfolk were unendurable. After
a few weeks in Washington he urged Frances Lucas Phillips, his
wife, to come up and choose a dwelling house; at the same time
he implored Cornelia to go to Raleigh, help his wife, "Aunt
Fanny," get off, and remain to care for his children.

Like a good sister, Cornelia obeyed, leaving behind her small
daughter June in the care of her grandmother and of the Negro
servants. From Raleigh Cornelia wrote this mournful news about
Miss Nancy Hilliard, who had moved to Raleigh in the great dis-
persion:

"Her house is going down every day. Mr. Utley gets drunk,
and the boarders had no fires all day last Sunday, no wood. The
few she has would leave, but Mr. Utley has borrowed money of
them, and they stay to eat it out."

About the Samuel Phillips household the news was more lively:
"When I went into Aunt F's [Fanny's] room and saw how much
there was still to do to get her ready, I began to think she wd not
get off in a week. There was a woman sewing for dear life on
a beautiful apron for Gerty [the baby], whose travelling dress
was not even done—None of her dresses home from the dress-
maker's—none of their clothes in from the wash, Aunt F's new

black silk not come home from Mrs. Scarlet's, and to crown all, a box from N. Y. (with three dresses made there and a new cloak) had not yet arrived by express. ... As soon as I had had a glass of ale and some ham and biscuit, I looked for my thimble and went to work you may guess. The first thing I did was to pleat a flannel skirt and sew it on the body, and finish it. Next to make 12 fine button-holes. Next to finish G's [the baby's] travelling dress. ...

"When I came in her room this morning it was after 8 o'c. Train left at 10. The black silk had not come home—the clothes from the laundress had not come. The woman was still sewing for dear life on G's white velours cloak, and not a thing had been put in the trunk.

"After the omnibus was at the door, I had to fix up the lunch basket. In the midst of all the hurry-skurry, everybody on the lot, and about twenty people off it, busy doing something for her, Aunt F. was as quiet and serene and deliberate as if she did not expect to leave in a month. ... Wonderful to relate, however, *she got off.*"

It was characteristic of Cornelia, this ability to pause in the midst of her campaign for the reopening of the University, her map-making, her care of her mother and her child, her anxiety about the poverty that seemed to be drying up the village of Chapel Hill at its very roots, to engage in the feminine arts of sewing and dressmaking, even of cooking; for on Thanksgiving Day, 1872, she sent food to no less than seven persons outside her home. "People in Chapel Hill are poorer all the time," she wrote to the late President Swain's widow. "Would you ever have thought of Miss Nancy Hilliard as an object of charity? and yet I fear she is. ...

"Gangs of negroes spend the night in Old South Building, rioting, shouting, drinking. You have no idea of the degradation. The halls and libraries are broken into at all times, and I am told that the Phi library which is especially in Mr. Pool's hands, has its books scattered all over the buildings. ...

"Old Dr. November lies on his death bed. He had made a profession of religion. He told me all about it. He said, 'Miss Cornelia, I liked to have been too late!' His principal pleasure is
having some old friend sit and talk about old times. He says he
knows he will see all the old faculty sitting up there in Heaven.
He means to look for 'em!'"

III

During this period, Cornelia, when not distracted by numerous
other interests, returned again and again to one of her favorite
subjects—more and better education for the boys and girls of
North Carolina. She wanted to see the state give more money and
support to the common schools as well as the colleges, and to
make education free. "We must educate upwards," she declared.
For two years she contributed articles to the daily and religious
press to proclaim this motto. She wrote to the state's leading men
to ask their opinion. To her warm letters ex-Governor Graham
replied coolly; he wrote bluntly that his preference was for educating downwards; that is, he favored building up the University
first and the schools afterward. Cornelia saw in this the danger
of a class division, and she appealed to ex-Governor Vance as
one closer to the people than the dignified Graham. Vance replied from Charlotte with a characteristic gayety and lack of
definiteness:

"My dear Mrs. Spencer: If I did not know, historically, that
you were of English descent, I would have made 'a Alfred Davy,'
as Mr. Riderhood would say, that you were a *born Irisher*, and
had an axe to grind! Your last was really the most outrageous
piece of flattery that I ever saw! You must not do so anymore;
you know my head is easily turned anyhow. I read it over to
Mrs. Vance, and she quietly remarked, 'Well, if the women of
N. C. don't make a fool of you, it will be a wonder.' So now being warned, I hope you will be more careful in the future. . . .

"Your article on the University, common schools, etc., was first
rate. I enjoyed the hit at the *commonality* of the former hugely.

By the way, referring to the question you ask, Where are the public schools of the State, Mrs. Vance bids me say to you that she and the ladies of our church here have a school going for the poor in this place, with 50 schollars [*sic*], who are educated and almost clothed by our congregation, called the Mission School. It has become so large and prosperous, that we are raising funds to build a commodious house, and for this purpose I am to deliver a lecture for them in a few days. So you see that private spirit is doing something without waiting for Ashley [state superintendent of public instruction]...."

Though Cornelia received small encouragement for some of her efforts in behalf of education, she continued to write for the papers, and in few articles did she fail to insert an artful stroke for the deserted University. For example, an account of a Sunday School picnic at Chapel Hill contained these passages:

"To my mind, cold chicken, apple tart, and bread and butter, judiciously interspersed with hard boiled partridge eggs, form not inappropriate adjuncts to the Sunday School cause of a June morning when introduced about 12 m.

"Your correspondent took occasion during the recess to stroll about the college grounds and buildings. Alas and alas! Some bold hand has written on the walls of a passage in the old West Building, 'Ichabod, Ichabod, the glory is departed!...' An old resident like myself walks through these corridors and groves repeopling them with the dead. Familiar faces look out at every window and meet me on the gravel walks."

This was Cornelia's way of saying to North Carolina, still inert but slowly recovering from its wounds, "How long? How long?"

18

Ring Out, Wild Bells

I

THE YEAR 1873 saw the village and Cornelia's spirits sink even lower than during the darkest days of the war. Then, an atom of hope might have been seen; now there was none. Poverty, weeds, sickness, and empty days sat at every street corner. Silence draped itself on every college wall. Not anywhere in town or on campus was there life or motion.

Late in the year Miss Nancy Hilliard, once so generous with food and good humor, died, destitute, in her little tavern room. "No minister in town, and no religious service or observances, unless you call such the tolling of our church bell," wrote Cornelia to her brother Charles. "Just as it began, and the little procession moved from the door, the *University-bell* joined in. . . . It was pitiful to see [deaf-mute] Lem Yancey following Miss Nancy to her grave with his head bent down." To keep up her spirits and to occupy a mind that might have become morbid had it been idle for a day, Cornelia resorted to her old love of teaching. She taught both a white Sunday School class and a Negro one, and organized sewing circles of little girls.

And then on a sleety day early in 1874 her brother Charles wrote her from Davidson College that he had heard there was hope the University might soon be reorganized. He had no details to give, but the mere hint was so enlivening that Cornelia was happy and uplifted even while the sleet of a January ice storm tinkled against her windows; and when her brother Charles sent some money to her for "old Couch," the village hermit, she was able to joke with Couch, saying if he didn't wash his face and make himself look like a white man, no woman would marry him. "You ought to have seen his old bleared eyes," she wrote. Later when Couch lay dying she went to his wretched shack, taking with her her little niece, Lucy Plummer Phillips, and herself washed his face. In a moment she exclaimed: "Why, Lucy, he's got blue eyes!"

Going on such errands was characteristic of Cornelia; she knew not fear and loved every soul that could claim Chapel Hill as home. She was capable of stopping any citizen to give either praise or reproof, and she could be emphatic with both. She once walked up to a leader in the Negro community and said without preliminaries: "No race can rise that does not value the chastity of its women—remember that." And walked on.

II

The year 1874 proved to be almost without meaning. It dragged itself to a slow end and faded, and then came the electric year 1875, destined to be vivid and memorable on every page of Cornelia's diary. It began with an event momentous in the Phillips household. Cornelia's daughter June was deemed old enough to go to a boarding school. She entered Peace Institute, the Presbyterian school for girls at Raleigh. In her diary Cornelia chronicled the news without a tremor. And yet to part with this daughter must have cost her an all but heartbreaking pang; for upon the bright-eyed June she had gradually come to pour out all the long-pent affections that elsewhere had found no outlet.

All that June knew or had, had come from a lavish, untiring mother. Seldom, for even a day, had Cornelia been separated from this only child, whom she had tended for sixteen years; rarely had June been out of her sight; yet now Cornelia was surrendering her, and withdrawing to a silent home in which for companionship there was only an aging mother in an empty and weedy village. Yet for Cornelia there was a partial compensation: if she could no longer talk with her child at will, she could at least write. And forthwith thrice a week, and sometimes daily, there poured out a stream of letters from mother to daughter, filled with village doings, with adages and distillations from the sages, with wisdom and not a little wit, mixed with gossip, sharp observation, and pungent comment.

III

All during these years of the seventies Cornelia's notes, letters, and newspaper correspondence that had so long pleaded for the reopening of the University were like seed sprouting in the slow soil of winter; outwardly there was no sign of germination, yet below the surface there was a slight but perceptible stir of life. Men had by now tired of hatreds and repression; they longed for days of peace and upbuilding work.

In the spring of 1875 word came to Cornelia that the University trustees had found a way to raise some money and the courts were being liberal. In early March she was able to write June about the exciting outlook. On March 20 a telegram from Kemp P. Battle at Raleigh brought the sudden and tonic news that the legislature had passed a bill permitting the reorganization of the University and even guaranteeing it a measure of support.

This day was her fiftieth birthday; but about that she cared nothing. She ran to her mother with the news. She ran to her neighbors with the same joyful story. She came back home to walk the floor and wait for the demonstration she was sure would come. Surely the happy villagers would turn out with fife and drum, parade the streets with torches and red fire. An hour, two hours, she waited, watching the streets. At last, no longer able to contain herself, she called to her daughter June, who happened to be at home. She and June collected two children of a neighbor, Susan and Jenny Thompson, and together they started for the campus. On the way they gathered the faithful villager, once the postmaster and University bursar, Andrew G. Mickle. Cornelia marched them all through the Episcopal churchyard and over the broad campus path to the South Building in which hung the college bell and rope. And finding all these silent, she climbed to the belfry and seized the rope. And then she rang and rang and rang. . . . She did more than ring a bell; she rang out an old world of defeat and inertia and rang in a new world of hope and belief. It was an incident that Frank P. Graham, in his speeches as president of the University in the depressed 1930's, used to dwell upon. His report to the trustees in December, 1930, ended with this paragraph:

"In the tragic era, Mrs. Cornelia Phillips Spencer, staunch champion of the public schools and University, received March 20, 1875, a message from the committee in Raleigh that the University was to be opened again. For five years the bell had not rung in Chapel Hill. For five years she had worked and prayed for that day. She climbed the stairs to the belfry and with her own hands rang the bell which has never ceased to ring to this day. The people of North Carolina were on the march again. Under God, we will not turn back now!"

IV

In May Cornelia wrote happily to Charles: "Kemp Battle and Mr. [John] Manning and Mr. P. Cameron were all here last week. Kemp staid with me. . . . Mr. Manning came down with his boy to see me after tea, and he and K[emp] and Mr. D[alton] and I and Mr. McIver, who, (I hear, stuck to the Trustees all the time they were here, like a tick!) sat on the piazza and agreed there were nowhere such *trees,* moonlight, nor air, as here. It was delightful to hear those old students talk. There seemed to be a constant disposition among us to be shaking hands all the time."

But by the time midsummer of 1875 had come, Cornelia, the first exhilaration having passed, was suffering from a psychic reaction; and she confessed to her brother Charles: "When I sit down and think about it all, I feel down in the mouth. I want to feel all glorious, and I cannot!" The cure for such spells of gloom was more activity and a new crusade. Cornelia knew this as well as anyone, and only a few weeks had passed before she had thought of a new enterprise that would benefit the revived but still impoverished University. It was a plan to induce the women of the state to outfit the scientific departments with new and improved apparatus. Outlining a clever propaganda campaign and revealing her cunning when she was about to do good, she wrote this characteristic letter to Kemp P. Battle in October, 1875:

"Please read the enclosed, and then read it to Mrs. Battle and Miss Nellie, and note if they are at all stirred by it. *Ex una, disce omnes.*

"I propose to send 15 or 20 copies to as many papers from Asheville and Morganton to the sea. And then I wish to write a private letter to some leading lady, old or young, in each of our principal towns, in my own name, to ask her to set the work going. ... I think every large female school in the State ought to be stirred up to contribute. Say each one of those in Raleigh gives $50. It would be a beautiful thing to do.

"I shall write little notes to accompany the circulars to each editor and ask his good word. Tell me the names of some of the prominent ladies of Wilmington, Fayetteville and Tarboro. I can indite them a pretty enough little note.... Good lack! how my heart beats to make 'em rise in their majesty and *do* something.... Don't you think a note from you, and from other gentlemen of the executive committee, to ladies here and there would do good? ... Our women, unless officered or encouraged in some such way, are timid of moving. And might be jealous of each other.... Do you not know that ladies care more for the wishes and good opinion of your sex than of their own?"

The circular letter mentioned here has unfortunately been lost; but it is known that the campaign as a whole was successful, as most of Cornelia's campaigns were; for it is on record that the University at this period was indebted to the "school for young ladies" kept at Hillsboro by the Misses Nash and Kollock for "Plateau's apparatus"; to the ladies of Louisburg, through Mrs. Joseph J. Davis, for a "parallelogram of Forces"; to Salem Female School for "Fortin's barometer"; to the ladies of Raleigh, through Mrs. Annie Moon Parker, for "Atwood's machine, galvanometer, and thermo-electric pile"; to the ladies of Hillsboro for a "Holtz electrical machine, giving a 20-inch spark"; to the ladies of Salisbury, through Mrs. May Wheat Shober, a "hydraulic press and turbine wheel." Thus did the women of North Carolina enable the young men at the University to begin the new era with a modern if modest collection of scientific apparatus. This was actually the second time in the University's history that the women of the state had risen to meet the same need, other scientific equipment having been presented by women during the presidency of Dr. Caldwell.

19

New Times and Men

I

"Y OU MUST COME home to take care of her . . . your dear generous mother," wrote Julia Vermeule Phillips, to June Spencer, in the spring of 1875, "for she is pressed into service by public as well as private imposition." Mrs. Phillips added: "Everyone is repairing their front fences."

Such were the signs of the times. The village, so long prostrate and somnolent, was now suddenly pulsating again with a new and eager life, and the Phillips house, long unused to any visitors, was a stopping place for important men in wide collars and broad white shirtfronts. The University was going to reopen in September —that was the word that brought life to every street, field, lane, and house; for the University furnished the heartbeat that poured living blood through the community's every artery. Cornelia even in her pride remained the thoughtful sister and friend, and she now hastened to advise Charles: "It is time for you to be making up your mind about returning to Chapel Hill. It is a sort of duty. You ought to return."

II

All that summer the village echoed with the joyful sound of hammer and saw, and smelled of fresh paint; for not only the University buildings but all the faculty homes needed repairs and refittings. Down from Hillsboro came the sturdy Paul C. Cameron, with a face like the map of Scotland, trustee, planter, and former slave-owner, himself to superintend the refurbishing and to make

153

new plantings of young trees to replace the campus oaks, which were falling and failing after wresting with storms for a century and more. An avenue of maples running through the campus from east to west still bears the name of Cameron Avenue.

Paul Cameron was then sixty-seven years old, a powerful-looking man with red hair and a great curving nose. On his father's plantation, Fairntosh, half a day's drive from Chapel Hill, more slaves were to be found before the Civil War than at any other place in the state. He and Cornelia came to be close friends, and whenever the University was in danger of suffering loss or damage, she learned to sound the alarm that brought Mr. Cameron to the rescue. His energetic labors had everything ready for the September opening. Fifty-nine students came. They assembled in the chapel where Cornelia and other village women had arranged the decorations. The central one was an evergreen motto made by Cornelia bearing seven letters: *Laus Deo*—"Thank God." And it was Cornelia who wrote the closing hymn sung at the triumphant reopening on September 15:

> Eternal Source of light and truth!
> To Thee again our hearts we raise.
> Except Thou build and keep the house,
> In vain the laborer spends his days.
>
> Without Thine aid, in vain our zeal
> Strives to rebuild the broken walls;
> Vainly our sons invoke the Muse
> Among these sacred groves and halls.
>
> From off Thine altar send a coal,
> As burning seraphs erst have brought;
> Re-light the flame that once inspired
> The faithful teachers and the taught.
>
> Pour on our path th' unclouded light,
> That from Thy constant favor springs;
> Let heart and hand be strong beneath
> The shadow of almighty wings.

Recall, O God, the golden days,
May rude unfruitful discord cease;
Our sons in crowds impatient throng
These ancient haunts of white-robed Peace.

So shall our upward way be fair
As that our sainted fathers trod;
Again the "Priest and Muse" declare
The holy Oracles of God.

III

And then, the exercises of this joyful day being over, Cornelia sat down and wrote for John D. Cameron, editor of the *Raleigh Daily News*, an account of the reopening:

"The day has been bright and beautiful, September was never more charming. The old college has donned her new dress, a delicate fawn relieved with brown. . . .

"At 11 o'clock a.m. the procession was formed according to the programmer, John Hutchins, Esq., acting as marshall, A. S. Barbee, Esq., and several of the newly arrived students assistants. The Salisbury Band afforded not the least item in the pleasure of the day. A band of gentlemen, they came promptly and generously at the call of the University and gave us the best music in the State without fee or reward. . . . Gov. Brogden, Judge Battle, Dr. Hooper, Gov. Vance, Dr. Phillips and Profs. Mangum and Redd occupied the rostrum, the Trustees and other distinguished visitors the area in front. About fifty of the *Horner* boys [from a leading preparatory school] occupied seats behind them with the students of the University, while the galleries were packed with friends from the vicinity and abroad. . . . The band gave *'Auld Lang Syne'* in beautiful style. There were hearts full and eyes overflowing at the memories awakened by that strain. . . .

"Rev. Dr. Hooper offered a prayer. This thrice venerable and beloved gentleman, who was himself a student more than 70 years ago, forms the only link now surviving with those early days, and it seemed a peculiarly happy circumstance that he should be present at the revival, after the long and death-like swoon of the college which he knew in its infancy. His prayer was devout, tender and trustful.

"Prof. Redd then read the opening hymn (which was sung to the good old tune, Coronation) composed for the occasion by Mr. W. A. Betts, a son of the Rev. Mr. Betts, of the Methodist Church, who graduated here more than twenty years ago, and married one of the prettiest girls in Chapel Hill during his Senior vacation. . . .

"Dr. Phillips then rose, making a short address as to the objects and aims of the founders of the University. It was said 80 years ago that they meant to establish a school of sound learning, *'without either politics or religion,'* that is without undue influence from party or sect. . . .

"Very few persons present were not agreeably surprised with our Governor's address. It was a speech full of animation, imbued with the best spirit of the age, wasting no time on vain regrets but pointing forward and onward. . . .

"Gov. Vance . . . remarked that perhaps his eyes were dim, but it seemed to him surveying the throng before him that the daughters were prettier than their mothers used to be.

"The Governor's eyes were doubtless dim as he spoke—dim for the moment, as many others were—but the accuracy of his vision is beyond all cavil, and especially where pretty girls are concerned. There were some in that old chapel to-day as fair as Commencement sun ever shone on—and I cannot say more. I have never seen anywhere finer types of female beauty than North Carolina has a way of sending up to Chapel Hill on these occasions. For delicacy of complexion, refinement of features and bewitching grace of air and manner, commend me to a thoroughbred North Carolina girl. . . .

"Judge W. H. Battle's was the tenderer task to awaken the echoes of memory, and bid us Remember, Resemble, and Persevere. . . .

"Col. W. L. Saunders, Gen. W. R. Cox, Messrs Horner and Graves, Maj. Bingham and Capt. Lynch, Maj. Hamilton, E. Morehead, J. S. Carr, A. W. Graham, H. Merritt, T. M. Argo, Capt. Ramsey, H. London, H. A. Nash, W. T. De Rosset, Jno. W. Graham, Thos. Webb, Thos. B. Hill, Major Duskin, and many other representative men were among the audience....

"Prof. [A. W.] Mangum next advanced and read the closing hymn, prefacing it with an elegant and graceful compliment to the lady [Mrs. Spencer] who had written it for the occasion.... This the band rendered finely to Old Hundred, the audience rising and singing with one consent. Our hearts were thrilled with joy and hope and a just exultation and gratitude."

IV

Other energetic men now came often to Chapel Hill. Among them was the young and courtly lawyer from Raleigh, Kemp P. Battle, whose cheerful talk and confidence in the future were cheering even to occasionally despondent people like Cornelia. One day in 1875 he wrote her that he had been elected president of the University.

"When the trustees decided that I was the 'best man under the circumstances,' I did not refuse. You will help me I know, you will always talk to me candidly and freely. Dr. Phillips will work with me as cordially as anyone could.

"I do not feel so burdened with *you* to help me, as I otherwise would, but my thoughts of the future are very solemn."

After such a tribute to her views and influence, Cornelia could not fail to respond; and indeed she was Dr. Battle's loyal supporter—and occasional critic—throughout the fifteen years of his presidency. Kemp Battle proved to be a leader in a line of great presidents. By birth and upbringing he was well suited to the post. His paternal grandfather, Joel Battle, was one of the University's earliest students. His father, Judge William H. Battle, was head of the University's first law school. Himself a graduate of 1849, Dr. Battle was first a tutor of Latin, then of mathematics.

He was in turn a lawyer, banker, railroad president, and planter. He was state treasurer in 1868. These occupations, he told Cornelia, "have trained me for the grandest of all trades perhaps." Dr. Battle's policy was to win the state's people back to the University. He was patient, careful, and considerate, and before he retired in 1891 to take the chair of history, he had reestablished the University upon a thriving basis.

v

The year 1875 was memorable, too, for the return of Cornelia's brother, Dr. Charles Phillips, and family to Chapel Hill from Davidson College. He was one of the three members of the pre-war faculty reinstated in their old positions, the others being Professor Kimberley and Professor J. DeB. Hooper. Dr. Phillips went to live in the Governor Swain house, almost opposite the old home of his parents and sister. To Ellie Swain Atkins, who was living happily with her captured ex-general in Illinois, Cornelia wrote this news: "Everybody is having a new front fence! I go in and out of your old home sometimes four or five times a day, just as if it had been Charles's home and this mine always. I don't think brother Charles likes to live there. He says the memories oppress him dreadfully."

Dr. Phillips was at once elected chairman of the new faculty, a post which he held for a year until Kemp P. Battle assumed the presidency. Great as was Cornelia's pleasure at thus being near her brother again, her delight in having the companionship of her sister-in-law, Laura Battle Phillips, was no less; for these two women had formed a friendship that lasted the remainder of their days. Cornelia's portrait of Laura, written about this time, says, "Laura is looking remarkably well these days, if not the prettiest one of us all. She is as plump and fair as you can imagine, her hair like satin and not a grey hair to be seen."

VI

In June, 1876, Cornelia wrote one of her happiest letters to Ellie Atkins:

"I have lived to see another Commencement. Have seen the college chapel crowded once more, and 750 fans in motion at once. Have seen the campus thronged and the procession marching, what time we heard the sound of the harp, flute, sackbut, dulcimer, psaltery, and all kinds of musical instruments. It has been a very gay and pretty and successful commencement, and I know your mother and you will be glad to hear it. . . . Tell your mother I had the following beaux to call to see me: Col. R. R. Bridgers, Col. Steele, Mr. Cameron, Col. Dave Carter, Mr. John Manning, Maj. Robt. Bingham, Dr. N. McKay, Dr. Pritchard— all the old fogies; but I was very well satisfied with my share of the fun. . . . The company for Commencement did not arrive in any great numbers till Tuesday evening when Nellie Battle led the train by driving in town in an open carriage with Mr. Duncan Cameron (looking beautiful). Next came another open carriage with Judge Battle and Bessie Batchelor and some young ladies from Louisburg. Next came John Watson's hack with my June and Alice Kerr and her brother. This, I guess, was the very happiest group of all. And then the Salisbury band—resplendent with six horses and just a-playing. Didn't I wish I was a little darky just then, so I could run along the sidewalk and *screech?* . . . Nellie Battle was the belle, of course. Fab. Busbee was flying around Nellie, also Mr. Cameron and a dozen other men. No one knows who is to be the lucky man. . . . Bessie B. is very much such a girl as her mother, Cary Plummer, was 25 years ago . . . Miss Mary Loder, also late of Chapel Hill, now of Raleigh, was quite a belle. Certainly a pretty girl and well dressed. She danced at the ball until broad daylight. So did several other Methodist girls. Tell your mother I want to know what modern Methodism is coming to. When I was a child Methodist members did not even wear artificial flowers."

In the same year Cornelia joined a group of Raleigh women in raising a fund to make and send to the Centennial Exposition at Philadelphia a banner to represent the State of North Carolina. This movement was at one time paralyzed by the rumor that a hundred captured Confederate flags were to be displayed in the same hall. But when this story was exposed as a canard, the fund was completed and the banner was painted by the Reverend Johannes Oertel, the only North Carolina resident (he then lived at Lenoir) who could claim to be a good preacher and a good painter, too. This banner was brought back to Chapel Hill where it is still preserved in the University Library.

20

No More Crumbs

I

IT WAS CHARACTERISTIC of Cornelia that as fast as she triumphed with one cause, she was bound to take up another. No sooner was the University once more open and thriving than she immersed herself in another thorny undertaking. The boys of North Carolina were now provided for; were the girls to have no more than the crumbs of education left over from male feasts? "Crumbs"— it was a word she often used indignantly. She wrote Ellen Mitchell Summerell:

"I think N. C. ought to give the girls of the state some attention as well as the boys. Co-education will never do in these latitudes, but don't you think the state ought to make some provision for the girls? When I think of what mere crumbs they have to pick up, I get angry."

With Cornelia Spencer to feel was to be moved to act; and it was not long before she was resorting to her characteristic habit of writing letters in order to disseminate stimulating ideas. One of the correspondents who exchanged views with her about the education of women was Major R. W. Bingham, director of a famous school for boys at Mebane, a few miles north of Chapel Hill. Only a few scattered pages remain of this correspondence, but these are enough to show that the sparks flew as steel met steel. The Major in a letter early in 1876 was not very sympathetic:

"More money is spent in North Carolina to teach girls to sing (to yell like hyenas) and tear the piano to pieces, both accomplishments being given up before the honeymoon is over in most cases,

161

than would sustain ten first-class male schools of 75 boys each
at $100 for tuition fees—and what a difference there would be
in results upon the State, its interest, its programs, its glory!"

But Cornelia declined to be discouraged by the fact that North
Carolina was backward even in male education. She continued to
send around her eloquent letters, and she talked often with leading men, pointing out that her young daughter June and her young
niece, Lucy Phillips, were having no great difficulty absorbing
Horace and Racine and botany under her tutelage, proving that
the feminine mind was just as capable of learning certain things
as the masculine one. One man who listened to her pleas was
President Battle, who lived only a few minutes' walk from Cornelia's house.

II

In the spring of 1877 the University announced that it would
that summer sponsor a summer normal school and that women
students might attend and enjoy the same privileges as men. ("The
Board of Education took the ground and the University con-
curred," says Battle's History of the University, "that while the
public money could not be paid to females, there could be no objection to their attending the sessions.") The sensation caused by
this announcement was enormous. Not only was this the first summer normal school ever attempted by any state university, but
it was felt that in admitting women to its lectures and classrooms,
the University was setting an example that was certain to have
momentous consequences. When the summer school opened, pro-
gressive citizens like Cornelia and Kemp Battle were delighted
by the lift in the air; but conservative minds felt that the University had plunged into a dark abyss and that the foundations of
the republic were being swept away by reckless and dangerous
innovations.

The University trustees in that year formally thanked Cornelia
for her labors in its behalf, but they did not credit her with launching the project of a summer normal school. That, indeed, was a

product of many minds, and its immediate success at Chapel Hill was chiefly due to the enthusiasm and care of President Battle. But to Cornelia belongs the credit for first obtaining the University authorities' permission for women to attend a series of classroom lectures in regular term-time. The subject was botany. The lecturer was Professor W. H. Smith. The women who won this momentous privilege were Cornelia, her daughter June, and her niece, Lucy Phillips. They were admitted under an agreement that they were to occupy the rear seats and with the tacit understanding that they were to keep very quiet!

This was some months before the summer school opened. When it did open in July, 1877, with a distinguished group of teachers and lecturers (Walter H. Page, subsequently editor in Boston and New York and ambassador to England, lectured in 1878 on philology and Shakespeare), Cornelia blessed it and listened to its speakers—though she could not hear a word—and wrote columns about it in the state papers, assuring parents their daughters would be properly safeguarded at Chapel Hill, where room, lights, and board could be had at the leading hotel, John Watson's, for $12.50 a month.

"The lady teachers who contemplate attending," she wrote in the Raleigh *Observer*, "may come feeling assured of welcome, encouragement and protection. And when such a woman as Miss Mitchell, of the Simonton Female College at Statesville, announces her intention of joining the school, and such a man as Maj. Bingham, of the Bingham School, teachers of both sexes may rely upon it there will be something worth coming for. For our female teachers especially I feel interested that such a golden opportunity, unparalleled in the history of North Carolina, should not pass unimproved by them. . . . Let no one stay away through want of courage or want of faith." Although Cornelia was later uncertain about some aspects of coeducation, she wrote at the end of this summer: "I think the Normal School demonstrated that *for a normal school* co-education is a good thing, and need not be feared. . . . Young people of over 20 may be trusted to take care of themselves under the conditions of such a school as this. They usually have by that time gained some sensible, and more or less serious, views of life...."

This normal school had other noteworthy influences. Among the students just entering the University at this time was a young man named Charles D. McIver. He found a wife at the University Normal School; at the same time he imbibed teachings that afterwards caused him to journey throughout the state saying: "Educate a man and you educate a single person. Educate a woman and you educate a family." This crusade, in which other educators joined, resulted in the establishment at Greensboro of the State Normal College for women, where one of the largest buildings was later named Spencer Hall in honor of Cornelia; an example later followed by the University at Chapel Hill, which likewise named its first dormitory for girls Spencer Hall. At Chapel Hill there grew up a circle of lively young men who did not stay their hands until they had made schooling free and almost universal in North Carolina—C. B. Aycock, E. A. Alderman, M. C. S. Noble, E. P. Moses, and J. Y. Joyner. They were among the leaders who at the opening of the twentieth century brought about North Carolina's educational renaissance and made Chapel Hill a center of light in the Southeastern States. Some of these educators candidly declared they owed many good ideas to Cornelia Phillips Spencer.

By the time its second summer had begun the normal school was well established and Cornelia wrote of it wistfully in the Raleigh *Observer:*

"Miss Coe (kindergarten instructor) makes her first appearance this afternoon. We are intensely curious. She demands a carpet in the chapel, she demands flowers, she wants pictures; everything pretty and cheerful and striking. I wish I was a child again so I might be a Kindergarten scholar.... Calling on the Durham ladies at Dr. Roberson's I met the Rev. Mr. Harris of the Baptist Church. He was here last year. 'Madam,' said he 'this Normal School is the greatest work North Carolina ever inaugurated, the greatest charity, the best investment.' This is the exact truth.... When I sit in the chapel and hear them all singing I feel my heart so warmed and expanded that I love all the world, and could shake hands with the Republican party if it wanted to go to school."

And then she wrote a hymn of thanksgiving for the normal school. It was first sung July 21, 1878:

> Praise the Lord in joyful measures,
>   Let this love our song inspire;
> Kinglike, he bestows his treasures,
>   More than all our hearts desire.
>
> For our *sons* we asked that waters
>   From the desert's rock might burst.
> Lo! His love hath bid our *daughters*
>   Grace the feast and quench their thirst.

III

At the commencement exercises of 1877 Zebulon B. Vance, now governor of North Carolina for the second time, came to Chapel Hill to give a memorial lecture on the life of President Swain. According to his usual habit when he had an important speech to make, he sent the manuscript to Cornelia, praying her advice and correction. She went up to the chapel to hear him deliver it and wrote to Mrs. Swain:

"It was nobly done. He allowed me to read the manuscript, and although I could not hear one word, yet I could enjoy the occasion. I saw so many of Governor Swain's old friends and neighbors hanging on Vance's words. Many a handkerchief was pressed to eyes at his close, and I just leaned back in my place and cried heartily, the sweetest tears of mingled joy and pain of my whole life."

Cornelia began now to worry about Mrs. Phillips, her mother, who was often restless and fractious. "Ma has been very poorly— as I too have been—with a terrible cold," Cornelia wrote to Mrs. Summerell in Salisbury in the spring of 1877. "June too has not been well. She and I are both undergoing a course of quinine and iron which will I hope fit me at least for sundry tramps this spring to Otey's Retreat, Cave's Mill, and the like. Marg^t [Mitchell] announces that she is getting 'too old' for these delights. It is only because she has left off the habit so long. With a bunch of laurel or a tress of jessamine in view, I could tramp it as gaily now as thirty years ago."

And then just as summer days began to appear, a new affliction came upon the Phillips household. Cornelia's mother, now nearing eighty-two, fell and suffered an injury to her hip from which she never recovered. And now Cornelia must be nurse to a crippled old lady as well as to a convalescent University. But she found the time to write one of her longest and most eloquent songs. It was written especially for the students who had just organized a glee club and was sung by them on University Day, October 12, 1877. These are three of its stanzas:

O Carolina! well we love
The murmur of thy dark pine grove,
Thy yellow sands beside the sea,
The lake beneath thy cypress tree.

We love thy stately groves of oak,
Thy vines that hang o'er broad Roanoke,
Thy mountains from whose rugged steep
Catawba's rushing fountains leap.

Where on the hill the wild bird sings
Or jasmine's golden censer swings,
Where maidens loitering through the glen
Hear love's sweet story told again.

21

Newspaper Editor

I

FOR YEARS—in fact, almost ever since reaching maturity—Cornelia had been a part-time journalist. She had for years contributed more or less regularly to the chief daily papers of the state; but she had had no official connection with any newspaper except as a paid contributor to the *North Carolina Presbyterian*. Now she became an editor in full plumage. Her name appeared at the masthead of the Chapel Hill *Weekly Ledger*, April 26, 1879. Mrs. Spencer's letters of this period are scarce and what few survive contain no reference to the *Ledger* or her experiences there. The publisher of the paper was J. A. Harris. He employed two students as assistants, F. D. Winston and R. P. Pell. The former was for years a Superior Court judge. He was a brother of George T. Winston, at that time instructor in German at the University and subsequently its president. Pell later became president of Converse College for Women, Spartanburg, South Carolina.

Cornelia was succeeded as editor in September, 1879, by C. B. Aycock, then in his senior year as a student. Aycock subsequently became one of North Carolina's famous governors and leader of a passionate crusade for more and better schools. The *Ledger* was much like other small-town weeklies of the period; it consisted of four pages more or less filled with reprinted matter and personal paragraphs. What remains of its files shows little pungent writing of the sort characteristic of Cornelia. Perhaps she was not entirely happy as the *Ledger's* editor, and this may explain why her connection with it was comparatively brief.

At the end of this year Cornelia's brother Charles Phillips, who had long been intermittently ill with a rheumatic complaint, resigned as professor of mathematics and became professor emeritus. "Poor dear old soul!" wrote Cornelia. "He has been caring for other people and doing for them to the exclusion of his own interests and his own affairs, till he feels as if he would be a castaway if he omitted attending to everybody in turn."

II

In the autumn of the next year came a blow to Cornelia for which she had long been prepared, but which nevertheless brought her some of the sharpest suffering of her life. It was the departure of her daughter June to enter the art school at Cooper Union, New York, where she was to ready herself for earning her own living as a teacher. Upon June Cornelia had so long lavished the affection of an overflowing temperament that when she was deprived of this natural outlet for the fountains of her heart, she was bereft and shaken. She had not wanted her daughter to grow up in the lonely village; and, although she saw the separation as bound to give June an opportunity to develop her latent gifts, the actual parting hurt like a wound. There is no mistaking the cry of anguish that echoes in this letter to June written by Cornelia in September, 1880:

"I stood at the gate a long time after you drove off. Not thinking of anything—just standing and keeping myself from breaking down. . . . Then I went up stairs. Everything of yours that hung there was a fresh dagger. I took every thing and folded them up and put them away. Then I went to the bureau and opened every drawer—took up your little ribbon trunk and sat down on the bedside with it and kissed it over and over—took up the bits and bows of ribbon and kissed them, and smoothed them out. . . . How everything stabbed me. . . . O my child! my child! how my heart cried out for you!"

This was the beginning of a truly remarkable series of love-letters from mother to daughter, written two and three times weekly for many years. Most of them were about small matters, but June preserved them all; so that in them we have a day-to-day picture of Chapel Hill; and the vivid minutiae of life in a post-bellum college village in the South are set down with such warmth and wit as to reproduce every mentioned thing and person with a convincing life-likeness.

Hitherto Cornelia's letters to Mrs. Swain, to Laura Battle Phillips, and to Ellen Mitchell Summerell, have been our chief reliance; but from now on we will be drawing heavily on the rich and eloquent letters to June. During the early eighties they contained many aphorisms and pungent comments. These are specimens:

"Do you know what it is to have something to look forward to? Something all to yourself, with which nobody can intermeddle—an almost secret pleasure shared with only one? That is the way I feel when I know I am going to write to you, or feel sure of getting a letter from you. . . . So in an infinitely higher degree one is able to feel at times in prospect of an hour's communication with God. Only at times, I fear, I cannot always feel so, nor always be ready to say, Fade every earthly joy."

"This is a great country—so much room for idiots to career around in."

"I have always loved David. Some of those old Old Testament good men I have felt I could never have taken to: Samuel, for instance—just, upright judge—but I am not fond of him, nor of Jacob, nor of Samson. But Abraham, Joseph, David—noblemen all of them."

"Dislike as few people as you can. It is not good to criticize those we love, if we mean to be lovely and loving ourselves."

"I observe that when all *other* arguments and statements fail it affords support to the feminine mind to fall back on '*scat*.' 'Scat' is worth a world of logic and fact. It rounds up a controversy so neatly and so victoriously."

"God reigns. Let that thought be a support. He cannot do but what is right."

"Last evening after I got back from P.O. it began to rain—hard all morning—also all night—and all day today. I am so happy in it!"

"Both my brothers are better, more amiable, men than I am a woman."

III

In the summer of 1880 the University authorities, in view of the approaching centennial, decided to compile a revised list of alumni, and they employed Cornelia, assistant to her brother Charles, who was the alumni secretary, to do it. Whenever there was a task of such a nature to be done, requiring intelligence and energy, Cornelia was usually chosen as the burden-bearer. For such services she did not always receive adequate pay. Luckily for her, she had a way of finding enjoyment in such labors. To June she wrote:

"I got a lovely letter from an *old* lady last week, sending me dates for her brother, a youth of extraordinary promise who died the year after he graduated *forty-three years ago.* And she mourns for him still—for the rare promise unfulfilled! Faithful heart! It does one good to come across such instances of love stronger than death. I *had* to write back to her, and told her he had been forty-three years, as men count time, in the bosom of Eternal Mercy, while his friends and contemporaries had been battling and struggling and enduring trouble and toil and pain—and I thought he had had the best of it."

In these sentiments lay something characteristic of Cornelia. Fidelity was a thing she admired above almost all other earthly things; but as she became older she found less and less to admire in contemporary human life. In a later letter to June she wrote further in this disillusioned vein about the life around her: "It seems to me nothing short of Gabriel's trump will waken our Southern young people, *boys and girls*, to a sense of what they are throwing away. To a sense of their frivolity, indolence, ignorance, and want of ambition. Our immersion in *politics* is a dreadfully poor business. It is the only thing we take any interest in, outside of drinking, and dressing, and dancing. The three d's."

To ballroom dancing Cornelia could never quite reconcile herself; the Puritan and Calvinist in her were always raising their heads; but she was like other supporters of the strict ideas of the period in not being quite so severe as regards the first of these three d's. Mentioning a visit from her brother, Samuel F. Phillips, who had come down from Washington to receive a degree from the University, she wrote: " 'They that water shall be watered'—and I suppose it holds good with whiskey.... When Uncle S[am] came in last night, before he took off his hat, he handed me a bottle of very fine whiskey, saying Col. Ruffin had given it to him, and he presented it to me. I smiled a private smile as I took it."

Meanwhile Cornelia was giving daily lessons in composition, geography, and arithmetic to her small niece, Susie Phillips, youngest daughter of Charles and Laura Phillips.

IV

And then there occurred a threat that enabled Cornelia once more to go to the rescue of her beloved University. Her weapon, as usual, was a pen dipped in the handiest ink. In November, 1880, it was decided that certain tracts of land belonging to the University would have to be sold to satisfy debts due to Miss Mildred Cameron, sister of Paul Cameron, and to the estate of the late President Swain for money lent the University for building purposes. The Cameron debt, with accrued interest, amounted to about $15,000. When Cornelia heard of this proposed sale, she put on her war bonnet and wrote to her daughter June :

"I do not know when I have been so angry . . . as if I would like to whip somebody or something. *Tomorrow* the University lands are to be sold! North Carolina sits still & allows it to be done. . . . Given for a sacred purpose, and every square foot of which should be precious. . . . Askew is coming up from Raleigh to bid. Think of such buzzards as he and Jim Mason, possessing the Roaring Fountain, Newton's Grove, Piney Prospect. The census returns say that North Carolina spent for liquor last year $8,000,-000. And she is too poor to save her University from spoliation! . . . I couldn't give up hope. . . . I could not speak of it to Mrs. Battle without my voice breaking. . . . I despise North Carolina!"

The upshot was that late that night, November 10, she sat down and wrote to Mr. Cameron at Hillsboro, begging him to save the land. Three days later she wrote: "I went in the lovely moonlight to P.O. . . . and got a letter from Mr. Cameron. . . . *It did one good* I tell you. Next day down came Mr. B[enehan] Cameron [a son], and Mr Jno. Graham *to buy the land in for Mr. Cameron*. I felt like screaming with joy when I heard it." The sale in question was not actually held until February 4, 1881, when Mr. Cameron did bid the land in. The University was never able to get out of debt to Mr. Cameron and at length his heirs took the money out in scholarships. Mr. Cameron, some years later, was courtly enough to will a slice of this land to Cornelia, no doubt as a souvenir of her rescue of it.

v

Soon after the first of the new year, 1881, the village buzzed with the story that Mrs. Spencer, Mrs. Mallett, and some other prominent ladies of the village had committed a sensational assault on municipal employees. Another version said Cornelia had struck Town Commissioner Cheek on the head with a broom. A third account was published by a Hillsboro paper, which said that "a couple of irate females" had tried to prevent the improvement of the city streets. The event in question was detailed by Cornelia herself in a letter to June, January 23, 1881. Her state of mind was indicated by the number of underscored words in her letter:

"I have been very angry for a week or two over something that I did not intend to aggravate you with, but as so much public feeling has been aroused, I suppose somebody will mention it and make it worse to you than I want it to be. So I will tell you myself that a fortnight since the Town Commissioner Cheek, you know, and *id omne genus,* took it into their heads to *trim up the sidewalk elms.* They set Dolph Crabtree, Ed and Jim King and Creel with ladders and saws and axes to cutting down stray oaks and sawing off elm branches. They made such havoc of the elms on Mrs. Hendon's sidewalk that I went out and spoke civilly to Creel and remonstrated with him (he was *superintendent*). Not one of them has (indeed *very few* men in town have) any ideas about trimming a tree. He said he didn't know nothing about it, but must do as he had been ordered. He promised, however, to let the trees on my sidewalk alone—promised it *two or three times over.*

"I went to Mrs. Battle's last Monday morning. When I came home I found *all my trees sawed off in stumps*—the ground covered with the long sweeping limbs and branches beginning to bud for spring. The Kings and Crabtree and Castleberry, etc., all up—sawing away and chopping. [Prof.] Winston had tried in vain to stop them. Had been running after me in every direction—had gone to the Commissioners himself. He had prevented them from touching his trees, and had sympathized with me in my rage and abhorrence of the whole move, and so had [Prof.] Simonds, but because I was away from home that morning the deed was done. . . . I am so sore about it all I can't express myself. However, such a storm was raised in town—the various business men came down here to see what had been done—that I am told the Commissioners do not dare to go on. That is some comfort. How they must enjoy the thought that they ruined my sidewalk, however!

"Dr. and Mrs. Simonds spent an evening here and could not talk of anything else. They were going into his yard to cut the limbs off his great oak by the gate that stretches over the sidewalk. He put up a legal notice warning them not to trespass, or he would prosecute them.

"Prof. Venable called yesterday afternoon, and began upon the subject at once. I told him I had been trying to reconcile myself to it—thinking maybe there was some hard horse-sense in the measure that I could not understand. He said he had 'never seen anything so barbarous in his life'—*never*. I could cheerfully see everyone of those men strung up to a whipping post and scourged for it. *Creel* most of all—for he promised me not to touch my trees.

"Winston says he is now convinced that republican governments are a mistake—that wherever the rabble have rule there is desolation and ruin."

VI

The winter of 1880-81 was one of the sharpest and most prolonged ever endured in Chapel Hill. In the middle of it Cornelia's mother, now eighty-five years old, was stricken with the fullness of age and required almost constant waiting on. Early in 1881 Cornelia wrote to June:

"I and Grandma are getting along in as small compass as possible. . . . I have had only one N[ew] Year visitor, and him I hailed and made come in—Mr. C[harles] W. Johnston. . . . Here I had to stop to attend to Gr[and]ma who in such weather requires constant attention to keep her warm. I got up at two o'clock last night to go to her and heat the bricks over again and see that she was warm . . . to get up again at light and go through the same process and make a cup of tea in addition. . . . Then she went to sleep and I got my own breakfast—two boiled eggs, a slice of toast, and a cup of tea. I could not go out to grind the coffee."

One night in that month, January, Cornelia, escorted by her cook Bettie, went to the postoffice to look for a letter from June and found there a group of fifty students watching a young man astride a machine which Cornelia inquired the name of. She was told the thing was called a bicycle. "I never saw one before," she wrote to June. "The fellow flew up and down the sidewalk perched upon it at a great rate."

In another month Mrs. Phillips was sleeping almost all the time away, but Cornelia suspected no danger. On February 22, however, her mother died quietly in her sleep. Cornelia wrote to June: "We three went in and stood by our mother. She lies on the lounge in the middle of the parlor. O my dearest I wish you could see her. The sweetest loveliest picture of an old lady asleep, without a trace of care or pain, tranquil and lovely and at rest. I sent to Mrs. Newton to make her a cap and she made it of sheer muslin with wide pleated borders and wide strings. . . . I put a shawl round her —she has a white lace handkerchief, wide ruffles round her hands— and is covered with lovely flowers, violets and primroses! . . . After I had dressed her and laid her in the parlour, I went and sat down by her. She looked so natural and yet so sweet and almost radiantly serene, I spoke to her. . . . I told her I had dressed her as nicely as I could and had done my best for her, and she was dressed as I had always wanted her to be every day, 'but that was your little mistake, Ma, yes, it was your little mistake. You never would dress up nice and I used to scold you. You know I did. But it was all in love.' . . .

"When Grandma lay in her coffin just before they shut it down, Mrs. Wiley Henderson went and stood by her and said aloud (before everybody) 'Mrs. Phillips, you have been one good woman. You have helped the poor and instructed them. You have been a friend to me and mine, and done us good, and not a bit of kin to you, neither, and you are receiving your reward now, and I know it.' Then she stooped and kissed her, and Mrs. Newton and some others. Last of all Uncle Sam went forward and gave her the last kiss. And then they put the lid on, and grandma's pale half-smiling face disappeared forever from the earth. . . .

"Uncle Sam went away at one o'clock, and I have been wandering around the house in a sort of subdued agony, picking up this thing and that, folding up some things of grandma's with fast-dropping tears, going upstairs and coming down without any aim, looking my last upon all our little arrangements, with my heart in just such indescribable pain as I suffered the day you went away....

"Everybody came. A good many of the students and all the respectable people of the town. A good many Negroes, too."

When, after her mother's funeral, Cornelia got home from the church, she found Dilsey Craig, "Aunt Dilsey," her father's former slave, sitting by the fire. Dilsey was now a free woman, but the call of distress had brought her home, and thereafter she was never long separated from Cornelia. Dilsey was not the only consoler. A few days later Cornelia was alone in the house when Mary Baldwin, the Negro cook, came in. "Seeing me," wrote Cornelia, "she showed her sympathy in a way that I shall never forget. First, she came up and begged me not to stay here all day, but to go to my brother's and stay. When I shook my head, she looked round for a poor chair, and brought it, and sat down by me in silence. I was touched by her action—and after a little I began to talk and read to her, and had a comfortable hour, cheered by her humble sympathy and evident attempt at consolation."

VII

Cornelia once confided: "I feel lost and shipwrecked when men talk business to me. I cannot reply. The reasons I have to oppose them are, or seem to be, sheer childishness." The old feeling of bewilderment came over her when her brother Samuel informed her that their mother had left a little estate of some $3,000. Part of this, he thought, represented Mrs. Phillips's earnings as head of the girls' school she had conducted in Chapel Hill during the thirties. Cornelia had never seen so much money in one lump, and confessed she knew not what to do with it. Her brother Sam offered to put it out on loan for her and Dr. K. P. Battle took it, paying her $180 interest annually, at the rate of $15 monthly. Cornelia enjoyed this small income for the rest of her life. It was the steadiest revenue that ever came to her, her earnings from her writings and other activities being liable to ups and downs. Cornelia sold most of the family furniture, gave her father's old books to the University; gave up the house to her brother Charles, who owned it, and prepared to accept her brother Sam's invitation to visit him in Washington.

"I shiver at the thought of going away from Chapel Hill," she confessed to June. "I am not young enough to be able to take any pleasure in the prospect of new scenes, or a new mode of life. My deafness deprives me of the only pleasure I could look forward to—that of hearing. I do not want to go to W. C[ity] at all. If I could go away somewhere alone with you, and we two could be to *ourselves* for a while, I could perhaps recover the tone of my mind."

She yielded at last to her brother's insistence and in March, 1881, she departed for Washington. She hoped she would be able soon to return to Chapel Hill, but it was with foreboding that she wrote this threnody:

"So farewell and adieu to you, hills and valleys, rocks, streamlets, and flowers—well-trodden paths and fountains, cushions of moss on hillsides, liverworts and houstonias just peeping from among them, and dogtooth violets nodding above.

> " 'Where on the cliff the bluebird sings,
> The jasmine's golden censer swings.'

"The *past*, at least, is secure. . . . *Deus benedicat illi.*"

About her departure, her brother, Dr. Charles Phillips, wrote to June: "Mr. Watson has taken your precious mother from us. They have just gone in a one horsed rockaway. The trunk went on this morning, and your mother had a lap-ful of last things to take to Aunt Dilsey. [Cornelia herself wrote later: "I made Mr. W. let me get out at Aunt Dilsey's and went in and gave her some last things and a last hug, and left her crying and lamenting out loud."] Somehow I did not realize that my sister was going till last night, and this morning I went over to see the last and the longest of her. . . . She went out to the graveyard to carry some flowers, and meeting Dr. Mallett on the way he turned his horse and took her there in his buggy.... [On her return to the house] Wifey and Lucy and Susie were there with me. Uncle Ben was in the kitchen, but missed the coveted goodbye and so did the cook Mary.... The tears would start in your mother's eyes, and her lips trembled every now and then, but this morning, she preserved a calm exterior, until she got into the rockaway."

Regarding her visit to the cemetery, Cornelia herself afterwards wrote to June:

"I went alone to where your grandma and grandpa are lying, and put some flowers on each of their graves and knelt down between them and committed myself and my child to the care of our covenant-keeping God."

Dr. James Phillips, English-born father of Cornelia. He was professor of mathematics in the University of North Carolina for many years

Cornelia's mother, Judith Vermeule Phillips, daughter of an
old Dutch family long resident in New York and New Jersey

Samuel Phillips, brother of Cornelia's father, James; buried in upper Trinity Churchyard, New York

"Mr. Sam" Phillips, younger brother of Cornelia, on whom she "loved to lean." President Grant appointed him solicitor general of the United States. Previously he had been auditor in Governor Vance's Confederate cabinet

Professor Denison Olmsted (1791-1859). Professor at the University of North Carolina and later at Yale. He built the house that Cornelia lived in longest

Dr. Elisha Mitchell, versatile and beloved professor who lost his life on the mountain that bears his name in Western North Carolina. His children were intimate friends of Mrs. Spencer

Mrs. Spencer when she was Cornelia Ann Phillips at the time
of her marriage

"How dear he was"—James Munroe Spencer, Cornelia's husband "Magnus."

Photo by Siechrist

The James Phillips house (also known as the Widow Puckett's house and the Olmsted house) on East Franklin Street, Chapel Hill, which was Cornelia's childhood and girlhood home. It was for some years called the President's House and later was occupied by Chancellor R. B. House

A group of Magnus Spencer's friends and fellow students at Chapel Hill in pre-Civil War days

Student marshals at the University of North Carolina Commencement in 1855

East Franklin Street, between the campus wall and the Presbyterian Church, as it looked in Cornelia's time

The same street at the same place as it looked in the summer of 1948

Upper left, Blind John Mincey and his wife Sal. *Upper right*, Mrs. MacNider and her granddaughter Sallie Foard. *Lower left*, "Uncle" Ben Booth, a Chapel Hill character, who let University students break boards over his head at twenty-five cents a try. *Lower right*, Aunt Easter, cook at Dr. Battle's

Old postoffice at Chapel Hill where Cornelia called every day for her mail. It was on the site of the present postoffice

Kate Fetter (Mrs. Whedbee), one of Cornelia's pupils, daughter of
Professor Manuel Fetter, long a neighbor

Miss Nancy Hilliard, Chapel Hill's boarding mistress for many
years—a friend of the friendless

"Her hair like satin . . .

Above, Laura Battle Phillips, Cornelia's sister-in-law and her confidante for years. *Below, left,* Margaret Mitchell, daughter of Elisha Mitchell, Mrs. Spencer's close friend. *Right,* Mrs. J. J. Summerell, the former Ellen Mitchell, long a friend and correspondent of Mrs. Spencer and mother of Mrs. Hope Summerell Chamberlain, the author of *Old Days in Chapel Hill* and *This Was Home*

Governor D. L. Swain, President of
the University of North Carolina, who
was called "Old Warping-bars." Cornelia speaks of his "look of infinite
benignity." *Below*, his daughter, Eleanor Swain Atkins, who married the
invading General

The Charles Phillips house as it looked when Cornelia lived in it with her mother. It was her home from 1869 to 1881

The same house today. In later years it was the Presbyterian manse

Professor B. F. Hedrick, the only University of North Carolina
professor dropped for his opinions. He was a friend of Mrs.
Spencer, who always remained loyal to him

The little Presbyterian Church which Mrs. Spencer toiled to keep alive. The
steeple came later

The hated Governor—W. W. Holden, Reconstruction Governor of North Carolina, whom Cornelia blamed for closing the University in 1870

Above, Abram Rencher and his wife, old Chapel Hillians and old friends of Mrs. Spencer. *Below, left*, Mrs. Fordyce Hubbard, wife of a University professor. She, too, was hostess to the invaders. *Below, right*, Dr. Johnston B. Jones, the University physician (with "face like a cameo") who after the Civil War was, like many others, obliged to quit Chapel Hill

Left, Will Maverick of Texas, one of Mrs. Spencer's boarders and pupils. *Right,* W. H. S. Burgwyn, Captain in the Confederate Army and one of Cornelia's favorite pupils

"June" (Julia J.) Spencer (*lowest, seated*) and her circle of friends at Peace Institute, Raleigh, North Carolina. Among the other girls are Alice Wilson, Emma Scales, Lizzie Watkins and Kerr Morehead

The cedar walk, bordered by a stone wall, cedars, and elms, leading down town from Mrs. Spencer's home at "Seven Gables" as it looked in the nineties. *On facing page,* the same cedar walk today—little changed

Upper left, Dr. Kemp P. Battle, post-Reconstruction President of the University and long Cornelia's friend and counsellor. *Upper right,* "Bart" F. Moore, one of Cornelia's aides in reviving the University. *Lower left,* Professor Charles Phillips, D.D., Cornelia's older brother, professor of mathematics and long chairman of the faculty. *Lower right,* Paul C. Cameron of Hillsboro, who helped in the reopening of the University. Cameron Avenue is named for him

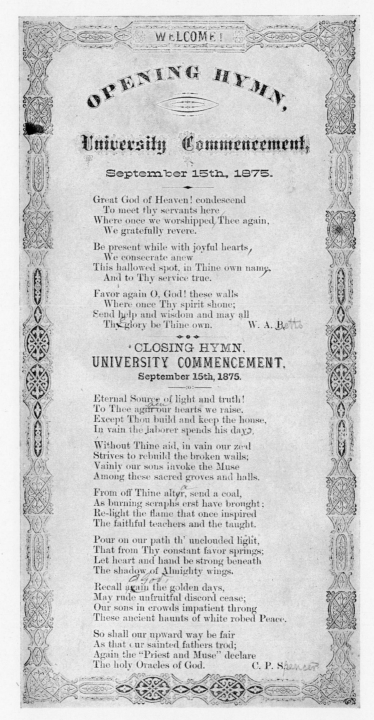

WELCOME!

OPENING HYMN,

University Commencement,

September 15th, 1875.

Great God of Heaven! condescend
　To meet thy servants here
Where once we worshipped Thee again,
　We gratefully revere.

Be present while with joyful hearts,
　We consecrate anew
This hallowed spot, in Thine own name,
　And to Thy service true.

Favor again O, God! these walls
　Where once Thy spirit shone;
Send help and wisdom and may all
　Thy glory be Thine own.　　　W. A. Betts

CLOSING HYMN,
UNIVERSITY COMMENCEMENT,
September 15th, 1875.

Eternal Source of light and truth!
To Thee again our hearts we raise.
Except Thou build and keep the house,
In vain the laborer spends his days,

Without Thine aid, in vain our zeal
Strives to rebuild the broken walls;
Vainly our sons invoke the Muse
Among these sacred groves and halls.

From off Thine altar, send a coal,
As burning seraphs erst have brought;
Re-light the flame that once inspired
The faithful teachers and the taught.

Pour on our path th' unclouded light,
That from Thy constant favor springs;
Let heart and hand be strong beneath
The shadow of Almighty wings.

Recall again the golden days,
May rude unfruitful discord cease;
Our sons in crowds impatient throng
These ancient haunts of white robed Peace.

So shall our upward way be fair
As that our sainted fathers trod;
Again the "Priest and Muse" declare
The holy Oracles of God.　　　C. P. Spencer

The closing hymn of the University Commencement of 1875, written by Mrs. Spencer. This is a proof with her corrections made in her own handwriting. The opening hymn was written by W. A. Betts, a University student and friend of Mrs. Spencer

June Spencer when an art student in Germany

Piney Prospect, Chapel Hill, in the nineties. This was the end of a walk often taken by Mrs. Spencer

Upper left, James Phillips, oldest son of Charles Phillips and nephew of Mrs. Spencer. *Upper right*, Susie Phillips (Mrs. Jewett) Cornelia's niece and pupil, who was "baffled by predicates." *Lower left*, Nora Phillips, Mrs. Spencer's handsome niece often mentioned in her letters. *Lower right*, The Reverend Alexander L. Phillips, Cornelia's nephew, who "made Aunt Dilsey shout"

In the nineties the college boys at Chapel Hill played tennis in their galluses

"Senlac" in Cornelia's time. The Kemp P. Battle home where Cornelia often
sought conversation and consolation

The Kemp P. Battle family. Dr. Battle and his wife, "Miss Patty," are seated in the center, with their sons and grandchildren' as they appeared in Mrs. Spencer's time

The Old Well, the oaken bucket, and University football players
as they appeared about the time Cornelia left Chapel Hill for
Cambridge, Massachusetts. *Below*, Students at the University of
North Carolina in the Gay Nineties

The University Faculty in 1884, all personal friends of Mrs. Spencer. *Seated, left to right*, R. H. Graves, A. W. Mangum, J. deB. Hooper, K. P. Battle, Charles Phillips, John Manning, and T. W. Harris. *Standing*, E. A. DeSchweinitz, A. L. Coble, J. A. Holmes, J. W. Gore, F. P. Venable, and W. T. Patterson. Taken in the yard of the James Phillips home. *Below*, House of the Seven Gables, Franklin Street and Battle Lane, where Mrs. Spencer lived with Professor and Mrs. James Lee Love and did much of her writing

The campus walk leading from Franklin Street to Old East as it looked in Mrs. Spencer's time. At left is the old John Watson Hotel. *On facing page,* the same walk in 1948. The Graham Memorial building occupies the hotel site

Upper left, Lucy Phillips Russell, one of Mrs. Spencer's favorite nieces. *Upper right,* Dr. W. B. Phillips, professor of chemistry in the University, nephew of Mrs. Spencer. *Lower left,* "Nelie" Vermeule, Mrs. Spencer's cousin and correspondent in New Jersey. *Lower right,* Chapel Hill's "glamor girl," Mary Anderson, considered the most beautiful girl in the village in Mrs. Spencer's time

A group of faculty members and students in 1894, the year Mrs. Spencer left
Chapel Hill for Cambridge

Cornelia Phillips Spencer, her daughter June, her granddaughter Cornelia Love, and her grandson J. Spencer Love (now chairman of Burlington Mills Corporation). Little Cornelia is wearing a challis dress and a guimpe made by Mrs. Spencer's own hands. Mrs. Spencer was seventy-three years old at this time

Professor James Lee Love and his children, Cornelia and
Spencer, grandchildren of Cornelia Phillips Spencer, when
they lived in Cambridge

Above, Dr. C. F. Deems, founder of
New York's Church of the Strangers
and Cornelia's first publisher. *Below*,
Dr. E. A. Alderman, president in turn
of North Carolina, Tulane, and Virginia universities, and one of Cornelia's correspondents

Cornelia Phillips Spencer as she appeared in 1898 when she
was seventy-three

The graves of Cornelia Phillips Spencer and her daughter, Mrs. James Lee Love (June), side by side in the Chapel Hill cemetery in 1948

Graves of James Munroe Spencer (Magnus), his father, William Spencer, Sr., his mother, Candis Spencer, and his brother, Dr. J. M. Spencer, in Pleasant Hill Cemetery, Clinton, Alabama, in 1944

The Liberty ship "Cornelia P. Spencer," launched at Wilmington, North Carolina, April 24, 1943. Sunk by a German submarine off East Africa a few months later, with loss of two lives

A Taste of Cities

I

AT WASHINGTON Cornelia found herself in her brother's house at 1119 K Street, whose comforts and luxuries far surpassed anything she had seen before; for as solicitor-general under President Garfield "Mr. Sam," as he was always known at Chapel Hill, had an income that enabled his large family to enjoy the best of everything. The number and variety of his books were to Cornelia particularly impressive, and she thought it "a refreshment to stand before them and look and look at them." Her first few days at the capital gave her a series of thrills.

"What a sensation," she exclaimed in a letter to June, "to see the Potomac! I don't know anything I would rather have a prospect of than to travel with you—go where we could see rivers and mountains together. No one who has never seen a great river can form any idea of what it is, and you lose the idea after living a few years away from one. To see that magnificent stream majestically gliding on, is an everfresh delight. It looks fit to bear the navies of the world.—And to see this city lit up at night! I believe it is more beautiful to look out then than in the day." To Laura Phillips she wrote: "Did you ever find it *restful* to be where no one knew you? After living a long time in Chapel Hill where your next door neighbor knows what you have for dinner if he wants to know, and where every little darky expects you to speak to him on the streets, I find it *delicious* to walk along and meet nobody I know or that knows or cares for me."

She particularly enjoyed roaming through the streets and

markets and stopping wherever she found a novel cluster of colors
and odors. She wrote this of Forepaugh's circus parade: "Thirty
wagons of every description, from a gorgeous imitation of Alexander the Great's war chariot (as I suppose) down. The foremost
team of ten pair of creamcolored horses mostly took my affections,
though there followed 8 pair of Shetland ponies—6 pair of calico
horses—horses led singly with gorgeous grooms. Camels arrayed
in purple and fine linen, elephants in every style, ladies in every
style—on horseback, on tops of the cages and chariots, on tops
of the elephants. I got tired of looking at last. Finally, and at the
end of the vast array came two or three 6 or 8 horse teams con-
veying immense cars, painted and gorgeous with devices and en-
treating the people not to mind Forepaugh, but wait till Easter
week [when Barnum was coming]."

And she who loved cats and had just left a favorite, Bob, at
Chapel Hill, was delighted with the numerous sleek specimens
she encountered at the capital. "I met a most conversible cat in
the market-house. He belonged to a market woman and sat on a
shelf. A fine tortoise shell. He responded to my advances like
a Christian. Got up and mewed and mewed and rubbed against
me. I was compelled to stoop down and kiss him just between his
eyes for Bob's sake."

Scarcely less did she enjoy a summer tour of the New Jersey
homes of her mother's kindred. At Lebanon she saw the Roes.
At New Brunswick she roamed over the great River Road farm
of the 18th Adrian Vermeule and admired his sprightly wife,
the former Maria Veghte, whose family had belonged to the old
Dutch settlers of the Raritan valley. There, too, she saw her
mother's unmarried cousins, Phoebe Davis, ninety-two years old,
and Katy, who was a mere eighty-five. They showed her a Dutch
Bible, published in Amsterdam in 1657, that had belonged to
Peter Brokaw, her mother's great-great-grandfather. At Plainfield
she visited the Cadmuses, cousins who were living in the house
built by her mother's father; and then went to New York to stay
with June; and there, at the age of fifty-six, she began to take

lessons in painting, particularly china-painting. This became the consoler and balm of her later years. She used to paint whole china sets which she gave away, and in the course of years she painted on china, wood, or canvas virtually all the wild flowers found in the Chapel Hill region. Little value, at the time, was attached to these things.

II

Returning to Washington, Cornelia took in the sights, including the trial of Charles Guiteau, who had recently assassinated President Garfield. "Guiteau is not uninteresting apart from his crime," she wrote. "He has some smartness—has good address —good easy manners—gets furious, however and seems to care for nothing then—but O, what a wild, wasted, friendless-looking creature." In October of 1881 she saw her first opera. Gerster was then in Washington playing in *La Traviata*. Cornelia was handicapped because she could hear none of the music, neither the voices nor instruments. "I was very much amused with all I saw. I laughed and laughed and *laughed*. The crowd of painted and powdered rips—men and women—the painted passion and sentiment, the exquisitely absurd idea of *singing* everything, the doctor singing his prescriptions and opinions, the heroine singing her dying farewell, the lover singing his anguish and despair.... I could not hear the exquisite notes that would have half redeemed the absurdities.... [With a glass] you see the powder and rouge and *wrinkles* behind all. I think the whole *troupe* was a set of old harridans."

Sometimes in the very midst of these diversions, her thoughts would go back to North Carolina, sometimes critically, but more than ever she confessed to June she was having a touch of homesickness. *"Tanta media via* after all is best," she wrote. "Perhaps it is that North Carolina (unconsciously) aims at. It is good to say 'wait awhile,' it is good to say 'taint no use,' it is good to say 'I don't know.' North Carolina forever—let us write it *in sand*.... I declare (privately) I have a very great notion to write a set of letters to the 'Times' or the 'World' about certain things in North Carolina. How I scorn them—as much as I love the old State."

Just what set off this outburst does not appear from her correspondence, but she was at this time addicted to frequent resentments against the narrowness and stinginess of some of the state's official actions; and then she would rebuke herself by incorporating such aphorisms as this in her letters to June: "Nothing prevents loyalty like a disposition to criticize. I wish you had never heard me indulge in it." And she who was so prone to melancholy, and to behold beneath the surface of things the *lacrimae rerum*, would relieve her feelings by writing thus to her daughter:

"Can you tell me why you are so very blue? It is not natural and shows that something is wrong, mental or physical, if there is really no private cause. . . . Perhaps all young women are given to making blue estimates of life who are away from home and compelled to act for themselves. You need some warm good friends of your own age to compare notes with and get comfort from. . . . A habit of looking out upon life lugubriously, captiously, unhopefully, leads to envy (which is hell on earth), distrust of the Almighty's goodness, and a paralysis of the faculties for any high and noble purpose." Yet soon after this she was ending a letter to June by writing, "No love to anybody.—C. P. S."

III

In April, 1882, came the 17th anniversary of the entry of the Federal troops into Chapel Hill; and now there came General Smith Atkins, their commander, to dine with Cornelia at her brother Sam's house in Washington. She had not seen him since he had carried off Ellie Swain as his bride. She wrote: "I should never have known him—, he looks *common,* having lost the little gloss and glamour thrown over him by his short military career. However, he was clever enough. Told me about Ellie's death; Mrs. Swain, and his children." She and the general kept up a correspondence for several years; he wrote her after the death of a small son: "I supposed that I had experienced every phase of suffering inflicted by death upon survivors, but I have suffered more in the death of my heroic little boy than in all former experiences combined."

One consolation of Cornelia's for her long stay at her brother's house was the affectionate friendship formed with her niece and namesake, Cornie Phillips. Cornie was frail where her sisters were vigorous, delicate where they were hearty, and one could see even then that she was not to stay long on this earth. Some of Cornelia's best and tenderest letters were written to her in the course of the six years that followed this visit to Washington; for the fragile and clinging Cornie took in some degree the place of a daughter, and Cornelia's heart warmed to her namesake as the pale girl became more and more dependent on her.

IV

There was another source of deep enjoyment to Cornelia at her brother's house—his library. Naturally a booklover, she had never before had her fill of miscellaneous and unregulated reading. Now from Mr. Sam's laden shelves she could at leisure take down and enjoy whatever she chose—fiction, science, philosophy, history, poetry, biography. Biography fed her love of and curiosity about people while poetry ministered to her solitary and imaginative self. But a naturally orderly and conscientious mind would not long permit her to read at random or for pure pleasure, and in 1882, when she was in her fifty-seventh year, she started a large new green-bound diary in which she made notes and wrote quotations from those authors that interested her for more than a moment. This diary became her companion and confidant, and she continued to write in it and find pleasure in it long after more material pleasures had ceased to interest her. These are specimen extracts:

"Things to be noted about all the charters granted to the English colonies in America:

"They certainly allowed *self*-government to an ample extent.

"They invited *emigration* upon this ground, expressly or tacitly conceded.

"They conferred a much larger religious and political freedom than was at their day enjoyed in either England or Europe.

"No clear distinction made in any of them between the imperial rights of the Mother Country and their own municipal rights. . . ."

"An education which *merely instructs* will *encourage crime*. The example of this found in Prussia—one of the most highly educated people in Europe—yet one of the most criminal."

"Death is not a single act; it is a process."

"A woman may always judge of the real estimation in which she is held by the conversation which is addressed to her."

" 'Old rusty Christian!' Phrase from Don Quixote, quoted in a book I lately procured from the University Library: 'Conventional Life of Charles V.' I found it interesting. All books are so to me that present *individual* life."

"*Catherine of Russia Autobiography*. She was a woman of whom I have seen types even in C Hill. . . . Women of personal beauty— estimating their charms coolly, and with reference to their commercial value. Women voluptuous without softness—good-natured but flinty—pleasant and gay, and apparently devoted to dress and to pleasure, but concealing under this a selfishness and cold-blooded indifference to the rights or wishes or opinions or sufferings of other people that would not stop at crime to effect its own purposes. . . . Satan himself glares out of such women's eyes."

Illuminative of the complexion of her own mind was her commentary, sometimes only a word or line, on quotations taken from influential authors. For example, Sir Walter Scott was quoted in this line: "A democrat in any situation is but a silly sort of fellow." Just below she wrote her comment: "This is the opinion of a Tory, 1825." The author of this quotation is not named: "Poetry is the expression, in beautiful form and melodious language of the best thoughts and the noblest emotions which the spectacle of life awakens in the finest souls!" Her comment was: "I should substitute the word *experience* for '*spectacle.*' The man whose thoughts of life merely as 'a spectacle' are given us, is not likely to give us thoughts of much depth or much savor. Are poets mere spectators, chanting only what they see?"

v

Her ability to read and enjoy Latin now came back to her with a new freshness at a time when she had many empty hours to fill, and she spent much of her leisure writing in her journal and making new translations of Horace. Of one of her Horatian favorites, "To a Beloved Fountain," she wrote several new versions. These are two:

> "O fountain of Bandusia, clearer than crystal,
> Well worthy of a flower-crowned libation of sweet wine,
> Tomorrow thou shalt be honored with a kid
> Whose forehead, now swelling with his first horns,
> Shows him ready for love or for war, but in vain,
> Since soon his wanton blood shall tinge thy stream.
> Never shall the fierce influence of the flaming dog-star
> Touch thy wave. Still the wandering flock,
> The wearied cattle, shall taste thy refreshing coolness;
> Thou shalt ever be the noblest of free-flowing fountains,
> While I sing of the oak overshadowing the rocks
> Whence gush thy prattling waters."

> "O fount Bandusian, more lucid than crystal,
> Of sweet wine well worthy, encircled with flowers,
>   Soon a kid I'll devote thee,
>   Whose horns now a sprouting
> Show him equally amorous and petulant,
> Tho' in vain: for thy cool gliding streamlet
>   His blood flowing shall crimson,
>   Wanton pet of the sheepfold.

The hour of the fierce flaming dog star shall never
Know where to find thee; thy shade and sweet coolness
    Wearied cattle shall comfort,
    Wandering flocks shall refresh.
Thou noblest of fountains, be ever free flowing
While the poet shall sing of the oak over hanging
    The rock whence thy prattling
    Sweet waters gush happily."

23

Back to the Village

I

AFTER NEARLY two years in her brother's comfortable Washington house, Cornelia had had enough of city life. Although she no longer had a home in Chapel Hill, that village was to her still the center of existence; and it was with a sigh of complete content that she returned to it in the late autumn of 1882. More than one home was opened to her, but she preferred to keep her independence and took lodgings at the house of her friend, Mrs. Selina Thompson, mother of four girls who had been Cornelia's pupils, Ida, Jenny, Susan, and Flora Belle. There Cornelia settled down to the most secure period she had known in years. She was free of housekeeping cares and the burden of family life. She often looked back to this part of her life as singularly blessed.

"I think sometimes it is a *duty*," she wrote in her greenbacked journal, "to put on record, the gentleness and mercy that mark the daily Providences of my life. It is wonderful to me—this *halcyon* calm. . . . Our situation here with our amiable Mrs. Thompson and her amiable girls is certainly all things considered the best that Chapel Hill could afford. We have 'all things and abound.' . . . Day after day the routine is the same. I dress leisurely. I open the door for *Bob* [the cat] to come in—I rub him down and talk to him as I dress. Then breakfast at 7½. . . . Then I come to my rooms and clear up and set to rights." After describing her mornings filled with sewing or mending clothes, and her afternoons dotted with visitors, she concluded: "At 9.9½ I prepare for bed. Often I sit by my fire reading till late. Then I sleep—night after

187

night—month after month with nothing to molest—wake day after day in perfect health—in peace to another quiet day of employment and comfort. *Laus Deo*."

II

She was especially glad to be back in time to attend Commencement. She came home from the exercises to write in her diary: "At 3 we had dinner, and at 4 Will [W. B. Phillips, her nephew] had a phaeton at the door to take Min [his wife] and me to chapel to see the prizes given, especially the Phillips Math. Prize, which was gained by a very smart fellow named Love." This was the first time this name had appeared in her writings, but in another year or so it became very prominent, for young Love contrived to meet June Spencer and soon afterward he became a steady caller at Mrs. Thompson's. In September, 1883, Cornelia wrote of June's return from an absence: "I met her with a carriage at our junction and we had a charming drive home together through the woods and fields of goldenrod. How we did talk! She looks very well and has gained several pounds. Has been busy all this week flirting with the young professors and that latest *Love* of hers." A few months later Love and June were regarded as an engaged couple. At the prospect of losing her only child to a suitor, Cornelia showed no unease. On the contrary, she went over to Love's side so completely that presently she was writing to June: "When I see a strong man on his knees, so to speak, before a frail, tender, unformed girl, placing all his hopes for life upon her love and truth, idealizing her in every aspect, idolizing her, I say it is a pity she is not all he thinks she is. There is a great deal of deception in the first flood tide of a newly awakened love." And again she wrote: "We shall miss the nice set of young men who have made our congregation so long—Bryan,[1] Love, White, Harris, Rouse, Warlick, Sr. But especially Love."

In April, 1884, June Spencer sailed for Europe to study the

1. He was afterwards the famous "Brother" Bryan, Presbyterian minister of Birmingham, Alabama.

arts of drawing and painting which she was to teach, and she wrote back long and blithe letters, many of which her mother revised, copied, and sent to the *North Carolina Presbyterian* for publication.

III

The year 1883 made itself memorable to Cornelia through the deaths of old friends and neighbors. Among them was Mrs. Swain, widow of the old governor and Cornelia's correspondent for many years; Mrs. S. F. Phillips, wife of brother Sam; Mrs. Eliza Grant, daughter of Dr. Elisha Mitchell; Ben Craig, former slave and husband of Aunt Dilsey; William J. Hogan, an old Chapel Hill neighbor; Miss Sally Williams, and Mrs. Felton. These deaths gave her long thoughts and made her feel lonely. She recorded in her journal that Mrs. Felton was the last of the White sisters: Susan, Emma, Eleanor, Betsy, Sophronia. "I remember sitting round the fire in Miss Susan White's bedroom with all five of them . . . all old women then." Thereafter her diary entries were often prefaced with the words, "I remember. . . ."

IV

Of an intended visit to Miss Sally Williams, who had been a nurse in ante-bellum Chapel Hill, Cornelia wrote a long letter November 1, 1883, to June. On a day when the sky was "as blue as in June, the sunshine golden, the air delicious," she and the frail Cornie Phillips, who had come down from Washington, engaged a one-horse phaeton, loaded it with gifts of coffee and flannel, and with a one-eyed old Negro as driver, started out for the Williams home on the Eno River sixteen miles distant, between Durham and Hillsboro. They first stopped on the edge of the village at the house of Aunt Dilsey, who had broiled two chickens and cooked some biscuit for the lunch basket. They went out by the old country road past the Robert Patterson farm and Mt. Moriah Church, watching the fall colors stain the gums, maples, and hickories. They stopped several times to pick the pods of the honey-locust, red-checked haws, and muscadine grapes. They were tranquilly happy.

A passerby told them they would find the Williams place a mile the other side of Guess's mill. They were close to the mill when they met two women afoot. Did they know Miss Sally Williams? Lor', they had knowed her mighty well, her and her sister, Miss Matilda. "Ain't you heard? They both of 'em is dead—died last July."

There was nothing to do but to go on, and this Cornelia and Cornie did, in silence. They found the mill with its dam and rocks, crossed the river, and after another mile, found a house inhabited by an old woman, some dogs, and some children. The old woman spoke to them familiarly, and then they recognized her. She was Annis Williams, elder sister of Sally and Matilda. "She used to come to Chapel Hill in the old days, knew us all, and loved us." Annis told them what had happened in the previous July. On the 19th Matilda fell dead from her chair. Ten days later, Sally, who had been poorly, just "wilted away" and also died.

Although ill and feverish, Sally had dressed herself within three days of her death, and when a delirium came on, she had begged Annis "not to unpin my underbody whatever you do." This request, though puzzling, was respected. And then when her thin body was being dressed for the grave, a secret hidden for years came out. Sally had died from a cancer of the breast. For at least three or four years, in the doctor's estimate, the enemy had been eating into her flesh. Meantime she had said nothing to her sisters, going on with her daily labors as nurse to the sick and doing her share of the housework. Annis explained that discovery might have interfered with her employment. After Sally's burial, the linen and ointments with which she had daily medicated her secret were discovered. Annis had moved across the road to her daughter's home; she could no longer bear to live in the old house.

After they all had talked themselves out, Cornelia and Cornie got back into the phaeton and plodded home. The journey had taken eight hours and they were quite exhausted. After this Cornelia and Cornie took many other trips together. Cornie had to lean on someone, and Cornelia liked to be leaned on.

v

About this time Cornelia began to realize she was becoming middle-aged and a little more, and she began to abhor the thought of change in whatever she loved. When Professor George T. Winston tried to install a hydraulic ram to pump water into his house from the Roaring Fountain, she wrote him a poem of protest supposed to come from the nymph of the spring, and when the thing broke down, she rejoiced as if over the defeat of a sinister enemy. Her letters to her brother Sam now often harked back to old times and remembrances. "I remember seeing Mr. Waitt, of the old days in Chapel Hill [the University carpenter born in New England] walking past our house one day reading a small book as he walked. I went to the gate to see what had so absorbed him, a hard-working man. It was 'Watts on the Mind.' Mr. Waitt was a Yankee. When shall I see a North Carolina carpenter thus employing a leisure hour?" In June, 1884, she wrote to Sam: "This is the 23rd anniversary of Mr. Spencer's death. It was a very bright hot day—the lagerstroemia and the pomegranates and the cotton being in full bloom all around us." Later she added: "Though I can recall very few deaths in our circle of friends and neighbors for ten years past, yet the population of the place . . . is changing wonderfully. . . . In the Methodist Ch[urch] not long ago I could see but four or five faces that were familiar. Poor old Jones Watson looking up at the preacher with dim and bleared eyes, and then looking over the cong[regation] as if in want of some face or faces there. . . . He and John W., the Carrs, Mrs. F. Barbee, F. Utley, Mrs. Jennings . . . theirs are the only ante bellum faces. At the B[aptist] ch[urch] it is still more strange—and at the Ep[iscopal] the Malletts and Miss M[ary] Smith are all."

From this time on, the shortness of human life was often the theme of her letters. "And O, the next world to which we are all hurrying—where is it. . . . And what shall we do there? Anything of more permanence than here? . . . Such queries are often in my mind these days, and there are times when I would like to go and begin that new life, and, it may be, join those members of *our* life's party who have preceded us thither. . . . The old White place, [Mrs. Swain's old home] in R[aleigh], is advertised for sale. 'None abiding.' "

VI

Early in 1885 Cornelia went again to Washington to witness, in company with her brother Sam, the inauguration of President Grover Cleveland. Her brother was well aware that the incoming of a Democratic president meant the end of his twelve-year service as solicitor general; yet outwardly he kept his serenity.

". . . to our good brother all this means defeat—dispossession," she wrote her brother Charles. "This handsome apartment will know him as proprietor no more. (His future is all uncertain I feel sure.) Yet as Mrs. Maury says, *'Doesn't he take it beautifully?'* Yes, he certainly does—doing the honors as gaily and cheerfully this minute—dear old fellow. . . .

"The show—the troops—the marching—the music—the uniforms—the fine horses and equipages. Cleveland, Arthur, Ransom and Sherman in such a gorgeous vehicle—such cheering, such waving of handkerchiefs, such glory! . . . The *civil* display is as impressive as the military. It befits a great nation of freemen and fills one's imagination—satisfies completely."

In the winter of 1885 June Spencer, having returned from Europe, was married to James Lee Love in the Presbyterian church at Chapel Hill. For a wedding journey they went to Alabama, where June visited her mother's old home at Clinton, and Cornelia wrote to them there: "At intervals today I have been thinking of you *in Clinton.* It seems strange—*incredible* that *June*—my June, my baby sh[oul]d be there without me. I think of *your father.*— Does he know that the little creature who brightened his last days of suffering, as nothing else could do, for whom his last prayer on earth was breathed—is *there*—among those scenes so familiar, so dear—; standing by his grave . . . I enjoy all your happiness,—

enter into it,—and thank God for it." On their return Mr. and Mrs. Love lived at rooms above Cornelia's at Mrs. Thompson's. Cornelia confessed to being "miserably jealous" only about her daughter's change of name, not of status, for as a son-in-law Love was consistently thoughtful and considerate; and Cornelia soon learned to be so fond of him that she wrote his mother to thank her for him. And this high opinion she never abated.

VII

The year 1886 was one of some disaster in the village. Christmas Day saw the burning of Governor Swain's old house, which to Cornelia had once been as familiar as her own. Its occupant was Professor Thomas Hume. "Dr. and Mrs. Hume had just settled in it with every circumstance of comfort and elegance," she wrote. "The house just repainted and papered, and they had furnished it beautifully. . . . by sunset nothing was left of the stately old residence but three tall chimneys. . . . I mourn for the house as for an old friend." Yet at the end of the year she was able to write: "I have only good and pleasant things to chronicle concerning myself and mine. God has been good to us. I place it on record here."

There were other griefs and losses in that year, and Cornelia wrote many consolatory letters. One of them was to Paul Cameron after the death of a beloved sister:

"Your friends in Chapel Hill have often spoken and thought of you in the past week, sympathizing heartily with you in your recent great loss and grief, and wishing they could by any means alleviate it to you. Not one has felt more than I. You have given me your friendship, and while I prize it, and feel rich in it, I must in some degree share every trouble that befalls my honored friend —feeling with him, and for him.

"I had not the pleasure of a personal acquaintance with Mrs. Mordecai, but it is allowable to estimate character from common report; and thus I know that she was a noble woman. The tears that fall upon her grave are sincere, the eulogies are merited. I know that to you the loss is that of a lifelong friend, counsellor, sympathizer, trusted and beloved beyond what is usual, these many years, one whose place in your confidence and affection time could never restore. The death of such a sister, or brother, in advanced life closes a chapter, turns a page, never to be reopened.

"But it is something that we all are to look forward to. He who lives longest has most of loss to endure. It is the common lot, and must be met bravely and in silence, praying God that when our turn comes, we too may be mourned tenderly and eulogized justly, having done what lay in our hands to do wisely and well. . . . Thank God for the life just ended, so long spared to you and to her family and friends; trust Him with childlike confidence, believing as we must believe,—or go mad—that at the end of this tangled maze which we tread so often in doubt and darkness, we shall find light."

24

The New House

IN AUGUST, 1887, Cornelia wrote one of her cheerfulest letters to Nora Phillips, daughter of her brother Sam, saying, "I cannot help wishing for you, or some of you, to be here right now, enjoying the freshness and cleanness and prettiness of 'Seven Gables' while it is all fresh and clean and pretty. It is such a pleasure to walk around the piazzas and rooms, the nice halls, the pleasant yard. I want to share the pleasure with everybody I love."

So did Cornelia make it known that she was in a new home, her married daughter's, just built by Professor Love on a lot immediately above the site of the Governor Swain house and diagonally opposite her own old home. She told about her pleasure further in a letter to her cousin, "Nelie" Vermeule, at New Brunswick, New Jersey:

"I guess your father and mother will understand . . . my feelings of thankfulness on taking possession of my pretty, comfortable room in my own child's house. I had lived nearly 5 years with Mrs. Thompson and no one could have enjoyed that situation more than I did. . . . I am writing now on the front piazza, before breakfast. It looks north, commanding at night a fine view of the North Star and its attendant constellations. . . . The piazza runs across the front and round to the eastern side, and my room opens on it on that side. I enjoy it prodigiously."

195

II

Two other events of importance to Cornelia took place that year
—she was able to begin her second book, *A School History of
North Carolina;* and her favorite niece, Cornie Phillips, fell ill.
It was to Cornie in Washington that she now wrote an eloquent
series of letters; they were about the woods and fields which Cornie
loved, and about old Chapel Hill, which Cornie loved no less. This
is one:

"June's front parlor window where I am writing looks straight
down the Hogan lane into the front door of the Episcopal rectory.
I was thinking just now as I gazed at the house that 37 years ago
your sister Katie was a baby there, not a week old. How proud and
happy your mother was. And how angry with Mrs. M. A., whose
first remark on seeing the baby was, *'What ugly ears.'* . . .

"She was a very beautiful child. I remember taking her down
street when she was about three years old into Pomeroy's bookstore. He took Katie and stood her up on the counter and talked to
her. I have a vivid recollection of her eyes and hair and peachy
cheeks. She was a shy child, but didn't show it by crying or struggling. She would be perfectly still and self-enclosed. Seemed to sur-
round herself with an invisible veil of reserve and silence. Susy was
a great deal more demonstrative, tho' not so handsome. . . .

"Why do I sit here thinking of those little ones? It is 33 years
since they heard the call and passed on, leaving that small house
desolate. I look at it sometimes and reproduce certain scenes that
there is no one now to recall but me. Nobody."

III

After such moody reflections, it was often a comfort to Cornelia
to walk down to Aunt Dilsey's cabin and sit with her. The faithful
old Negro servant was sometimes fractious—she herself called it
being "outdone"—and needed humoring and petting. Cornelia
would sweep out the cabin and read aloud to her. Aunt Dilsey's
yearnings were often whimsical, and she could seldom say what

she wanted beyond "bitters," and "something good." By these she
meant whiskey toddy and flour biscuits. One day Cornelia sent her
nephew, Alex Phillips, down to see her, and Alex, who was a
ministerial student, prayed with her so eloquently that the old
woman shouted. Nor did other members of the family forget her.
An entry in Cornelia's journal for March 13, 1887, says: "I went
to see Aunt Dilsey this p.m., carried her $7 from bro[ther] Sam.
Peach trees in bloom for a week past. Dogtooth violets, arbutus,
anemones and hepaticas for 2 weeks. . . . Have been reading of late
various books: to-wit—

Proctor's Pleasant Ways in Science
Darwin's Voyage round the World 1835
George III
Dr. Claudius (a good novel)
Coleridge's Lectures on Shakespeare
Life of Byron
Lang's Letters to Dead Authors
Pettigrew's book on Spain (2nd time)
Lodge on American Colonies
Lord Teignmouth's "Life of Sir Wm. Jones"

Cornelia often complained now that her mind sometimes failed
to retain what she read; but this had its advantages because she
could read a good book over again with the original enjoyment.
At the end of 1887 she had to record the death of a friend for more
than fifty years, Mrs. Ellen Mitchell Summerell, and she saw 1888
come in with foreboding, for the prescience so characteristic had
warned her that events of moment were impending.

IV

When spring came to Washington, Cornie Phillips was no better,
and Cornelia, who was busy making silk caps for fraternity boys
and re-covering a sofa for the Di Society, redoubled her attempts to
cheer her by long and graphic letters of village life:

"Last evening I went over to Mrs. Hogan's and sat with her and her sister on their long side piazza—when I came home I found our piazza full—; Pres. and Mrs. Battle, Prof. Toy, and Rev. Mr. Taylor, all in full blast. Mrs. Welling and her sister [these New York State friends had taken rooms for the winter in the Love house] say we have the most agreeable little circle of friends they know of, in any place of this size. . . . Mr. Cameron spent an evening with us last week, and as he insisted on sitting on the piazza, and as he is as deaf as I am, of course the neighborhood had the benefit of all the conversation."

"July 1, 1888. This is $10\frac{1}{2}$ o'clock of a Sunday morning, the same being the first day of July. Everybody is gone to church meeting except your Uncle Charlie and me. . . . It is a fine day for July to begin with. Quite cool and dazzling bright at 6 o'clock, and now the sky is lightly clouded.

"After I was dressed—say 7 o'clock (nobody else awake but Beck)—I walked off to Mrs. Battle's garden and got a bunch of citarena and geranium and roses and a cape jasmine. Then I went and sat in their front piazza a while and thought of *many* things. All so solitary there—so peaceful—so dewy; the grove, the grass, the shade, the deep sweet shade."

"The ear trumpet is . . . a very *fatiguing* instrument. . . . It strains my nerves in some way, and after $\frac{1}{2}$ hour's exercise with it, while my friends are all congratulating themselves that I have it, I am so nervous, and so tired, and so fractious, that I have to get up and go somewhere to *cool off*."

[On a trip to the Mason farm] "I wished for you to enjoy the look of the woods—the plum-trees along the road, full of red and yellow plums—the blackberries shining out, the pink and purple pea vines—everything limp and wilted through the day, and standing up straight and dewy of a morning. I went to my room at night and found two immense feather-beds ready for me. I tumbled one

of 'em off on the floor, and slept on a mattress as hard and unyield-
ing as a plank. I opened every window blind and lay looking at
the lightning that lit up the whole landscape every second or two—
all the wide fields and distant woods. How awfully lonely it looked
in the glare. At breakfast we had hot fried ham—ditto chicken,
ditto middling. Hottest of large soft biscuit, ditto of cornbread.
Boiling hot coffee. Plenty of good buttermilk and butter. . . . When
I came home their overseer Andrews drove me. He is without doubt
the *ugliest* young man I ever did see. I think he is *impressively* ugly.

"However, he is rising in the world, owns a nice horse and buggy,
and so I hope Miss Sally Barbee will set her cap at him."

And then the news about the sick girl must have worsened, for
Cornelia wrote to her, "I can only commit you to God. I do pray
for you that he would care specially for you now, would give you
strength to suffer, strength to submit. His will be done. . . ." And
then came a letter from Cornie's father in Washington: "I talked
with her about herself; and then led her quietly to her beloved
topic of 'Chapel Hill'—telling her about the olden times . . . so
fragrant with pennyroyal—and other spicy weeds which my bare
feet have so often bruised, . . . filling the air with scent." This
letter was a few days later endorsed by Cornelia: "She lived till
Tuesday, 9:30 A.M., and passed away without a struggle, conscious
to the last."

v

Cornelia and her daughter and son-in-law had scarcely settled
down to the even flow of life at Seven Gables when a menace arose
in an unexpected direction from the campus. The spurt taken by
the University after its reopening in 1875 had by now begun to
spend itself, and although outwardly affairs seemed to be going
well, the old institution was running into rough financial seas. A
decision to jettison part of the cargo for economy's sake, because
of the cutting off of the state appropriation, became known in 1888,
when it was announced that the younger professors, W. B. Phillips,
nephew of Cornelia; Atkinson, and Henry would not return the

next year, and that Cornelia's son-in-law, James Lee Love, then assistant professor of mathematics, though granted an extension, would have only another year to stay. Thus was the new household to be disrupted before it was fairly established. Cornelia received this news with sinking spirits.

Before the year was gone her brother Sam, now well established in a private law practice in Washington, came down for a visit. His arrival was joyfully greeted by his ailing brother Charles; and although the two men, now gray, portly, and partly bald, had much merriment together, Cornelia, usually so eager for fun and able to hold her own in any witty company, joined in the laughter with an effort, for something that tightened her throat told her that she and her brothers, these three children of James and Judith Phillips, were now together for the last time. She went down to Aunt Dilsey's and told her, "I feel as if my heart would break." The old servant tried to console her, but vainly.

25

Historian Again

I

CORNELIA'S SECOND BOOK, *First Steps in North Carolina History*, appeared this same year, 1888. It was written expressly for the children at those ages which she loved to teach and whose welfare was always on her mind. "Its author," she wrote, "would be glad to know that not one of them from ten to fifteen years old, will fail to read or to approve of it." She explained her story as follows:

"Ours is the story of a quiet, contented, somewhat unambitious people, not studious of change, not easily provoked—a people loyal to Law and to Religion, steady, modest, sincere, and brave; generous but not enterprising; prodigal of their best when called upon by others or in defence of their own rights, but moving too slowly and cautiously when not under the strong stimulus of special occasion."

First Steps in North Carolina History, finished when she was sixty-three years old, was not one of Cornelia's best productions. She possibly wrote it from a sense of duty, and at the urging of educators who knew how great was the need of a school history of the state. Certain chapters smell of the kerosene lamp she used, and have an air of having been written from the surface part of her mind and not her whole heart. In the endeavor to adjust her thoughts to childish minds, she lost the warmth and pungency that always made even her more prejudiced expressions readable, while the apt phrases and image-making words characteristic of her private correspondence are scarcely found in this pocket-size history.

In those chapters where she had most knowledge of the period dealt with, notably the Civil War period, she pleased neither the unreconstructed Confederates nor those who had rediscovered the Union. Probably this dissatisfaction on both sides was to be expected, for the ground she trod upon was barbed and planted with old and sullen mines.

Particularly did she encounter criticism for her references to three controversial s's—secession, slavery, and states' rights. She gave great offence in the first edition by saying that secession "was absurd on the face of it" and by references to "fiery seceders" and "arrogant and overbearing slave-holders." She was also severely handled for certain minor historical inaccuracies and occasional slips, such as any writer on history is liable to, because of imperfect sources. Altogether this history was a source of vexation to her, and at no part of its career, either in the script or in the published form, did it give her any satisfaction. She received just $100 for the completed manuscript.

II

Yet this little book went through several editions and has had extra ones since. It has its charms, and is in certain particulars unique. It is probably the only history ever written which is interlarded with poetry, the poetry being in general better than the history. The poems were intended for declamation or reading aloud, and included authors native and not. In rescuing some of the selected pieces from oblivion Mrs. Spencer did her state a service. Best in the book is that portion of the narrative devoted to the Revolution. Cornelia was well versed in the lore of this period, and her love of Revolutionary characters and anecdotes make these chapters highly readable. This is one of her stories of 1776:

"The Rev. Mr. Debow, minister of the Hawfield church, was preaching that day very earnestly on the goodness of the Almighty, to whom alone he ascribed the victory. One of Caswell's soldiers was present, an honest and brave but rude fellow. He got up in meeting and said if that was to be the way, and Dick Caswell [general and governor] and his men were not to have any credit, he wouldn't stay there any longer. And so he went out."

Her last chapter but one presaged what did occur only a decade or so later: "One natural gift points out that our greatest prosperity is yet perhaps to come from manufactures, and that is the enormous water-power distributed over our whole territory except on the seaboard. . . . All these magnificent resources and means of power and prosperity lie yet in a great measure undeveloped, unthought of. North Carolina is never in a hurry even when she is pursuing her own advantage. Our people have always been slow in co-operation. The different sections stand too much aloof from each other, not considering that the prosperity of one aids the prosperity of all."

Unfortunately for Cornelia, she had not full access to the North Carolina colonial records just then being copied and published, as taken from the official papers and archives of the British government. Nor did she have the advantage of the social and economic studies which came in the twentieth century to strengthen the political and military histories which the nineteenth century favored. Her bibliography was scant, and the state historians who had preceded her were often partial or romantic. But what she had aimed to do she did as well as the resources then open to her would permit, and the product was a condensed history highly useful to North Carolina school children until they were able to get a better.

26

Sunderings

I

EARLY IN THE next year it was decided, at the insistence of their children, that Dr. Charles Phillips and his wife, Laura, should give up their house in Chapel Hill and go to live with their sons, Dr. William B. Phillips and the Rev. Alexander Phillips, in Birmingham, Alabama. Cornelia was opposed to this removal; but in view of her brother's growing invalidism and the strain of nursing and housekeeping on her sister-in-law, she said nothing, watching in silence the long labor of packing up and the sundering of old ties. Dr. Phillips stood the transfer from house to train cheerfully, and even remarked that during the night journey he was glad of the sight of the stars, which he had not seen for many years. But before the train had traversed more than a small part of South Carolina, it was seen that he could not endure the journey. He was taken to the home in Columbia, South Carolina, of his son-in-law, Colonel John S. Verner, where he died in great pain.

"He was the most *living* one of us all," wrote Cornelia to Laura, "the brightest, strongest, most vivid, most interested in all, most sympathetic—the one to whom we all looked, and turned. . . . June thinks of *Cornie's* joy to see 'Uncle Charlie.' Aunt Dilsey says nobody will be gladder than *Ben.* The old woman came and spent the day with us yesterday. She is deeply hurt—deeply. Says she *rested* so on Mas' Charles and Miss Laura. I rose before the sun, Friday and went down to see her—and cry on her old shoulder."

To June she wrote: "I have been reading old Matthew Henry

on Paul's letter to Timothy. Paul was not afraid to anticipate his 'crown.' He almost reached out after it beforehand. I think of your Uncle C[harlie] in his company. He loved his writings so much, studied them so constantly and so devoutly. What a joy to see the writer and talk them over. If we are going to enjoy heaven we ought to be as much as possible in communion with the saints here. The Poets, the Philosophers, the Historians, the Scientists—how do we know which of them we shall meet there? ... I can imagine your Uncle C[harlie] or your grandfather in converse with Paul very well—but not with any man or woman of whose inner life or religious belief here we know nothing or merely conjecture and hope.—What questions!—What replies!— What pressing on to know more and more and more of the fullness of God. 'O glorious hour! O blest abode!' ' "

II

During the University commencement exercises of that year, 1889, a melancholy pleasure came to her—surviving members of her husband's class, 1853, were having a reunion at Chapel Hill and they all came to see her—Capehart, McIver, Morehead, Shorter, and Worth.

That year Mr. Love decided to go to Harvard for graduate study and the next year did so, leaving his wife, June Spencer Love, with her mother. Once more Cornelia, having complete possession of her daughter, was happy; but it was not to be for long. After a year at Harvard, Mr. Love was appointed an instructor there and in September, 1890, Cornelia was once more bereft and alone, for Mrs. Love felt bound to say goodbye to Chapel Hill and go to Cambridge to join her husband. Cornelia remained behind at Seven Gables with only the Negro cook, Beck, for company.

Hitherto when June had left home, her mother could feel assured that, however wrenching was the separation, it would not be for long. Now she could not be sure. And in the intervening years since June had left her to go to Raleigh or New York,

Cornelia had become much more dependent on her; for the mother, though scarcely less vigorous mentally, was physically no longer a young woman; and after several lonely years had begun to enjoy the people, the going and coming, that her married daughter and her husband had brought to the house. For example, she had just written to a friend, "June has some old students or other people to every meal: this morning at breakfast Judge J. J. Davis, Major Bingham, Dr. Beall and Mr. Cook; last night at tea Dr. N. McKay, Col. Steele, Gen. Barringer, Rev. Harding.... Maj. B. told me after breakfast it was admirable. And Southgate and Jones both told her yesterday they had never eaten as good ice cream in North Carolina as hers. So on the whole, she feels like old Mrs. Turrentine when her biscuits 'got the praise.'"

Now all this gaiety and stir of life, valued all the more by Cornelia because of her deafness, was to end abruptly. After June had departed for Cambridge, she wrote to her:

"I wandered to and fro in your room. Everything stabbed me— everything. I simply fell flat for two or three hours, and made no attempt to rally. Here was an old muslin belt which I made for you in '85—I held it up—I kissed it over and over...."

"It is standing *alone* for the first time in years that I find so hard, so unwelcome. How I wince at having to interview the boy with chickens—the man with beef. Even Lou Mack with her 1 lb. of butter and 1 doz[en] eggs...I have the most curious sensations whenever I go into *your* rooms. These are *her* things.... Here are the toothpicks in the little vase...the flat candlestick, and candle lying across it."

The descent into the valley of despond was very deep, but after a time Cornelia's natural vigor and independence came back to her and she was able to do battle with Beck, the cook:

"I have just escaped from the pantry and kitchen and Beck!" she wrote to June. "Beck wants to order and direct me a great deal. Snatches things up when I put 'em down—'Law, Mis' Spencer, Miss June don't allow *that* to set *there*.'... She is slightly derisive of my doings. Comes into the pantry and takes things with such an air of knowing better than anyone else where everything is and how to do. Waves me out of the kitchen with both hands and remonstrates with me at every turn—affects the confidential servant *left in charge* of things and doesn't wish to be interfered with by dotards! "

III

In a few weeks more, having taken in Mr. Fogartie, the Presbyterian preacher, as a roomer, Cornelia had recovered her poise and was able to survey the situation with her customary sanity and balance. To June she wrote:

"I believe it is a great mercy and kindness *direct from heaven* that took you out of C H and sent you so far away! . . . Enjoy your fortunate circumstances as much as you can, and don't brood over the unfortunate. Be brave and cheerful, and wait patiently God's will. . . . I think you have formed some very nice acquaintances already. Don't you notice that the higher you go in social life, the more quiet and simple and unpretending people are. No effort about their good manners. The good-breeding is ingrain[ed]. . . . Incessant activity and industry mark the Yankee proper, activity of mind as much as of body. . . . Our ladies are not idle with hands, but I fear their minds are very torpid. And our better class of married women give their whole time to their own affairs. They do not work for humanity. . . . The Yankee disposition to *help others*—what we call '*public spirit*'—is what we lack in the South. We are *kindly* enough, but we are not *actively* interested."

A little later she had entirely recovered her sense of practical necessities and could write: "This morning I have been over everything. Put clean things on Mr. F's bed. . . . Cleaned up pantry. Filled lamps. Bought beef and butter and s[weet] potatoes. Had Mr. Woods here for an hour fixing my clock. He brought me 4 big potatoes 'from my mother.' Says Mrs. W. says she *feels like that much kin to me.* Have cut up and salted a jar of green tomatoes. Have mended a pillow case. Have taken off one leaf of the screen in Mr. F's room and placed it by my washstand. Mr.

Woods will make me a *foot* for it. . . . Now I have three pr. of socks and 2 of stockings to darn." She also described some millinery experiments; how she took Mrs. P. H. Winston's four caps made in New York "as large as bonnets and made 'em all over— cut 'em down from 75-gun frigates to modest sloops of war. She is so grateful and happy."

It was characteristic of Cornelia that she could write a history, compile a catalog, translate Horace, advise governors, darn socks, and carry on the daily jobs of housekeeping without feeling any clash between the one thing and the other.

27

Village Annals

I

DURING THE FOUR years between 1890 and 1894 Cornelia did some of the most brilliant writing of her life, and virtually all of it was contained in notes and letters to her daughter in Cambridge. Her letters to June, sometimes written daily, made up a faithful and graphic chronicle of village life; for Cornelia, who no longer cared to be active physically, could sit at her window on the porch and invest every passing and passerby with a penetrating interest.

One of her vivid descriptions dealt with the death of a young married woman who had been ill but who was believed to be recovering. Scene, her bedroom:

"Her father said he must go down stairs and read his papers and go to bed. She was in high spirits and begged him to stay a little longer. Then he said after a little he was tired and got up and kissed her goodnight. Her mother remained. Presently M. asked her for a fan. 'What in the world do you want a fan for, when it is so cool?' 'Oh, I feel somehow faint. Fan me, mama.' Her mother saw a change in her look and begged her son to go for the doctor, whom he fortunately found on the street. M. was still perfectly conscious, begged he would not give her morphine or chloro—she hated their effects so. She called for her husband and said, "Mama, don't leave me. I feel as if I was going.' Became unconscious and died without a struggle.

"Mrs. F., Mrs. M., and I dressed her; put on her pretty underclothes and a handsome white nun's veiling made up with white silk and trimmed with white ribbons. I never saw anyone so perfectly white, so fair as she looked; perfectly round and plump, and without a particle of color, like marble precisely. And when dressed, she lay languid in repose, looking like a bride. When all was ready, the men came up and took her in their arms and carried her downstairs and laid her on a couch in the parlor with a cluster of white roses at her throat. Her hands were like snow. Her mother came in to see her.... and fell down on the floor beside her."

This is a jotting for one day in November, 1890:

"I went into the pantry which, alas, is much in the condition these days of Mother Hubbard's; and looked and looked for something that would do to take to a sick woman. Do you remember a country woman coming here perhaps in June and asking for light-bread or anything for a woman who had been bedridden for months, a Mrs. R.? She has been brought to town to be near the doctors.... Kings' Daughters and others have been tending to her, and I thought I ought to go. So I got up some bread and butter and some of Mrs. Hogan's canned apples and a few chrysanthemums and walked down there. The woman is young and quite pretty tho' she has had 8 or 10 children. That is what ails her now. Then I walked past Tenney's and part the way down the hill looking at the glowing shrubs and forests. I met four little Negroes each carrying a dead rabbit. They had a dog and gun among them. I walked back by way of the back street, strolling along looking at Williams and company playing tennis, looking at this tree and that.... Isn't the fortitude of women wonderful in such circumstances? Think how the sex has borne it—what young, delicate girls, what sickly women, what wretched wives. Think of going through it all, for a drunken brutal husband, for an unfaithful husband? Think of going through it all alone, with husband gone, mother, friend, all gone. It is a daily, hourly, miracle how women go on calmly—yea, joyfully, proudly—having babies."

Her search of a scant pantry made Cornelia think of her current expenses, and a calculation showed her that her food for three weeks and two days in 1890 had cost her $5.50. "I have not had an egg in a week," she wrote. She was outraged that the price of eggs should have gone up to 20 cents a dozen. "I won't give that," she declared firmly.

Fortunately for Cornelia, she was able to obtain roomers, some of them students, who kept her from feeling lonely, and she considered herself in immense luck when a Mrs. Willing, of New York State, who was in search of a mild climate, came to live with her each winter. Mrs. Willing was an intelligent, well-educated woman and Cornelia took much comfort in her.

II

Cornelia was not of a temperament that would permit monotony long to weigh upon her, and there were many little adventures that whiled away the march of days. One day in 1892 the ladies of the village were set a-flutter by the news that Professor Albert Bushnell Hart, the Harvard historian, was coming to town to visit and lecture, and that a desirable home was sought for him. At once a quiet but vigorous struggle was set in motion by several willing hostesses. But Cornelia's name and presence prevailed, and she easily carried off the prize. Professor Hart proved to be just what the ladies of the village would have ordered. He was not at all shy like the native professors, but dramatic, complimentary, worldly, and well-dressed, and Cornelia watched him carefully and wrote a daily bulletin to June about him.

"Today," she wrote, "he took a nap sitting by the fire! *'This is rest,'* he said. . . .

"This morning directly after br[ea]kf[as]t Prest. [Geo. T.] Winston and his brother, P. H., came in—and after some pleasant talk they carried H. off, and we have not seen him since. I laugh inwardly when I think of Hart walking off so innocently between those two sharp razors. . . .

"Mr. Hart came in about 5 o'c this afternoon, Mr. Winston having taken him to see Aunt Dilsey. He was delighted to go and

says she was about as interesting a person as he has met. He says
he means to go again. . . .

"What arrests my attention in observing northern people, such
as he and Mrs. W[illing], is their greater *seriousness* as compared with us. They seem so dreadfully in earnest. They seem
to have business in hand—something to do, to think about, to
study upon and arrange for—and they show this objective purpose
all the time. Our people are so much more easy, gay, careless. . . .
They are ready for a good laugh at all times, ready to 'sink the
ship,' and disport themselves. . . .

"Yest[erday] afternoon I went to see Mrs. Hooper. . . . I told her
of the Harvard Prof., and she was awe-stricken. Wondered much
at his coming, or wanting to come here—'thankful' he was where
he could be handsomely entertained! etc.

"Very much pleased with the tea wh[ich] I told her came from
you. Sends her love to you and best thanks—proposes to 'enjoy it
greatly'—as she loves black tea and had been wishing for some.
Mrs. Hooper has the old-fashion of expressing gratitude for small
attentions warmly, and with apparent humility that always seems
pathetic. I took her hand as she was wondering why people were
so good to her and said, 'This dear generous hand has been filled
full, and opened wide to the sick and the poor ever since I have
known it, and why shouldn't people be eager to offer you love and
kindness?' . . .

"We got home in time for supper, finding Mr. Hart busy con-
ning his lecture. . . . We all proceeded in the soft warm moonlight
to the chapel. I did feel a glow of gratitude to Mr. North as I went
in that hall, chaired and carpeted and brilliantly lit, and in all
respects what it sh[ould] be. A good crowd. Boys pretty generally
out and behaved beautifully well. All the *gentry* from the village—
faculty ladies, etc. Mrs. Hume looked *elegant,* Mrs. Towers handsome and bright. Lecture on political geography of U. S. Lots of
maps. . . . I sat and gazed at the maps and thought I could understand very well the general *trend* of his talk. He had *dressed* from

top to toe and looked splendidly. We don't often see a man so well dressed—in C. H.

"Everybody strictly attentive and all passed off perfectly well. . . . and then we all came along home through the heavenly groves —every twig on the trees outlined against the moon and stars. Mr. Hart asked for 'a glass of milk and a cracker,' and soon went to his room. I stayed up and read his lecture (typewritten) clean through. . . . I asked him at br[eak]fast if he read all that about the slave territory, & the Kansas struggle, and *old John Brown!* He laughed and shook his head—'No, no.'

"The typewriting was faulty and the interlineations numerous, and it all marred his delivery. As you say—It takes Southerners for oratory. . . .

"H. is so undemonstrative, and says so little, you cannot tell what he does or does not care for. I believe he is all the time thinking how he shall advance himself in his profession. He has no fire of genius—no ready adaptation, no swift comprehension. . . . But he is not *dull.* . . . He told me just now he was in love with C. Hill —had had a most enjoyable time here, and was truly grateful for all the kindness shown him by everybody. . . . I must comfort your mind by telling you I had just made me three nice little caps before the H. prof. came! I took comfort in 'em myself."

And this is a sketch taken from an account of a University commencement in 1891. Referring to one of the visiting young ladies, she wrote:

"This girl was no beauty, but certainly elegant, in a costume that would have been elegant in any assembly. Cream-colored dress with gold-colored ribbons, sash, bonnet, gloves, and fan. Such exquisite gloves and such tiny hands, and such graceful, assured, self-poised manners.

"The bonnets all very small—mere caps, black lace capes and flounces on front breadths and trains. The fashionable clutch to the skirt seems designed not so much to lift the dress from the ground, tho' it does that effectually, as to exhibit the leg and thigh and hips as clearly as possible. I saw one girl who pulled on her skirt so vigorously as to show the whole leg *ab initio* and the behind just as plain in outline as if she had on only one garment. And she must have known that it was so, for she walked very slowly and with an air of being on exhibition. Some women are so. I don't say they are not modest women, but they look immodest, and there must be some taint at the core or they couldn't do it."

III

In the midst of these routines, Cornelia had to respond to the usual demands on her talents. One day Professor George T. Winston came in and asked her to write a cantata for the children to sing at the approaching decennial celebration of the Goldsboro, North Carolina, graded schools. She complied and received the following from Superintendent J. Y. Joyner:

"Thank you very sincerely for the songs which you prepared for our decennial celebration. We think them beautiful in conception and execution, and peculiarly appropriate to the occasion. . . . It would be a great pleasure to me to have you attend our celebration on May 22d [1891]. I should feel that the occasion was rendered more complete by the presence of one who has been for so many years so staunch and able a friend of public education, of everything that makes for the good of the 'Old North State'."

Cornelia's attentions to the unfortunate, especially to Negro families, did not go unacknowledged. One day she got the following from a colored client:

"Mrs. Spencer—I have been sick ever since 3 weeks before Christmas and I had Dr. W. coming to see me and he did not do me any good and Dr. R. come and attended me a while and now Dr. Whitehead is attending on me he says it is dyspepsia and change of life and since it has been so warm for a day or two i have been able to go out doores and Mrs. Spencer I never will forget you for your kindness to me I enjoyes your confectionaries so much when I get able to walk about I am coming down to see you—please mam give my love to Miss June when you write to her and please mam tell her how long I been sick if you please mam. Your humble servant, Rilla Strowd."

There was another note of thanks received about this time that must have pleased Cornelia no less:

"My dear madam—Nothing has touched me more during these busy weeks than the tender and constant regard you have shown for me and my little family. But for your kind aid and watchful care I sh'd have been o'erwhelmed in the sea of duties that swept me along."

This was from George T. Winston, the new president of the University. Belonging to the "razor-sharp" Winstons, he was a positive and vigorous young professor who loved executive power and throve on opposition. Cornelia, whose temperament was similar, much admired him and he fully returned her regard. At times he was almost a daily visitor at her house, where he often sought her counsel, even though he seldom took it or anyone else's. Contemptuous of slackness and incompetence, he was a symbol of the resolution that was returning to a once-prostrate state.

IV

At this period, which might otherwise have been a lonely one, Cornelia was pleased to have the younger professors drop in, as they often did, not only to pay their respects to Chapel Hill's greatest personality but to hear her pungent comments. One of them was H. Horace Williams, who was later, as the "gadfly of Chapel Hill," to acquire a reputation scarcely second to Mrs. Spencer's. In one of her letters to June containing the small coin of village gossip she wrote:

"After Mrs. Winston left and it stopped raining, I went down to Mr. F.'s and carried Mrs. F. a pretty booklet for New Year's, and she sent me home with a plate full of splendid black-cake. It was much too fine for me to eat by myself, and this afternoon H. Williams called, and I produced my cake and a bottle of sherry upon which we made merry. W. was very pleasant. Had a delightful time in N.Y., but it was fearfully cold. Went out very little, to the opera and concerts mostly. He has taken board at Mrs. Mallett's."

She also received frequent visits from the young professors Venable, Holmes, and Gore, all of whom subsequently established their fame in the fields of chemistry, geology, and physics, respectively.

But amid these small adventures and gayeties, she often felt the ache that lay under old scars, and when June 20, 1892, came 'round she wrote:

"This is my wedding day. I went into the garden before breakfast—attended by the Captain [her cat], and got a bouquet of white jasmine and rose-pink-phlox, and adorned the br[eak]fast table by way of remembrance.—Of all who were at my wedding, how many are left?—Brother Sam, Sister Laura, Miss Margaret [Mitchell], Mrs. Selina [Thompson]. O memory! Memory!"

Cornelia's letters to June at this period contained frequent references to three things: religion, continuing war with Rebecca the cook, visits down the hill to Aunt Dilsey, and sometimes to her spells of depression. Just after the Presbyterian preacher, Mr. Fogartie, had departed, she wrote this review of memories:

"I felt so cast down all yesterday afternoon. Mr. F's departure seemed to sever the last link between my life with you and the new one alone. I felt prodigiously alone and sat with my head against the back of my rocking chair thinking over everything. How distinct the separate acts of my life. I look back to the years when you were a child going after chinquapins with the Fetters, and your little cousins, and the Miss Martins. Then with the Mason girls and Nora or Lucy or Cornie or Alice Kerr. Then your school days at Peace and the glad comings home. Do you recall that ride through from Morris with the Masons and John Morgan driving you? Poor John Morgan! Then the walks with your little scholars, and the college boys—and the normal schools. Your going away to New York, the beginning of so many goings away. Then the great change caused by grandma's death. Then the life at Mrs. Thompson's. What recollections I have of long walks over

these hills with that family—What returns home laden with spring
flowers—fall flowers—dresses covered with seeds—worn out and
weary but happy and triumphant. Poor Cornie; what luxury to
her these tramps. I remember so distinctly some I took with her and
Mrs. Kerr that winter, '86-'87. Shall I ever go out on these hills
again—or are the hills and the streams really as far gone out
of my life as those friends and followers who roamed over them
with me? I doubt if I ever climb *Bolin's* Hill again, or cross the
creek at its foot in Tenney's meadow—if I ever see Tom's den
again, or Glenburnie. Those walks with Mr. Battle were so pleasant.
Do you remember the last one we took with him and the little
Lewises to the mill-dam just before they all went home in '86? ...
The tide has ebbed and left me stranded on the shore."

To Laura Phillips she wrote:

"What have you been reading today? I have had good Matthew
Henry's comment on Romans. Oh, how comfortable Henry is, and
how my mind and heart enjoy the old way of discussing Bible
truth. Addison Alexander's sermons are most precious. The two
volumes I have brother Charles gave to Mr. Spencer the last visit
he paid Chapel Hill. I feed upon them continually. They satisfy
my soul. ...

"Lyman Abbot [editor the New York *Outlook*] has come out
squarely as Unitarian. He has been coquetting with that doctrine
for years. I remember Grandma saying of him 25 years ago and
since, 'Lyman Abbot is not sound.' ... Abbot says openly, '*I dare
not say Jesus Christ is God as well as man*'. If Christ be not God—
God manifest in the flesh—then he cannot be the Savior of men.
If he is not God, then to whom shall we go? ...

"For my part I do not know how a woman gets along in such
circumstances without some sense of religion, some leaning upon
the unseen to help her. I guess all women *are* more or less religious
—they do—though unconsciously—look for—and do get—support
from beyond themselves and their surroundings. They may not
know it, but they are supported by the powers of nature—which
is only another word for the Father above."

But as often as she was in a state of grace, she was likely to be brought abruptly to earth by the mundane inhabitant of the kitchen: "I bought a gobbler two days ago for my 22nd [Washington's birthday] dinner and this morning he was found stiff in the coop. I should not have thought last night cold enough to kill a turkey in a coop. But there he was dead—. I never can trust Beck about anything, you know well. I found a teaplate broken in three pieces and laid upon the shelf yest. 'How did this happen, Beck?' 'I don't know nothin' t'all about it.' ... I discovered one of my best towels hanging dirty on her washstand in the kitchen. 'What is this towel doing here?' 'I just br[ough]t it out to wash it.' "

v

As for Dilsey, increasing age had made that small black slave-woman more and more indifferent to food, and on certain days Cornelia found her lying in bed, conscious and in full possession of her faculties, but silent for hours at a time and neglectful of all food. At such times Cornelia would exert herself to entice Aunt Dilsey's appetite; she would take her broths, milk, butter, whiskey, hot rolls, jellies, and other dainties, and sometimes sit down with her and compel her to eat. One thing, however, would always rouse Dilsey from her dreary state; that was the spectacle of Cornelia in a nervous or depressed state. Then the black woman would take the white woman in her arms and comfort her as she would a child.

" I rose early and went to see Aunt Dilsey before breakfast," Cornelia wrote one day. "Found her just making up her bed. She was dressed so clean, looked so decent. Was so glad to see me and ask about you and hear everything. Sends you her love and blessing. Showed me her new bed-quilt she is piecing, with pride. The morning was delicious. I had to stop on the hill and take a long look on the blue horizon ... the delicate greens showing against the dark pines, dogwood showing white here and there, all so fresh and tender."

Although Cornelia always wrote cheerfully to her daughter, she sometimes confessed to Laura Phillips an occasional sense of loneliness and depression. She was particularly liable to be depressed on anniversaries, which she remembered with extraordinary acuteness. For example, on March 1, 1892, she noted: "Twenty-five yrs ago today Mrs. Fetter died. I am sole survivor here of the circle of that day in C. H. The years have fled past like a dream. . . . I think of our departed friends a great deal at this season of the year, tho' I don't dream of them as you do. Those whose remembrance is most associated with *nature*, with her flowers and woods and streams, seem to come back to our minds more constantly and more clearly than those whose memories are not so intertwined."

VI

The spring came on and one day in May Cornelia got a letter from Laura Phillips beginning: "My dear Cornelia—I came near saying 'dear grandmother'—for that you *are* a grandmother is the uppermost thought in my mind and has been ever since I received a note from Mr. Love announcing the arrival of 'Miss Cornelia Spencer Love.' "

28

Grandmother

I

AND SO AT the age of sixty-seven Cornelia Phillips Spencer became a grandmother. Her first letter to the new mother exclaimed:

"My dearest: It is too much to believe that you really have a baby! ... *Isn't it precious?* I do believe the suffering beforehand makes the little one all the dearer to its mother. What you pay a great price for is inestimable.... Oh dear, dear, I feel like laughing and I feel like crying when I think of it all."

Later in that year, 1892, mother and child came down from Massachusetts on a visit, and for the first time Cornelia enjoyed the sensation of having in her lap a grandchild. And this visit was repeated the following year. Meantime Cornelia kept on living at Seven Gables, alone except for the daytime presence of the surly cook, Beck Mason. "Every day passes so quietly, and with such steady monotony, it really looks as if things might go on just so for 20-40 years."

II

Early in 1894 Cornelia commented again on this procession of uniform days; and nevertheless with the prescience characteristic of her, she was moved to add:

"Yet I know well this is only a momentary lull, so to speak, such as is often the precursor of great changes.... I feel now as if change was approaching." Her clairvoyance did not fail her; she had reason long to remember the events of 1894.

In the spring Mrs. Love at Cambridge thought her mother had been alone long enough and wrote to her asking if she were not ready to give up the solitary life in the cottage at Chapel Hill and come to live in Cambridge. Cornelia replied, "My going to you must be dismissed from your mind at once. It has never entered mine as even a possibility." March 20 was her birthday and she confessed to June: "I guess I am not as young as I was. I am easily fatigued and have lost the ambition to undertake and do, that I once had. Exertion is no longer the pleasure it used to be. . . . Let me look, however, upon this beautiful morning and thank God for green pasture and still waters. . . . The oaks are tasseling. Peach trees out of bloom. Distant woods have a greenish hue. Butterflies abound. Robins and jays, bluebirds and red birds and brown birds fill the yard."

III

In April she got the news of Senator Zeb Vance's death. "Another old friend is in the secret; I shall always think Vance one of the really great men of North Carolina," she wrote June. "And now I have marked Vance in my centennial catalog as among the dead."

In the same month she found that Aunt Dilsey was no longer able to sit up and cook herself corn-cakes in the little fireplace skillet she had used for half a century, and she asked Dr. Whitehead to see the old woman. The doctor came away shaking his head, saying he could only relieve her pain. Dilsey rallied, and on Cornelia's next visit "she was up and dressed by her fire, and John's little girl Sarah was giving her her bit of bread and cup of coffee. Talked of you and was just as usual, sensible, cheerful, sympathetic. Talked of Gov. Vance, remembered him well." But this show of strength was only temporary and it soon became evident to Cornelia that Dilsey would scarcely live beyond the spring.

"I have come back from Aunt Dilsey's and have read a while, have walked to the west-end gate and looked at everything, and now I will try to get some comfort out of a letter to you. I have to repress myself, harden my mind, and so keep from feeling the death of our dear old woman too keenly or irrationally. . . . I like to think I have never given the old soul an impatient or unkind word in my life, nor had such a thought of her, though in these later years she had necessarily been something of a burden on my slender finances, a care and a responsibility. No human being could have been less so than she."

In the midst of these broodings she was glad to have a chance to go out on May Day to Laurel Hill, two miles from Chapel Hill, and pick spring flowers, including clusters of laurel blossoms.

"The laurel—the laurel!" she wrote. "Never more beautiful and luxuriant. That drive to Laurel Hill was in the nature of a refreshing shower to my mind. I think sometimes I stay at home too much and live in too trifling and *undersized* a round. I dreamed of the hill and the rocks and the laurel and the rushing creek all Monday night. . . . I am going presently to take Aunt Dilsy some rice for her dinner. I shall sit and sing for her. All the women sitting round begin to wipe their eyes when I start, 'And Must This Feeble Body Fail?' or 'Over There.' She lies quiet and placid. . . . The other day Aunt D. was anxious for me to be shown a square of pink mosquito net which Tilda Atwater, out of her poverty, had bought to put over Aunt D.'s face while sleeping. They keep her as clean as if she was a lady. Think of poor Tilda's charity. . . . Do you know these lines? I say them over and over to myself often these days:

> "As a vesture shalt thou change them, said the prophet;
> And the raiment that was flesh is turned to dust;
> Dust and flesh and dust again the fashion of it,
> And the gold threads woven and worn of youth are rust.
> Hours that wax and wane salute the robe and scoff it,
> That it knows not aught it doth, or aught it must;
> Day by day the speeding soul makes haste to doff it,
> Night by night the pride of life resigns its trust."

II

Aunt Dilsey's last faint breath came on May 25, 1894. She was conscious and serene almost up to the last moment. A few hours before her death Cornelia came and leaned over her. She hardly noticed me," Cornelia wrote, "except to squeeze my hand. When I said goodbye she said, 'I lean my head on Jesus' breast.' I kissed her and she nodded her head and pressed my hand again."

Cornelia looked into Dilsey's trunk and found that Dilsey had prepared and laid in order there everything needed for her burial. For *The White and Blue,* the student non-fraternity paper, Cornelia wrote a short article in the June 5 issue, saying:

"Chapel Hill has lost its oldest inhabitant. 'Aunt Dilsy,' widow of old 'Uncle' Ben Craig, . . . died in her own house on the 25th inst. at the great age of 93 years. She had been for more than seventy years a member of the Baptist Church, and for a large part of her long life was the faithful and trusted servant of Dr. James Phillips, professor of mathematics in our University for forty-one years.

"At the 'surrender' Aunt Dilsy declined to use her liberty but remained true to 'old master' till his death in 1867. . . . Let not the rising generation be impatient of a short and simple annal like this. They will never know the sweetness of attachment that exists between an old servant and the family to whom the loyal service was given."

III

Cornelia came back to her house, sighed, and returned to work, for the University had asked her to letter in the names of the graduates on the parchment diplomas to be awarded at the approaching commencement. For this labor she was annually paid $10. The month of June, ominous June, had come, and after this her letters to Cambridge mentioned her occasional loneliness more than ever before:

"I am at the west window of the study," she wrote. "And feel afraid to go about the house, all is deadly silent and still, *deadly.*"

But a postscript, describing a visit at the University president's house, was more cheerful: "Not so deadly lonesome after all. Mr. and Mrs. Winston came by and insisted on my going to dinner with them. And I went. And had good talk with 'em both and an excellent dinner. Roast chicken and ham and rice and snaps and squash and all sorts of pickles and condiments, iced milk, peaches and fruit-cake and wafers and preserved ginger."

There followed a chronicle of losses from Cornelia's circle of old friends. Foster Utley, the old University carpenter, died suddenly. "I have known Mr. Utley for more than 50 years," she wrote. "If there has ever been an unkind or impatient word spoken of Mr. Utley in all these years I never heard it." Then Mrs. J. Pleasant Mason, of the Mason farm where Cornelia had so often visited, was stricken, and Cornelia went out several times to visit her. Mrs. Hooper, another old friend, was also ailing.

On June 19 Cornelia wrote Mrs. Love a usual letter of news and gossip, but did not finish it. When next day she resumed, she mentioned she had been reading a life of Dean Stanley. "It is striking to see how dependent he was on feminine sympathy. First his mother's. . . . He married Lady Augusta Bruce, one of Queen Victoria's most intimate friends. She was a very homely-looking woman, if her portrait is true, but seems to have been just what he needed." And then there was a sudden change in the handwriting and then came the sentence:

"And now I have something serious to tell you." Followed the story of a small hardness in the left breast, the attempt to ignore it, an eventual appeal to Dr. Whitehead, his verdict that it was cancer, and should be immediately excised. "Think of me as comfortable and not unhappy, except when I think of you as you will feel after reading all I send." In reply she received a prompt telegram from Professor Love requesting her to close the house at once and take the next train to Cambridge. To this she answered: "I am greatly relieved to have some one decide for and order me.

Greatly relieved. . . . I can hardly tell you how demoralized I have felt all this week—like a child. . . . I will do just as you say."

Very few people knew of her departure. President Winston escorted her part of the way. In Cambridge Professor and Mrs. Love took charge of her. The operation was a success, the healing quick; within a few weeks she was writing to friends in her old sprightly way. By October she was visiting at the Warwick, New York, home of her former lodger, Mrs. Willing. But the shock of all that had happened had told upon her and she was very quiet; for she was nearing seventy years and she did not believe she would ever see Chapel Hill again. "I am quite passive," she wrote June from Warwick, "and try to behave and be good and do as I am told."

29

Cambridge Friends

I

THOUGH HER daughter June and her son-in-law, Professor Love, had easily adjusted themselves to the life at Harvard University and had acquired absorbing interests and friends in Cambridge, Cornelia at seventy was necessarily slower than they in coming to terms with what to her was an alien existence. She was at first acutely sensitive about her deafness; and always hating to make explanations, she shrank from meeting new people or even going out. She was at times beset by a benumbing loneliness. Yet there were at least three great compensations for having to accept this new life. First was the unvarying care and affection she received in the home of Professor and Mrs. Love; second, the delight of having her grandchildren daily in her lap, for soon a second child was born, James Spencer Love, who was afterwards one of the youngest majors in World War I, and then a successful textile manufacturer in North Carolina; third, her pleasure in having unlimited access to the great libraries and bookshops of Harvard and Boston; for as she grew older, books became even more her daily refuge and consolation.

Bit by bit she warmed toward Cambridge life and found there excellent friends whose hospitality rivalled that of Chapel Hill. Yet often in the midst of the new pleasures, some old memory, some anniversary of the heart, would flame across her mind, and for relief she would go to her journal and write: "I spent greater part of today on Castle Is[land] (City Point) in Boston Bay, with June and her little ones. The children had shoes and stockings off and waded in the Atlantic, while I and June sat on the rocks or on the benches and nibbled candies and Saratoga chips and drank ginger ale and watched the ships. . . . One immense ocean liner (Leyland's) came in while we sat. . . . Today 11 years ago we laid *Cornie* by her mother in Chapel Hill. *I often wish for Cornie!* She was part of the old C H life and retained to the last of hers a warm vivid interest in all that pertained to it and to the people who made it." This entry was made August 1, 1899. On the 11th she made another: "Thirty-one years ago Gov. Swain and Mr. Fetter thrown from carriage today (1868). . . . How vividly I recall that day."

Sometimes in her journal she reproached herself for broody thoughts: "The melancholy that comes of such considerations is largely constitutional, I imagine, and is an inheritance no doubt from *English* blood. Aunt Ann Phillips (bless her!) [wife of her father's brother, Samuel Phillips] told me once that it dwelt largely in her, and she could never look over even a little box of broken trinkets or toys of her former life without pain—'And yet,' she said, 'it is a pain that I cherish, often voluntarily invite and yield my mind to at intervals.' "

II

In Cambridge Cornelia—"Grandy" she was to the children— occupied a comfortable room on the second floor of Professor Love's house on Walker Street. Here she spent much of her time in front of a bay window, sitting by a small mahogany table particularly beloved because it had come from her old home in Chapel Hill. Reading, writing, and sewing—these were her favorite occupations. Letters to her scores of friends were always written on a portfolio held in her lap. She used a fine-pointed steel pen, writing with an unfailing clarity and legibility, with never a smear and rarely a correction, and observing every nicety of spacing and punctuation. Some of her correspondents, like Mrs. Charles Phillips or Miss Margaret Mitchell, were so regular that her granddaughter Cornelia—called "Ne" when small—soon learned to recognize their writing, and she would run upstairs shouting, "It's from Aunt Laura!" or "It's from Miss Margaret!" Shout she must, for Cornelia could by now hear none but her daughter June's voice, and communication with her was often done with pad and pencil.

To one with the natural independence and dignity of Cornelia, this condition must have been galling; but to none of the household did she complain. There was another handicap of which she made no complaint. It can now be surmised her deafness was perhaps due to an infection of the ear that was never discovered; for at intervals she suffered from severe head-pains which prostrated her or made her very nervous. Her daughter June knew what to do for such attacks, and this no doubt explains why the mother hated to be separated long from Mrs. Love, especially as she aged.

Cornelia was never so content as when having children in tow, and she early took a hand in the education of her granddaughter. With "Ne" listening, the classic stories and the novels of Cooper, Dickens, and Scott, were read aloud. The listener was not permitted to sit idle, but was encouraged to have a piece of "fancy-work" or hemstitching in hand. Although deaf, Cornelia was a thrilling reader and knew how to impart the proper dramatic touch to such tales as Dickens's *Christmas Carol,* including the Cratchit dinner, which was ever in demand on Christmas Eve.

She abhorred idleness, and when not otherwise employed, she sewed, usually by hand. She made black and white caps for herself, both the "best" and the "everyday," and she liked to make gingham dresses for little Cornelia, ornamented with "hamburg" edging, or ruffles, or with bertha effects and guimpes. Because she was so deft with her fingers, she did much of the family darning, and any small jobs of mending were brought to her as a matter of course. Although immaculately neat, she never seemed to care about her own clothes. She was satisfied with black and white; yet when she saw a pretty woman tastefully dressed, she was delighted and could take in a costume with a sweep of her eye.

For food, too, she cared little, though she was fond of a fresh cup of coffee. At chicken dinners she always took a wing, whether from choice or self-abnegation was not known. But she loved hard, round peppermints, and kept them in her room for herself and small visitors.

III

One of her chiefest pleasures was to receive good visitors from home. A stream of them passed through Harvard. If they were Southerners they were welcome; if they were North Carolinians and Presbyterians she beamed upon them; and if they were from Chapel Hill she came to meet them with face alight. Young men studying at Harvard drew her particular attention, for among them she dreamed of finding those who would honor and uplift their state.

She also took keen pleasure in the brisk and talented New England women she met in Cambridge. Her letters home often mentioned Miss Maria Gardner, whose sister Elizabeth (Mme. Bouguereau) was a famous artist, and Mrs. Charles F. Cushman, who was the former Sally Adams, sister of the opera singer, Suzanne Adams.

In these days Cornelia seldom went to church, but she knew and liked the Reverend Alexander MacKenzie, pastor of the Congregational Shepard church, which the Love family attended, and every Christmas she helped to prepare the eggnog which was sent him, and enjoyed his little note of thanks saying, "The beverage was very sustaining."

IV

A year after Cornelia left Chapel Hill, the University, over which she had kept a maternal watch so long, celebrated its one hundredth year, and among the honorary degrees awarded was one for Cornelia. It was the first honorary degree ever given by the University to a member of the sex which still was not allowed to vote or to send students to its classes. She had already labored for eight years on the University's centennial alumni catalog.

She now wrote to the air of "Rosin the Bow" the words for the 1895 centennial song, and also, to the air of "Auld Lang Syne," a song for the alumni banquet, June 5, 1895.

Soon afterward she received this request from Josephus Daniels, editor of the *News and Observer* at Raleigh, North Carolina: "Dear Madam—please do us the kindness to write a short letter for publication in answer to the question, 'Should women wear bloomers?'"

v

When the last day of 1899 came, she recalled that it was the end of the century in which she had been born and in which she had most vividly lived, rejoiced, and suffered.

"Thank God, the Almighty disposer of all things," she wrote, "for his mercy to me and mine this past year. Yea, and for many years preceding."

Another compensation that removal to Cambridge gave her was the opportunity oftener to see her kindred, including her aging brother Sam at Washington and the Vermeule family in New Jersey. She was awe-stricken when on the hundredth anniversary of her mother's birth she was able to go to North Plainfield, New Jersey, and gaze upon her mother's childhood home in the substantial old Jersey farmhouse built by the Revolutionary militia leader, Captain Cornelius C. Vermeule.

In Washington Cornelia, ever a connoisseur of attractive people, was delighted to be able to make a congenial friend of her brother's second wife, Sarah Maury, of Leesburg, Virginia. To June she wrote, "Such pretty ways she has, graceful, playful. . . . There are so many handsome things about the house—paintings, vases, bric-a-brac generally. . . . She keeps the reins over the establishment. Regulates and looks around and is watchful."

When she had returned to Cambridge, her brother's letters to her dealt almost entirely with old Chapel Hill. In fact, she noted that one long letter from him failed to mention any member of his family, but was concerned almost entirely with recollections of Dave Moore, Burnett the barber, Dave Barham, Uncle November, Uncle Ben Craig, Fred Lane, and other Orange County old-timers, nearly all Negroes. But he did not forget the old white families.

"I shake myself," he wrote to Cornelia, "and recall what the Orange County farmers would have to say in the good old days about summer rains in their neighborhood. 'Tommy Hogan says that he hasn't had enough rain to wet a man *in his shirt-sleeves. . . .* Ithiel Atwater says that they had a *good season* at Mt. Pleasant last Thursday afternoon.' All that has gone entirely out of my human intercourse. Its echoes sound like old music. I should like to be present at one of those old dramas about the Hargrave's store—with *stage directions* at my pleasure: as 'Enter Thos. Hogan'; 'Enter Geo. W. Purefoy'; 'Enter Chas. W. Johnston, Sr.'; 'Enter Billy Burgess, bearing a wild turkey,'—or even 'Enter Mrs. Adams with blackberries'; or 'Miss Jennie Pendergrass with spectacles'; or 'Miss Dilly P. desirous of talking or a little coffee and sugar.' "

VI

The best summary of Cornelia's quiet life at this period was written by herself in a letter to a Negro friend, Cinderella Shepard, who was living in New Jersey after having left Chapel Hill at the end of the Civil War. Cinderella was seventy-five years old when she got this letter:

"Dear Cinderella: Nothing in the way of a letter could have pleased me more than did yours of the 7th which was sent to me from Chapel Hill. . . . I am happy here, of course. Mr. and Mrs. Love are both as good to me as they can possibly be. I spend my time just as I did at Chapel Hill—reading, writing, sewing. In winter I never go out. The snow and ice are too much for me. We have snow upon snow, a blizzard is raging now, and the snow is about two feet deep. At such times I do long for old North Carolina. Yet my health is excellent here.... I like these Yankees. They are good people, every bit as good as folks in the South and with ten times as much push and snap and energy.

"I get letters from one old Chapel Hill friend or another every week.... My maid, Beck Mason, lives in the house Mr. Love built, with the family that bought it. She sends me a letter now and then, and tells me about my colored friends. My dear old Aunt Dilsey died the spring before I came away, also Aunt Carolina Jones. Uncle Simon Battle died soon after. Thomas Dunston is still the college barber. I never hear anything of Roman Jones, of Charles Snipes, or Rilla Strowd.

"Cinderella, I have always lived in peace and friendship with colored people, and am proud now in my old age to think they are my friends and remember me with kindness. I hope to meet many of them on the other side of the dark river, on whose shore I am now standing. I am an old woman, to be sure, but I trust I shall not be afraid to go when I am called.... Affectionately your friend, Cornelia P. Spencer. I put in for you a Boston handkerchief for remembrance, and with my love."

VII

At the new year, 1901, Cornelia designed for herself a course of reading which included the most popular novels of the day in order that she might sample contemporary tastes—among them *Richard Carvel, Janice Meredith, Red Pottage,* and *When Knighthood Was in Flower*. But she had to report: "I read the opening chapters, then my attention flags. The characters don't take hold of me." She fell back on the English biographies, diaries, and books of letters, which were more to her taste. She made notes of and extracts from these books which she put down in the green-backed journal she had brought from Chapel Hill. These are specimen entries:

Matthew Arnold's description of [Cardinal] Newman: "Who could resist the charm of that spiritual apparition, gliding in the dim afternoon light through the aisles of St. Mary's, rising into the pulpit, and then in the most entrancing of voices, breaking the silence with words and thoughts which were a religious music— subtile, sweet, mournful?"

Sweetest line Virgil ever wrote: "Sunt lacrymae rerum et mentem mortalia tangunt."

Nothing finer than these lines:
"Thou overwhelming armies whose command
Said to one empire, 'Fall', another, 'stand';
Whose rear lay wrapt in night, while breaking dawn
Roused the broad front and called the battle on."   (Young)

"And 'mid this tumult, Kubla heard from far
    Ancestral voices prophesying war".   (Coleridge)

"Quoted by Swinburne from *Sordello* as the 'two finest lines in the language':

            "As the king-bird with ages on his plumes
                Travels to die in his ancestral glooms."

" 'What is there wanting in Goethe which Dante has?' asked Fitzgerald of Tennyson one day in presence of the busts of the two poets. *'The divine,'* was Tennyson's reply."

She even reread some of Walter Scott, but felt compelled to call him "a Tory." When Lord Tennyson and Queen Victoria died, she mourned for them as for familiar friends. Confessing some recent indulgence in "literary trash," she wrote to Laura Phillips:
"I dropped 'em all and began Carlyle's *Frederick the Great* which brother Sam sent Mr. Spencer during the last year or so of his life and which we read together in 1859—a piece of well-flavored corned beef after a lot of confectionary. Some one sent me a 'study' of Browning's poetry which I like much. Mrs. Brown-

ing lowered her standing by espousing Spiritualism and by her advocacy of Louis Napoleon, but she was sound in her religious beliefs. And so was he, sound. Did you know they were Presbyterians?"

VIII

In the spring of 1901 there died at Greensboro, North Carolina, the Reverend Solomon Pool, Cornelia's old enemy in the postwar years at Chapel Hill. When she heard the news she could not repress the old vindictiveness and in her journal she wrote:

"An invalid for several years from a paralytic stroke. What a miserable story his so called presidency of U. N. C. was! How poorly it looks 30 yrs. after."

She could not attain the loftiness of her brother Samuel's sentiments when in 1884 he attended at Washington the funeral of John Pool, late United States Senator and Solomon's brother, whom Cornelia once detested only second to Solomon. At that time Samuel wrote her:

"You do not admire *any* Pool I believe, but supposing that you read my last to Charles [Phillips] about Mr. Pool's sudden death I wish to add that, as a pall-bearer, I saw his dust committed formally to the dust yesterday evening at Oak Hill on the side of the steep hill. The silver upon the coffin had upon it something which I decyphered as it was lowered, 'Our Father.' No other word or name. Some twenty friends were there. The grave is under a singularly beautiful specimen of cucumber tree, its fruit blooming with a delicate pink. To me it gave a North Carolina touch of color to the occasion. As the attendant took up some dust to emphasize the solemn transfer by the minister I leaned eagerly forward to see it lie upon the coffin, there it appeared, just *appeared*, not thrown enough to rattle—the 'exigui pulveris jactu' of which Virgil speaks as so potent in the fighting of bees and that has been so eloquently adapted. I think such dust falls upon the hearts of the survivors as well as on the head of the departed."

IX

Among Cornelia's musings at Cambridge there was one element that often rose to pester her thoughts; that was the cluster of errors and omissions belonging to the past. "Few things," she wrote Laura Phillips, "are more mysterious than the way in which people neglect to question *old* folks about themselves, their families, their youthful days, etc. I could have asked old Dr. Hooper 50 questions about his life, about Dr. Caldwell, etc., and never once did it. I am angry with myself when I think how little I ever talked with Mrs. Mary Hooper of things which are now important to know." In the same tenor she later added this reflection: "I get letters every now and then from some one I used to know, reminding of something I once said, or did, which 'did them good.' The emotion awakened by such letters is always rather akin to pain. My life always appears on any review of it to myself as utterly wasted, and I often repeat when I am alone Rossetti's lines, 'Look on me well. My name is might have been.'"

As Cornelia advanced further into her seventies, and griefs and losses multiplied, she found comfort in reading Dr. Samuel Johnson, whom she felt to be akin to her in temperament and cast of mind. "I have six vol[ume]s of Dr. Johnson which I go to as to an old long-tried friend", she wrote in her journal. "I also turn to Boswell's Life of him. Such *excellent clear sense* seems to support one's mind. Also the old poets—Campbell, Milton, Young, Gray. Their strong faith revives mine. And they are *of old*. They mingle with my past. I love to have them in my hand even if I do not read a line. I know so well the shelves in my father's old library where these old books stood for years—the exact places. I seem to get in some companionship with him when I handle his books."

X

On May 6, 1902, she wrote: "This is my ever dear and still fondly remembered husband's birthday. He would now be 75 years old—having died in his 34th year—so long ago. I always recall him as a young man. I wonder if he would know this old, wrinkled, gray woman."

In this year died Mrs. Sarah Maury Phillips, second wife of Cornelia's brother Samuel. Cornelia mourned doubly over this death because she not only had sincerely admired this capable and sweet-tempered woman, but she feared the effect on her aging brother. She wrote in her journal this from the poet Montgomery:

> "Heaven and earth
> Shall pass away, but that which thinks within me
> Must think forever; that which feels must feel;
> *I am, and I can never cease to be.*"

She added: " 'When I am a very old and respectable citizen,' writes Louis Stevenson, 'with white hair and bland manners and a gold watch, I shall hear three crows cawing in my heart as I heard them this morning.' "

During these quiet years at Cambridge, twelve in all, she was much given to musings on old, old days, and as often as recollection came strong and bold she made an entry in her journal, as this in August, 1902:

"Brother Sam has sent me, (having borrowed it from me 10 yrs ago) a bound vol. of the U. N. C. Magazine for 1844.... I recall those days of my first youth [she was then nineteen] with a sense of mortification, humiliation, and failure. I wonder if all old people survey their early *'teens* with the same disapprobation. I look at the papers contributed to that volume and remember more or less distinctly the young collegians who wrote and were applauded. It is probable that brother Sam is sole survivor of the editorial corps. And it strikes me that so many of them *died young*:

"*Virginius Ivy* (beloved, 'twas said, by *Anne Swain*), handsome, romantic-looking.

"*G. A. Stanfield,* supposed to be very talented, certainly ambitious—

"(E. DeB.) *Covington*, the gallant editor, bright and gay—

"*Rich'd Forbes*, promising, interesting, agreeable—

"*Geo. Strong*, red-haired and debonair—

"*Jas. Johnston*, more gifted, 'twas said, than any—very highly thought of—died very young.

"*Rob't Cowan*, handsome and gay.

"None of them lived beyond middle life. Most of them never attained it. Buxton and Strong both became judges.—Steele was M. C. [member of Congress]. Don Wilson committed suicide."

At this period Cornelia's mind was seldom free of anxiety about her brother Sam. His daughters could give little good news of him, for his frame was weakening and his heart was no longer strong. She noted that his letters rarely contained any contemporary reference, but dealt chiefly with the broody past.

"Looking back now, thirty years, what a mistake it all was— *his joining the Rep[ublican] Party*, his going away from N. C. *There* he should have remained, raised his children—lived among what the Bible would call 'his own people'—and died there. . . . And yet, what is my opinion worth?" But to this paragraph, she later joined an addendum in a different but firm handwriting: "Thinking the above reflection over, I feel that it is one-sided. Bro'. Sam lived a much larger life in W[ashington] City—He saw more, learned more, enjoyed more, and had infinitely greater opportunities for doing good, helping other people and enlarging his own heart than N. C. could have given him in thirty years. That he could *help others was one of his keenest enjoyments!*"

She wrote him two and three times weekly, trying to console him, and herself, for the growing infirmities of age. Of her sister-in-law, Laura Phillips, she wrote: "Laura [is] unhappy at her loss of memory. Dear old soul! A common calamity after 75 years. . . . What old people forget is what happened today or yesterday or last week. They remember what was said and done 50 years ago, yes, only too well."

At last brother Sam seemed to rally and he wrote his sister letters more cheerful than for some time. Then late in 1903 he weakened again, took to his bed, and sank gradually. One day in November he looked at his children around him, tried to rise, said "I must look after my flowers," and fell back, dead. He was buried near his first wife, father, mother, daughter Cornie, and brother Charles at Chapel Hill.

Cornelia, long expecting this separation, bore the news bravely, but to Laura Phillips she wrote:

"O Laura! How my heart aches and burns and swells and then falls back beaten and bruised and utterly limp when the truth strikes home again and again that I have no brother. . . . One thing especially among the many in which the loss of brother Sam continually weighs upon me, is that I have no one now to review days, dates, anniversaries and the like with. Henry Clay's birthday, Apr. 12 we always remembered—he was one of our youthful political idols. Brother Charles cast his first vote for Henry Clay, 1843, and drove 41 miles that day in order to get to the lawful precinct where he might. Who cares for Henry Clay now? Tomorrow is Lexington day. Bro. S[am] liked to recall 'the embattled farmers.' " And in her journal she wrote briefly: "I am now alone. The last of that family of five, so long united in the old Phillips house in C Hill. All are gone but this old trembling feeble woman who sits alone. Ad te clamavi, Domine."

XI

Although the shocks and losses incident to old age often weighed heavily upon her spirit, she had many little pleasures which she loved to record in her journal. Among these were personal visits from distinguished men with a North Carolina ancestry or connection, such as Walter H. Page, then editor of the *Atlantic Monthly;* Hannis Taylor, author and ex-minister to Spain; Herman Harrell Horne and Charles H. Johnston, college instructors. She wrote: "Charles H. Johnston, James Phillips, Wm. Kerr, S. W. Sperry, W. Page, B. S. Hedrick—these are six young fellows, all N. C. scions, grandsons or great-grandsons of valued men who were of old, and did good service to the State in their day, now long since past, but these representatives are coming on. All but one at work in Harvard. That one is my dear father's great-grandson. Every one of Presbyterian stock, except perhaps young Page."

To her niece, Lucy Phillips Russell, she wrote: "I spent the morning going over several trunks of *things*. . . . Lucy, the end of life presses rather heavily upon me at times. It is near, for I feel many things slipping away which once I clung to. The poets and the philosophers. How do we know about them? but the saints, we are sure of them. . . . You are to think of this old woman sheltered under the wing of her good daughter and thanking Heaven with great seriousness when she lies down at night for all Heaven's mercies. . . . You have the same turn of mind that your Auntie is gifted with. . . . Perhaps the month of March has something to do with the annual introspection, the living again of life's farewells, musing, brooding over days, scenes, woods, faces, long long ago passed. . . . Perhaps it is wrong, foolish, certainly it is unavailing, to indulge such memories. It is like pressing a dead rose's stalk to one's breast till you can feel the thorn pierce again. Still, I would not be *I* if I lost the habit."

To her niece, Elizabeth Maxwell, she wrote: " 'Brother Sam'. Oh, how sweet those words were to my very soul. . . . I sit thinking of the old days, of your mother in her Chapel Hill home, surrounded by her little ones, Cornie, John, Nora, and Lizzie. Fanny and Gertie as yet were not. You all, and Charles's four oldest, were as much in your grandfather's yard as in your own. Your mother used to wear white a great deal then, and I remember a neighbor who admired her very much, saying once, 'I saw Mrs. Sam Phillips coming out of his office this afternoon, all in white, with such lovely color in her cheeks and eyes and hair—she was beautiful—and I knew he must love her. . . . Only two old women remember much about it now, your Aunt Laura and I, and we will soon be laid on sleep. Our children must go on, play their parts, accept their lot, and do their duty till they too are hushed in sleep."

Although Cornelia's physical vigor was waning, her mental vigor remained strong, and she kept up a steady correspondence with North Carolina people, and was delighted one day to get a letter from E. A. Alderman, in succession president of the Universities of North Carolina, Tulane, and Virginia; and she marked with especial approval this sentiment:

"North Carolina has always been a hard state to serve, exacting much for little and subject to hurtful spasms of conservatism."

On receiving from Mrs. Charles W. Johnston a snapshot of a happy family group on the porch of her country home in Orange County, North Carolina, she wrote: "It is a real pleasure to me to know that you and Mr. Johnston had all your children together at home once more. Once more! It will not always be a certainty, you know. That household group will separate inevitably. East, west, north, south, those nine boys and girls will eventually scatter; and if you and Mr. Johnston have given each one the strong principles of religion—the truth and love and integrity and industry which are a common inheritance in both your families, then you will have sent forth from your old home nine little streams which are to water the city of God."

XII

In 1904 Cornelia entered upon her eightieth year. One of her first journal entries of the year noted that she had been "busy with glue and tacks and screw-driver." And then came a comment on a letter received from her childhood playmate, Margaret Mitchell of Statesville, North Carolina: "How different her handwriting now from the precise neatness that has always marked it. Every letter I get from her gives me a tremor of the heart, lest it be the last. . . ." And she sat down and wrote to Margaret:

"My first recollection of you, or rather of your father's house was about 1829 (I guess). I had been paying you all a visit—a heavy rain (which I dimly remember) led your Mother to send my attendant maid, *Caroline,* home without me and with the proposal I should stay all night with her girls (to wit: Mary, Ellen, and Margaret).

"All that I recall is that delightful getting ready to go to bed with you—and the sad sequence of my father's arrival to take me home—the taking me out of bed, bundling me up in shawl, and my father carrying me home. I have never forgotten the barking of dogs in the village and the sense of security I had in my father's arms as we went along through the grove. . . . I agree with you about those 'heavy *barouches*' which our mothers used—heavy and *ugly*. But as you say, they gave us a good deal of pleasure and so are to be remembered with gratitude. A favorite drive of my mother's (*Charles* driving) was around the *race track*. . . . I suppose the [R. R.] station must now be on that ground.

"Horse racing, cock fights, gambling and drinking, with here and there a murder seem to have been the amusements of the people in the early years of last century. A rough lot they were about Chapel Hill. . . .

"You wrote me that Mrs. McL.'s old 'Aunt Susie' said that if she could have her wish now it would be *to be strong*. Yes, yes! I long sometimes to *run* upstairs,—to *run* down,—to start out for a walk with a *relish*. Well, let me remind myself that Dr. Johnson advised against all references to illness or infirmity in our conversation.

> 'Think not of our approaching ills,
> Nor speak of spectacles and pills.' "

Miss Margaret's once-firm and perpendicular writing became more and more slanting and tremulous, and then in October, 1904, her letters came to an end. When the news of her death reached Cambridge, Cornelia could only write to Laura Phillips: "You and I stand alone."

Confessing that a gradual weakness was growing upon her, Cornelia in this year, 1904, made this last entry in her green-backed journal:

"Here I close this book, my companion for 22 years. . . . I lay the book aside with gratitude to the Dispenser of my life for the protection He has given me—the blessings and enjoyments and the time for *preparation*."

XIII

But life was not yet over for Cornelia, although she had so many times believed it to be. She lived for four more years, and made many more notes on life and people, and wrote many more brisk letters. Most of her sentiments were now tranquil and mellow; but once in a while there would be a surge of the old fire, a return of the old pungency; for although she was fully aware that she was nearing the bottom of the hill, she was too great a lover of life and of the human drama to surrender her vitality in any passive way. When 1907 brought in June, the fateful month for her, she wrote to Laura Phillips:

"You and I are all now. . . . Fifty-two years ago. I can still see some of the faces at the wedding. . . . Nobody needs to think I want to return to my old home and see the changes. No, no! 'It is not now as it hath been of yore!'

"Dear old bridesmaid, friend and sister, the best a woman ever had—may our friendship continue on through this *next* life!

"This month was Commencement day at the University of North Carolina. My heart warmed so as it turned to the memory of it. . . . I have such tenderness of feeling toward old Chapel Hill and the old folks now disappeared. . . . Do you ever meditate on the thought of how entirely the men and women of the preceding generation have gone? Nothing left but a house or two, but the wild flowers still survive. The liverworts, the houstonias, yellow jasmine, and white fringe tree, the rhododendron and the kalmia, flourish in their old haunts just the same. They were there before Columbus came, they are there now.

"A soft autumn day brings many memories of woods, fields, chinquapins, nuts, and wild grapes, and the companions of childhood, and even of later age; for many a long tramp did I take all through my sixth decade. I think of the old North Carolina woods, fields, and highways. How silent, how solitary, and how restful. . . . Perhaps it is but the old cry of humanity for rest and peace and permanency that seizes us, a hunger of the heart. I faint with it often. . . . I always recall my ever dear husband, still fondly remembered, as a young man. I wonder if he would know this wrinkled old woman?

"Two old United States senators from Alabama, who died lately, were contemporaries of my husband. If he had lived—but why think of it?"

On June 27, 1907, she recorded in her diary that it had been "13 years today [since] I left Chapel Hill." Strange to say, during all these years she had never been able to bring herself to go back to Chapel Hill, even in company with her daughter. She used to say: "I shall go back, but never in the flesh." On December 31, same year, she wrote, "Adieu. Thank God for all."

In January, 1908, Cornelia received a visit from the Reverend A. L. Phillips, her nephew and a son of her "old bridesmaid," Laura Phillips. He afterwards wrote to his mother: "I had a most delightful visit to our beloved kin at Cambridge (16 Francis Ave.). . . . June presents a fine appearance of a matron who in good health gives herself intelligently and successfully to the management of her household. . . . Auntie (Cornelia) looks well in the face. She is much broken, of course, but looks natural. . . . She walks with difficulty. She will not go out of doors for a walk. She was exceedingly tender and sweet to me, taking my hand in both of hers and blessing me. . . . Her mind seems as brilliant as ever. . . . She spoke of waiting quietly her summons from on high."

Soon after this she had an attack of what was called "la grippe." It left her suffering some pain in one ear and feeling very weak. Cornelia now prayed daily that she might "go gently." Her physical powers were failing rapidly, but her mind remained clear, her handwriting firm. "I go about the house and enjoy my unbroken sleep, my food, and my freedom from all ailments," she wrote Mrs. Loula Hendon Donnell, "but I have no strength. I have been going slowly, quietly, down hill for three or four years."

To the last, she was able to read with unabated enjoyment.

One of her favorite books was the Phillips Brooks Year Book, presented in 1895 to her daughter June by Mrs. Elizabeth Kerr Atkinson, daughter of Cornelia's old friends, Professor and Mrs. W. C. Kerr. She was reading this book daily when March, 1908, came in. She used to remark how formidable March was to old folks.

On the 8th she was attacked by faintness, and on lying down she became unconscious. She lay unconscious for two days and on March 11 she died gently. Her age was eighty-three. Her body was taken to Chapel Hill where the funeral service was held in the church for which her father had collected the funds, and where in the village cemetery she was buried close to her kindred as the last of the children of James Phillips and Judith Vermeule Phillips.

Her farewell had already been said to Laura Phillips in a letter written from Cambridge early in 1901: "Goodbye, Chapel Hill.—*That* it comes to for us all. But when I came away riding through the town with Pres[iden]t Winston, I did not say farewell.—I felt that I would return soon some way—some how.... I shall return, but not in the flesh. These eyes will never see it again—but I shall hover over the place and haunt those woods and hills, doing some errand for God, some work for his Kingdom under another form."

XIV

In April, 1943, a ship named the *Cornelia Phillips Spencer* was launched in the Wilmington, North Carolina, yards during the Second World War. Near by were two other similar ships approaching completion—the *Kemp P. Battle* and the *Walter Hines Page*, both named for men who were Cornelia's admirers and friends. Within a few months the *Cornelia Phillips Spencer* was sunk at sea off East Africa by enemy action. With the self-depreciation habitual to her, she would have said, "Just what I would have expected."

XV

Cornelia Phillips Spencer had the mind of a statesman; that is, she could see ahead of, around, and behind the things before her—could see it as a whole and in its relations. If she had been a man, she would have been an excellent senator, or University president. She was a natural teacher, being able to draw a principle from a mass of particulars. She was a philosopher of no mean ability in her capacity to grasp universal elements. In her ability to perceive and use the significant thing in any being or situation, she was an artist. Her intellect was powerful and creative, her nature selfless and catholic. Yet she was feminine, and was not above harboring occasional so-called feminine weaknesses. As a widow living on a meagre income in a village far from the active centres of contemporary life, her achievements were large. Yet it often seemed to her that she was a failure. "Faithful in few things," was her constant reproach to herself. This feeling may have been due in part to her life among a defeated and prostrate people in a lethargic state, or in part to her handicaps as a woman living at a time when women were not permitted to vote, to attend classes in a University, or to own outright themselves and property. As to whether or not she rose grandly above these obstacles, this book must be testimony.

30

Mrs. Spencer's Sayings

CORNELIA PHILLIPS SPENCER expressed herself naturally and freely in spontaneous sayings, aphorisms, and epigrams that were treasured, exchanged, and enjoyed by her contemporaries. Below are representative short utterances derived from her letters and diaries and from the recollections of her friends. These sayings perfectly illustrate the practicality and sensibility that were often found linked to a strong love of religion and poetry in her many-sided character. They also illustrate a complete blending of the feminine with the masculine traits of her mind. But these passages (many of them compiled by Hope Chamberlain) must be read with one reservation—they sometimes reflect moods rather than permanent opinions:

What tremendous mistakes people make who lead lives opposed to general custom and the voice of experience. The trodden road is the safe road.

C. is like a cat in having no gift of open expression, but if you notice her ways you will see more interest in you than you at all suspected. . . . There are plenty of people who say cats have no attachments. They are the sort who never observe nicely, or see clearly.

Never yet did anyone do God a service that He did not pay them for it, *well.*

246

(To her daughter at boarding school) A parcel of girls and women shut up together must necessarily get into an unhealthy state of mind and body. You ought to see men, to hear how men talk and laugh, and tell of the affairs of life and business and politics. I don't want you to be coarse, but I want a healthier, commoner fibre about you.

It is deplorable to set your heart on a thing and fight and worry and scheme about it till at last you do prevail. I think the Lord may give it in anger that it may turn to dust in the mouth.

Passing away is written on everything. Accept it, rise to it, and make the best of it.

X has had a fall and displaced his shoulder-blade. If he could dislocate his tongue, too, it would be a blessing.

Marriage is earthy and for this life only.

"Religion of a people is the effect of their civilization." That is, "looking at things on a large scale" (Buckle). Cart before the horse, I think. O pshaw! I don't believe what Buckle says. His notions of religion are the notions of a man who has never learned Christ. And certainly never read the Old Testament carefully.

(To a young girl who asked her how much she should charge for her services as a governess) "My dear, charge them a plenty. People take you at your own valuation."

If women and horses knew their strength, this world would be a different place for both of them.

(Of a young lady who had many admirers but never married) "She can catch fish but doesn't know how to land them."

Some people have peach preserves on their biscuit for supper; others eat molasses.

(Of a young girl whom she wanted to send on an errand) "Oh yes, she will do it. L. is like cold souse—always ready."

There she sat with her vacant face like a sleepy cat, but her claws are sharp.

(Of Rosa Greenhow, the Confederate spy) She is a large, soft, mournful-looking woman, by her pictures. Such women, such looking women, I mean, I have often found out to be Tartars!

Boys from some of the older families of North Carolina and Virginia could plan and execute mischief in college—cruel pranks, carried out with great cold-heartedness.

The Southern slave-holder will figure in history, will adorn the pages of romance, and will be held up alternately to the admiration or to the scorn of mankind, as tyrant, or patriarch, according as friend or foe shall depict him. God alone knows through what difficulties the Southern planter went forward to his duty. How fearfully weighted by his inheritance, how blinded, how hampered, how weakened by circumstances which neither he nor his fathers could control.

(To a lady who told of her intention immediately to study Schopenhauer) "How do your attic and your top bureau-drawer look? Would you be willing for me to see 'em? If not, you had better first study the life of Christ."

My deafness is almost unbearable with sickness in the house. It throws me back, and annihilates all opportunity for usefulness, because I am out of rapport with all around me.

No other topic has the same relish for narrow-minded people as their own affairs, grievances, or prosperity can afford. Over and over they discuss it, they turn it, they sit beside it, warm it over, re-hash it, and *slaw* it.

A man who would doubt the verity of the equinoctial, would not hesitate to speak disrespectfully of the equator!

If girls could foresee what married life entails upon them, could catch but a glimpse of their own future therein, how few, how very few, would marry. This is my deliberate opinion.

Life itself directs us to the life beyond death, for this earthly life does not satisfy the cravings of our spirits.

Melancholy is inseparable from poetry. The light of life does not consist in happiness, but in comfort.

In everything, in even our best things, the rule should be restraint. Over-devotion to religious duties produces fanaticism. Mysticism leads to insanity. Overwork in lawful callings to derangement and decay. Over-love to husband or wife or child, often brings disaster to the loved ones. The mind gets warped and weakened. Feeling usurps the place of reason, and we are unfitted to meet the trials and losses that must come to all.

Always leave a wide margin for the unexpected.

There are times and seasons with me, when the memories of the dead whom I have loved, and who loved me, do come with great freshness and strength. They seem to overpower me quite. Absorb and draw me away. Today, Sunday, Aug. 28, '86, I have been with my father and my mother once more.

Things of the mind and heart, with no definite material aims, are worthy. Simple living, brotherly kindness, and intellectual opulence.

Those women whose measure for all folks is, "They have always been lovely to me!"

Considering that the Virgin Mary was a Jewess, it is wonderful that anyone should ever have given her blue eyes and light hair. Yet somehow I always think of our Lord as having dark blue-gray eyes.

Chas. Sumner was as inevitably bent to his own ends, as hard, as self-inclosed, as the stairway of Bunker Hill Monument.

I am superstitious about anticipating pleasure, and about planting potatoes. Dr. Mitchell used to say, with a grin, that he planted his potatoes in the ground, not in the *moon*. Miss Annie Watson and I thought differently.

All books are interesting to me which present individual life.

People of petty respectabilities and pruderies, without inspiration of great realities. How uninteresting!

Everyone who has lived in a place where is a central object of interest like the University there, or the government here in Washington, feels the want of it, in other places.

I am reading five or six books at once—gorging, like a glutton.

Like Russell Lowell, I would not give up anything that had roots to it, even though it might suck up its food from graveyards.

Poor Mr. X. I do feel sorry and ashamed that so much intellectual force and ability, such acuteness of sense and perception, should be as nothing before the strength of his avarice, and inborn meanness of soul. It does seem sometimes as if to be smart was of very little account, when it won't keep us from grovelling. Suppose that a hog could calculate the sun's orbit? Is he any less a hog?

The world is certainly growing better. Compare the tone of society, as our books show it, to this day. The life of others, the charity, the warmth, the sense of responsibility for our brothers, the desire to do good, how it pervades literature. Lady Mary Wortley Montagu's career and the way the best people spent their lives a hundred years ago, how different. The Kingdom of God is coming, and not slowly.

The mind sometimes takes a cold or a chill, same as the body. I have had such a chill for a month past. I am subject to such turns of mind. If my old father suffered from it, as I seem now to understand that he did, how little sympathy he must have received. I go to Dr. Johnson, as a long tried friend, in Boswell's life of him. Such excellent clear good sense seems to support one's mind.

I got a foolish letter last night from a foolish young woman, inclosing a foolish bit of so-called poetry, of her own composition, asking me to *criticise* it, and to tell her how much to charge for it. Her *nervous system* had broken down in the school room, and she had taken to her pen, poor soul—I wrote her a nice letter, and comforted her, and advised her to stick to prose. What was it that "Mr. F's aunt" hated?

As to our political depravities, they are disheartening, but I do believe in the destiny of these United States. They are God's country. He will not let wicked men destroy them tho' they may assail them heavily.

I am pleased and proud of two acts of our Government lately— The relinquishment of all hold on Cuba. . . . And the prompt aid given to the desolated W[est] India Is[lands] (after earthquakes and hurricanes).

The true character of Napoleon is just now beginning to be unfolded. There was precious little good in any of the Bonaparte blood.

I am impressed, while reading the private letters of such men as Jefferson, Sherman, Franklin, Grant, and the rest, by the tone of melancholy underlying their confidential talk. They all seem to have neared death with a cloud over them, a burden of trouble, of disappointment in life, and no anticipation of happiness hereafter.

The older I grow, the more I do try to believe. I say the Creed over and over, as I sit at my sewing, or as I walk on my piazza in the twilight and watch the stars come out.

I am of the opinion that denominationalism is on the decline among Protestants. It has done its work, and should go. A larger life and hope awaits the living church.

Personal prejudice rarely outlives a generation. Nothing lasts in this world, not even a good strong enmity.

I cannot understand Tennyson's *In Memoriam,* I here confess. I cannot read Sir Thomas Browne. I cannot read Dante, I do not understand him. I do not like mystical enthusiasm. I cannot see into it. I cannot get through it. These saintly ladies in the High Church novels adore Thomas à Kempis. Very much of this is pretense, to my way of thinking.

There is a honey sweetness about Emerson. He attracted and has kept his disciples.

North Carolina is not a generous state to serve. Nor when she does open her hand, is she discriminating. She exacts much, and spends little.

H——whose handwriting reminds me of certain falsetto traits in her character. Would be *finified,* and can't carry it out. Her sister's writing is round and legible, with bottom to her letters.

(To a young woman) I am so *glad* you have put on a bustle [1884]. No young woman can be different from others. But I do hope it does not look so *very* awkward, or make your dress hike up behind!

Don't you get too enthusiastic over the Yankees, and all the prevailing fads, and lose your own identity, and swamp your individual raising in a general gush of, Hurrah for the New! Down with the Old! That cry has been raised before now. Keep cool and cast an occasional eye on the old landmarks.

Nothing has made more difference in the personal appearance of womenkind than paper patterns. Everybody is so much better dressed now than they used to be forty years ago.

New York city for three months will suffice for an eye-opener and stimulant to any confirmed North Carolinians. After that, they can go home and sit them down on a lower round of the ladder.

I have been reading Proverbs. Its worldly wisdom is consummate. The cautions to silence, to reserve, to prudence in speech —how striking! All oriental peoples are noted for reserve. They think the Western nations such chatterers. Gravity, self-respect, safety, all inculcated in these aphorisms.

The colonial governors of North Carolina were all carpet-baggers: men like Warren Hastings, Clive, and others whom we have seen in the flesh, who were distinguished from the people among whom they lived by having no sort of regard for the public opinion of the community.

My old friend's face seen after years, is that of one who has endured much, defied much, is still defiant. A quiet thoughtful self-collected face, with great power in respose. A strong face.

An uncongenial and not intimate set of people never do get on well, or enjoy themselves on a picnic or a country excursion.

There is a lot of time for a good talking over, in two weeks!

He had so little talent for drinking that they called him a tee-totaler.

(Written in Cambridge) I am opposed to snow, and I *p'intedly hates* wind. Oh the weary white snow!

I like always to mention the weather in my diary, to make sure how much good weather we really do have.

I really like most people, but I am deeply attached to very few indeed.

If you wrote 3-4 words to a line, and half an idea to every twenty-five words . . . . you can hope to go on [keeping up a large correspondence].

Oh money, money! How it melts in hands that are warm and open!

Take your life a day at a time, and have faith.

No one is so poor as he who is always wanting something.

She has no end of money, and no end of energy, and nothing escapes her. I asked her if she had attended the San Francisco earthquake.

Miss Nancy Hilliard used to say she loved to spend a day in the country—it made her feel rich to get back to her own house.

What's the use of being smart and cultured if you cannot organize and order every-day things?

One of Solomon's proverbs they omitted was this: *A little soft sawder—behold it is a good thing, and doeth good.*

Perhaps it is not best to be always thinking and talking about what is merely *sensible*.

I think a sense of humor is really important to the character. It helps out one's education, rounds off one's qualities, and fills up the cracks and interstices between the solider materials.

I hate *sensitiveness!* It is first cousin to jealousy and envy. It is a great mischief-maker among relations.

Our young folk are immensely selfish, and that's a fact.

Her face shows the want of culture. Nothing like *books* to refine the features.

I think sarcasm is never so misplaced as in religious discussion. Never does any good, irritates your opponents, and hardens the hearts of those who agree with you.

I think it is by the little unthought-of things we do and say that we are longest remembered, and perhaps most kindly.

Something old-fashioned, something before-the-war, in her methods of thinking, even though the thought itself is modern.

I do rejoice in a hearty rain. It comes so manifestly from heaven.

He has too many friends to be lonesome, too good a conscience to be unhappy.

I agree with Mrs. Gamp. She said, "Give it a name, I beg!"

It is never worth while to act as if you thought anyone meant to be impertinent. You ought never to seem conscious of the possibility of such a thing.

Poor John has been going about all day disconsolate as a wet rooster.

He is a man more like a cold potato than anything else I know.

To come slipping down, resisting, unwillingly, with rolled eyes, like the back-sliding heifer.

In the place where love once was, young people will always be by me so regarded.

I have a strong regard for the man who works with his hands, who loves hard work with oar, or pick, or plough.

I looked over the small library (in the Brooks house). Mostly ethical works, sociology, and economics. Hard, and dry. I am too old, and too ignorant to attack such things. "Give me my crust and hollow tree."

For myself I would prefer reading the multiplication table, to the subtlest disquisition of the human intellect on the subjective, and the objective, the *me,* and the *not me.* Yah!

... *something malign* about May. Old superstitions declare it an unlucky month on several counts: 'Specially unlucky for marriages. The poets have thrown a glamor over this month which is dispelled when you come to watch it well.

I have seen people keep themselves to themselves for a long term of years, and spend their money on their own comforts, carpets, curtains, silver, and dress. I have seen it all come to naught, and be scattered to the four winds; but one thing I have never seen —the righteous man forsaken, though he may have been improvident.

(Of an escapade) What a silly caper of a silly girl, which has plunged all her kin into mortification, exasperation, humiliation, and many other disagreeable states of mind, ending in "ation".

Money is always valuable. I should not advise any woman to marry a man who was not in a position to take care of her; but sometimes the fairest prospects crumble. Don't I know it too well! It is idiotic folly for a woman to feel that marriage is to shut up her talents in a box, to be opened no more, all her acquirements, all that she has spent money to acquire. It is always nice to be able to make a hundred dollars!

Keep up your French, by all means. It has been a great pleasure to me in my old age to *read* French. It has been sixty years since I knew any of the science of the language. My Latin I have done better with. My Greek has long gone to the dogs, and I never had but a smattering of Hebrew. Do you be sure of one thing, that whatever you learn of value will in some way, some day, prove valuable if you will but hold on awhile.

I like to hear about solitaires and sealskins, and hothouse grapes, and turkies and velvets. When I want a book, though, I like to choose that for myself.

These nineteenth century girls are never apparently impressed by anything shown them. They take themselves too seriously for that. They look on with gravity, purse up their little red lips, and fasten their bright eyes upon you, with kitten-like attention. Quite severe in fact. I am myself a little afraid of 'em.

Some old men's way of presenting their old friends is displeasing and wanting in good taste. They remember their college days only by poor jokes and nick-names. This is nauseous.

A Northern winter calls people to a strict account of how they spent their summer.

New England spinsters, the sort of women who make the real underpinning of society. As conservative as I am myself, but so thoroughly wide-awake.

June says there are two topics that make me mad, too mad to be able to discuss them soberly and righteously, namely the women, and the Negroes. It is true. I do lose my temper.

It is the foreign immigrants who pride themselves on their families into whose hands this country will fall in another generation.

I have been to Concord, and to Lexington again; reading the monumental inscriptions, pausing before the doors whence Emerson and Hawthorne issued. Massachusetts has nothing better to show than these grounds. No better tale to tell than that of 1775.

This is the time of year in New England when they are all busy tearing around in pursuit of *something,* either pleasant to the eyes, or to be desired to make them wise. Worry and gnaw they will, as one of George Eliot's characters says of the puppies.

(Of Walter H. Page editor and ambassador to England) He likes to hit, and hit hard. I dare say he does good. Wakes the slumberers. Personally he is one of the pleasantest men I have ever known. Modest, moderate, with plenty of edge.

Live to be seventy-five, and your mind will be staggered by the procession of the generations that pass.

I look on most of the moves that people make with disfavor. I do believe there is much virtue in good staying power.

We must not lose human interest in life, frail as is our hold upon it. Life is our condition, after as well as before funerals. Live on to the close, is the rule.

If one or at most two or three hearts hold me, when dead, in faithful remembrance, it will be as much as I ask, or expect.

Live to be over eighty years old, and your experience will be of many everlasting things dissolved, many engrossing things forgotten, many settled things set afloat again, and many things once denounced, and discarded, brought out again to be used in following the fashion.

As we go on growing older and older we outlive not only those we love, but also our interest in things. Do you remember those pathetic lines of Mrs. Browning's?—

> "For me, my heart that erst did go
> Most like a tired child at a show
> That sees through tears the juggler's leap."

Yes, the time comes when, whatever the show may have been, one is glad to go home.

31

Mrs. Spencer's Essays

SOME OF Mrs. Spencer's best and most characteristic writing was done in the form of short articles and essays for the *North Carolina Presbyterian* in the "Young Lady's Column." At a time when religious writing, especially for young readers, was too heavy and didactic to attract any considerable following, Mrs. Spencer larded her contributions with such humor and pungency that they were not only closely read and appreciated, but were cut out afterwards and faithfully preserved in scrapbooks. She gave her followers a strict Calvinism, but one made wholesome with a genuine piety and a deep sympathy with those folk commonly found only in the byways and hedges. The three specimens that follow were found in an old and yellowed scrapbook scented with dried fern leaves and the faded petals of roses.

SHORT AND SIMPLE ANNALS

There are various strata among our peasantry, and the coming in contact with them all is not equally pleasant. The class referred to last week is the one I prefer to visit. Self-helpful, and self-respecting, there is nothing of the mendicant in their tone, and we can go among them and learn lessons of industry and thrift and contentment. Among my nearest neighbours are a widow and her widowed daughter,—both widowed in the war,—than whom I really do not know two North Carolina women more to be respected. They are always at work—spinning, weaving, knitting, sewing, and working their patch of ground between whiles. I entered the cabin one day in June and they had all their humble stock of furniture out of doors and were busy "scouring and scalding." The old lady regretting that they could not whiten their walls, and that the chinking between the logs would keep falling out, I suggested papering them, and came home and sent her a bundle of files of the Philadelphia Presbyterian for 1859. The next time I called, the amount of "good reading" visible in that little room was astonishing. The mother remarked that she could lie abed and just put on her spectacles and get a sight of good. I don't think I ever saw that valuable newspaper "spread itself" to better purpose. Besides their incessant industry, these women are about as charitable as any people in my village. They share what they have with those who are in want, and there is no more welcome or frequent visitor at a sick bed then the elder widow. In her clean blue homespun gown and calico apron and white handkerchief tied round her benignant old face, and with a short pipe in her mouth, I don't know a more comfortable and soothing figure for the eye to rest on in the intervals of a fever dream.

I have another friend whose husband's body was found after the battle of Seven Pines with twelve rifle balls in it. She is a stanch little woman who looks as if she was made of steel springs. During her married life she had lived in almost abject poverty, and any one who had seen her in 1864, a new-made widow, standing barefoot with her four little barefoot ragged children round her, would have thought it a desperate and hopeless case. But she went out to work—such work as was possible to her—chiefly spinning and weaving—and she has prospered, she and her children. As gentlemen never see this column, I may remark to you in confidence, girls, that there are some men whose wives can get along a great deal better without them than with them. Their removal seems to be the signal of a change for the better among all their dependencies.

This widow is living to-day in more comfortable circumstances than she could ever have hoped for. And as to her buying a green veil and attending a camp-meeting, she says nobody has ever dared to name no such as that to her; and her eyes will flush up now when she speaks of "William". Which leads me further to remark that it is not always the best husbands who are most faithfully mourned.

When people don't get along well together in the married estate, bystanders and moralists should be careful which party they blame most. The one most in fault is not always the one most *apparently* wrong. Fifteen or twenty years ago I knew a couple among our very poor, whose wretchedness was the neighborhood talk. He was a drunken ne'er-do-well, and she a decent spoken woman who had seen better days and whose family were respectable small farmers in a neighboring county. They lived like cat and dog, in such poverty and want, as I trust, are seldom seen in our country. Everybody blamed him of course—but it has always been my private opinion that, though in the main a good woman, she was a shrew of the first water, and nagged him into his evil courses. Indeed she *had* a temper and a tongue. He neglected and abused and finally abandoned her and his little ones. Then consumption kindly stepped in and stilled her complaints. Her family took charge of her pretty little black eyed girls, and her last articulate words were, *"Tell Harry I forgive him"*.

He disappeared in a slough of debauchery, and emerged to my recognition some years afterwards lying in a typhoid fever in the house of the woman for whom he had abandoned his wife, and to whom he had never yet been married. He lay a long time, reduced to the last gasp, and suffering no doubt a thousand deaths. A friend of mine who had in former years vainly endeavored to induce him to return to his wife, and had ministered to her forsaken and dying —went to him now again with oil and wine—and when he began to return to life brought his sins to his remembrance, and urged him to do justice at least to this woman, a good tempered cleanly creature, and marry her. He promised everything during his convalescence, but when finally well hung back. He was sobered however, and six months after attending a Methodist revival in the

country church near him, he and the woman both professed to
have undergone the great change. Shortly after this, one Sunday
morning, a decently dressed couple entered my father's gate, and
accosting him as he stood on the piazza, the man said, with a most
hang-dog expression of face, while the woman pulled her calico
bonnet down over hers, "Doctor, we've come to get you to marry
us. We've been living together fourteen years and got a parcel
of children, and we want to do better and get married." My father
raised his chin and surveyed them through his spectacles, and said
briefly, "I think it is time." They were ushered into the parlor and
the ceremony was performed with three or four witnesses. After it
was over, my father addressed a few short and very plain words
of advice to them. They listened with every appearance of humility,
and then the man turned to the friend who had visited him when
"sick and in prison," and offered his hand, and burst out crying.
The woman wiped her eyes with the cape of the sun-bonnet—and
they both declared their purpose of leading a new life. And they
have done it. They live this day respectably, and have a little farm
and are sober, industrious, and, it is believed, *Christians*.

Most people believe it is the steady kindly nature of the woman
he has married that saved him from entire ruin. And though no one
should cast a stone on the grave of his first wife, I cannot but think
if the poor thing had learned to hold her tongue, he might never
have deserted her.

Look where you will, young ladies, you will find that men are
very much as women make them.

Woman's influence is almost wholly moral, man's intellectual.
I have never seen a man whose mind I judged to have been improved by his wife—even where she was a superior. But I have
known hundreds made better. And the reverse is true. Very few
women's morals improve by association with men—but it helps
their sense mightily.   S.

(Written probably in 1862.)

In June

(This essay was written in 1876 and contains an account of the wedding of Laura Nunn to W. Guthrie. The names in parentheses were written by Mrs. Spencer in the margin.)

There is no prettier month to be married in than the month of June. There is no prettier place for the ceremony than a village church. There is no prettier hour than 8 o'clock in the morning.

For in the first place, June is the month of the greatest glory and light and verdure. It is hardly the "month of roses", with us, as poets farther North call it. Our first crop of roses departs with May—but June is the month of the white jessamine and the blush roses. Still something of the grace and freshness of the Spring remains, while we have all the pomp of Summer, without its glare and stifling heat. Nothing can equal the delicious coolness of early morning in June. Nothing can be more beneficial than the influences of earth and air and sky. Sick people always are refreshed in June, and unless the dread summons has been dispatched for them —the messenger whom there is no evading—they take a turn to recover now. Gloomy and desponding people are reanimated—and people who are constitutionally cheerful may be said to become positively frisky as soon as June sets in. Now the mower whets his scythe, and now the golden waves of wheat go rippling over ten thousand hills, and now the birds begin to turn their children out of doors, and break up housekeeping and go on summer tours. I think June is the best month for a wedding. In the second place, the village church if it has been lately painted and whitewashed,—with all the windows open, and branches of trees swaying and bending outside and trying to peep in,—with all its solemn and all its happy associations—crowded with old friends and neighbors— everyone in high spirits—minister trying to look solemn, but not succeeding—sunlight playing on the doorstep and threshold like a benediction—the whole village in a broad grin, so to speak—black folks and white folks all hurrying to church, and nobody able to

keep his countenance when catching anybody's eye. The old familiar village church is surely the best place, and 8 or 9 o'clock in
the morning is just the loveliest hour from which to take a new
departure, and start for a new home—*via* the Centennial in these
days.

I was at a wedding the other day which combined the above
requisites—and as I sat in the church waiting for the arrival of the
happy pair, and watching the assembling crowd, I thought of my
absent girls, and wished they all had been there.

One of the best things about a wedding in church is that it brings
out everybody, old and young, and does them good. It has an interest for all sorts and conditions of men and women. Here comes
an old lady (Mrs. John Watson) with spectacles on her nose. She
tries to look as if she had only come to a prayer-meeting; she as-
sumes a look of mortification and resignation and patience, but
I catch her eye just as she has pursed up her mouth, and she
smiles. She cannot help it. She elevates her chin, and takes a good
look at the congregation through her glasses, and beams upon
them.—Next a crowd of little girls (little Mary Martin and her
little sister) from three years old to ten come hurrying in. They
are afraid they will be too late. They are breathless with excitement,
and sit down on the chancel steps so as to have a good look at everything. Poor dear little souls! they have quite an air of consciousness
too—their cheeks are rosy red, and their eyes are dancing with
delight. A little boy (John Guthrie) gets among them, but they
don't care for little boys—he is ignominiously hustled round, and
finally made to perch himself on the pulpit sofa, where he subsides
into solemnity, and drops his lower jaw in an imbecile way, and
lets the whole world see that he is shedding his front teeth. The
little girls appear to scorn him. There sits a whole row of young
ladies in the amen corner—; they are running over with smiles and
laughter. If you speak to one of them she blushes, and laughs
afresh. And there are two brides of a month or so. One (Mrs.
Algernon Barbee) looks calm and stately—the other dimples with
laughter (Jennie Newton Barbee). There are some single ladies,

who have passed the age when they may be supposed to feel any anxiety on the subject of remaining single all their days. They are smiling like the rest of us, but I think there is more of the *sentiment* of the occasion expressed on their faces than on any other. I have long been persuaded that the most of what is high romance, and pure and generous sentiment there is left in the world is to be found among single women who have outlived their first youth. They have never been disenchanted. The old dreams and illusions and traditions are still possible, and still retain their influence. The world does not know how much it owes to those, whom it is content to sneer at as "old maids."

And now the gentlemen come pouring in, business men and idlers, they all have an interest in a wedding. That young man (Robert Rogers) with a tolerable imitation of a moustache surveys the assembly with the air of a conqueror. I look at him with respect and lose myself in an abyss of speculation as to what influences have prevailed to produce a moustache so black, while his hair is undeniably red. It appears to me that the gentlemen all look decidedly more serious than the ladies. I see some married men near the door who exhibit a severely chastened aspect.

But here come the family friends, and here comes the bride. We all cease to breathe. The minister steps to his place and the few words that unite two hearts for better and for worse, are spoken. Meanwhile we scan the bridal attire. Every inch of that pretty grey travelling dress gets a good going over—the lavender chip hat and veil—the dainty necktie and gloves. We find it all correct. The bride-groom is always a nobody. We do not regard him in the least. He is a mere lay figure dressed up to afford us a bride and to afford the bride something to lean upon. On her all eyes are bent, and though I do not suppose she knows in the least what she is saying, or where she is standing, she plays the play out with a pretty grave composure and sweet self-possession that really seems heaven-sent to all brides.

And now it is all over—they turn to the right about and are out of the church, and we have shaken hands at the door, and they are in the carriage and gone. As I look after them I feel thankful that another orphan girl has found a protector and wish that her mother could see her. Perhaps she did.

"Prepared—as a bride adorned for her husband". There must be something worth noting about a marriage ceremony when the spirit of inspiration can find no higher comparison to make, in describing the glory of the New Jerusalem. A happy marriage is indeed the nearest approach to Paradise that remains. And yet, I don't say to you all that you should by all means marry. No indeed!

S.

A Candle on Christmas Eve

Now that Christmas is over, and gone for another twelve months, and nobody can possibly harbor the suspicion that this may be a bid for a contribution to anybody's Christmas, I would like to tell just how one little candle threw its beams on Christmas eve, 1888, round about the place where I live, and lighted up a walk undertaken by this present writer.

The candle in question was lit in Chicago. This was the way of it. I received a letter from that far city containing a small sum and directing that sum to be spent in charity, in remembrance of one departed.

Now the size of a sum of money depends entirely upon the point from which you view it. From my standpoint on Christmas Eve, I was a rich woman when I received that postoffice order transmitted into cash, and started out at once to put it where it would do most good. For I knew of three poor homes where a dollar or so would shine like the electric light, and there was no time to lose, for it was Christmas Eve. How bright and soft the sun and air were. How gaily the brown leaves flew. There is no place in North Carolina where a winter's walk is so delightful and can be taken under so many advantages as round Chapel Hill. We have a soil that will not stay muddy. We have the southwest wind for a constant visitor. We have the loveliest grey and brown hills and valleys all around, and the bluest horizon in the distance that eyes could wish to dwell upon. All you need is a clear conscience and a good pair of feet.

Now first I knew of an old woman near eighty, who fell from her doorstep two months ago and broke her poor old arm, and will probably never be able to use it again. Old and childless and utterly poor, if she has ever begged for charity I have never known it. She has lived in her cabin on what, when I was a child, we called *"Trustees' land."* This meant that it belonged to the University; and it was allowed to two or three poor people to perch here and there on some *"coigne of 'vantage"* and build a cabin where no one else would ever be likely to want to build. She told me with great pride, this time a year ago, that she had quilted seven quilts before Christmas, and the seven dollars she had made by it would "pretty nigh take her through the worst of the winter". I hurried there this Christmas eve. She was at her hearth, and a little black and white "fice-dog" sat by her watching with great interest the sizzling in a "spider" of certain scraps of food. The room was clean, the bed was neatly made! I think it is the poor who do most for the poor. What is a visit once a week, an occasional basket of food, an occasional fifty cents from a prosperous neighbour compared to the daily, almost hourly attentions paid by some poor kindly neighbour of the old and infirm and helpless.

She intermits cooking and looks up at me with a smile. She shows me her little old hand, the fingers quite stiff and immovable—her arm weak and unserviceable. Her white hair is straggling upon her face and neck, and her poor blue eyes look out but dimly on the hills. Still she smiles, and the Christmas gift that a friend has sent her from a distance looks larger, and will go further, and do more good than many a gift made by millionaires this very season. What would it not mean to her? Well, I fear it meant, in the first place, a box of snuff, and I hope nobody will begrudge her that bit of luxury on Christmas Eve. Then it meant a peck of meal, a piece of bacon, a pound of coffee, &c. It will be spent very carefully we may be sure.

Thence I hurried through the woods up and down some well-wooded stony hills and over a little brook along whose banks the dead, grey golden-rods stand stiffly nodding at the dry asters and the silvery eupatoriums who respond as if to say, yes, yes, we have had our day, our summer is over. The pines and cedars are sweet on the soft air, and just on the edge of a clump, facing the south, suddenly I beheld a freshly bloomed golden-rod, looking up quite fearlessly into the blue sky. A Christmas golden-rod! Think of that. I went my way, as the novelists say, up a pretty steep rise at the last, pleasing my imagination with the thought that I am conducting a little rill of charity all the way from Chicago, over these hills, into these humble abodes. The evening grew brighter and brighter. Here live a mother and daughter. The daughter's husband, and the mother's only son, both perished in the war, and the two women behind a breastwork composed of a loom, spinning-wheel and two pair of cards have kept the wolf from the door so far. I receive another smiling welcome. The elder woman sits alone picking the seeds out of a pound of cotton. Her right wrist is swollen from a bad sprain but she does not stop her deft turning out those seeds for a moment while I stay. She has some pumpkin stewing in a pot, and gives it a stir from time to time. The daughter is gone to town on an errand. There is a nicely striped rag carpet for somebody in the loom, and great hanks of yarn hanging all around. Every thing here too is neat and clean, and the old woman herself has a face fit to kiss and ask a blessing from. She is always cheerful, always smiling. "Eighty-one my next birthday", she says, "and well and hearty"—and then she laughs.

Then I open the little sluice and deposit the charity in her lap, and I give the stewed pumpkin a good stir to save her the trouble, and go out in search of the next old woman whom I find in the heart of the village. She is a colored sister, and the only one of the three who belongs to my church. She too lives alone, having neither chick nor child, and to her too this little rill from Illinois means a breathing spell all through Christmas week.

When I reach home the setting sun's "pathetic light" has faded into twilight and all the air is still. I put my bright bit of goldenrod in the very centre of a cup full of violets. Christmas Eve! Of the thousands spent this day in gifts more or less costly, and giving joy, no doubt, to thousands of hearts, there will not be many bestowed more gracefully, or that will rouse more gratitude than these few which came one thousand miles so gently and so timely into three North Carolina log-cabins.

C.P.S.

Chapel Hill, Dec. 26th, 1888

Mrs. Spencer's Journal

FROM 1882 to 1904 Mrs. Spencer kept a Journal in which she recorded not only random jottings somewhat similar to those of the Diary she maintained during her married life and the war years, but longer reflections which in form and spirit often became philosophic essays. The entries were highly varied. For example, what she called her Green Journal, so called because of its green cover, had on its first page a recipe for catarrh of the head given her by Dr. Burke Haywood of Raleigh, North Carolina ("ammon. muriat., potass. chlor., ex. glycyrrhiza, aqua ad") and on the next a long discussion on "The Resurrection of the Body" taken from the *Country Parson.* Below we give extracts which indicate the substance and style of her typical entries, many of which were made in Cambridge, Massachusetts:

Self-Culture by J. F. Clarke. A very readable book. Easy, discursive, and clear. What strikes me about such books in these later days of my life is that they are so *readable.* So sprightly and pleasant. Is that because they are superficial? One is apt to think so, associating the idea of *"hard reading"* and something of *difficulty* with all such works. Is this just, however? An English grammar may be an excellent grammar and yet agreeable reading. See *Cobbett's,* which I never saw till last year at bro' Sam's in Washington, and read as eagerly as I used to read novels. Watts "On the Mind" is another wonderfully agreeable book on a subject usually wrapped in dull obscurity. . . .

Instead of the *formation* of character, Clarke speaks of the *development*. Insists that there is in each man *a seed*.

Aug 31-Sept 1, '86. At 10 o'clock last night several distinct shocks of earthquake were felt in C. Hill. Charleston, S. C., was nearly destroyed, as we learn by telegrams today.

Lizzie and Gertie [daughters of Mrs. Spencer's brother, Samuel F. Phillips of Washington, D.C.] arrived from W.C. today. Board at Mrs Hogan's.

Mrs Eliza (Mitchell) Grant died in Statesville N.C. Jan. 5, 1883. Mrs Swain died in Raleigh Feb. 5, 1883.

Bro Sam's wife, Fanny, died April 21, 1883.

Mrs Felton died June 4, 1883. Miss Sally Williams died June 1883, born 1809. "Uncle" Ben Craig died July 5 1883. Wm. I. Hogan died Dec 1883. *Old neighbors all.*

1887, Mar 20, Sunday. My birthday. The last time it occurred on Sunday was in 1881. My mother having been thus dead just one month. It is now 6 years. . . . I think of my mother a great deal and with infinite tenderness and pity and longing. I remember going over in that six-years-ago-Sunday-afternoon to see poor Lizzie Mickle and tell her goodbye. She died in Aug. of that year while I was in N.Y. City. It was as bright a day as this but the season not so advanced. Now the fruit trees, peach, cherry, apple are in full bloom or past it. Lilac and y. jessamine in bud. Daffodils and hyacinths passed. Goldenrod passed its prime. Maples flushed crimson, elms budding.

I spent this morning first in reading. June came with beautiful bouquet at 10. Staid with me till Ch. time. (Prof. Holmes read). I went to see bro' C. Found him with swollen foot. Susie better. Went to see *Morris Atwater*, who is slowly dying at our gate. Got Dr. Geo. Mallett to go to see him. It is a most piteous case of suffering and poverty. These poor negroes—they seem ready to relapse into barbarism. Pretty bouquet from Laura. After dinner June came again (this time with jelly and cream). Mr Love came and he went up to meeting of Y.M.C.A. and she went to see her uncle C. and I went to inquire after Mrs. Winston. Returning by bro. C's, I took J. up and we came home & I went to Mrs. B's with her to get some old shirts of Lee's for poor Morris. Mr. Battle gave me the Epis. Ch. Parish register to look over. Bro't it home and have been looking at its entries since supper. (Thompson family all gone to hear Mr. Alderman, Bap. minister, preach his farewell sermon. He came here last July.) The Joneses, Fetters, Waddells, Hubbards, Wheats, Greens, Hilliards, Saunders, Johnstons, Mal-letts, Battles, Lucases, Smiths, Mickles—and how many more—whose names are in this book—all gone—dead or passed out of sight—once so prominent—so busy here. What a *memento mori* such a book is. *"Where once we dwelt, our name is heard no more."*

I note of all the strenuous efforts made by the *Chapel of the Cross* to convert and bring in and attach to its service (during the years '49-'87) such a class as the ———— represent, *no fruit what-ever remains to this day:* of all the members of these families duly baptized, *not one.* Similarly with the negroes, numbers of whom are registered—"belonging to" so-and-so—*none* remain with them. The same thing may be noted of our Pres. Ch. in regard to poor whites and negroes. We did not baptize 'em, but equally we have failed to attract 'em.

Easter Monday, April 11, '87. I went to the graveyard at 3 p.m. with Mr and Mrs. Thompson to the burial of Miss *Dorcas Barbee.* Aged 84. How many of these *old maids,* who have spent their lives in other people's houses, doing other people's work, I can remember in my Chapel Hill life. *Miss Betsy Dyer,* at Dr. Mitchell's, identified with the family for so many years. *Nancy Scott,* who came here among the Colliers, and died in Dr. Jones's house (as Miss Dorcas has done, only it is now D. Macaulay's). *Sally* and *Matilda Williams,* and in a lower sphere, poor *Betsy Toler,* who died in the poor-house. Well, they all sleep sweetly now.

Mrs. Rebecca (Franklin) Davis, Mrs. Sally Utley, Mrs. Seaton Barbee, and Mrs Gore, David McCaulay, Mr. Carr, Mr. Foster

Utley, and about enough men to fill up the grave, were all that were present. Not one person to shed a tear. Yet not one who could or would say otherwise of Miss Dorcas than that she was a good and useful woman all her life. . . .

[*After her removal to Cambridge, Mass., in 1894*] *Sept. 1, 1899.* I was on the cliffs at Nahant. J. and her blessed little ones [Mrs. James Lee Love (June) and her children, Cornelia and Spencer Love] were moving round among the rocks, I sat still and took out a letter rec'd from Mrs C. W. Johnston as we started from home, containing a newspaper slip from Tenn., giving sad information concerning the present condition of my old friend, Prof. A. G. Brown, formerly of U.N.C. and associated with my young life there from '45 or '46, till he left the Uni(versity) about 1857-8. Now passing his old age in a Tenn. County Poorhouse.

I looked out upon the wide ocean—the white-sailed ships, the beating surf, the beautiful scenery all around, thanking God MOST HUMBLY for His mercy to me and mine. Could one have whispered fifty yrs ago of the changes in store for that pleasant circle of friends in C.H.! Alas and alas for many of those friends! *Mentem mortalia tangunt.*

From Grant Duff's diary. A word of 11 letters. The first six Gladstone loves. The rest he hates. The whole said slowly he wd like to do. The whole said quickly is where he ought to be (Reform-a-tory). (1882, G. then very unpopular.)

An evening party in London. Lord S: "Are you going to X-House?"
Lady R: "No, I am going to my bed."
Lord S (who is very deaf): "Then we shall meet again very soon."

Bentham on Cobbett (in private letter)—"A more odious compound of selfishness, arrogance, insincerity, malignity, and mendacity never presented itself to my memory or imagination."

"Quant à cela, on change sa religion comme sa chemise" (Frenchwoman).

Mar. 20, 1900. My 75th birthday. Three fourths of a century completed. Wonderful that such a one as I sh'd be continued while others doing good service are called off. *Wonderful!* ... A box of N.C. wild flowers from Minnie P[hillips], one do, from Dr Battle, and from Mrs B[attle] a box of *beaten biscuit.* Most welcome all such signals.

Aug. 1, 1900. "Sidney Lanier's Letters". "History of Gypsies", which is commonplace, and padded to make out a thick volume. I learned nothing from it. Lanier's blended *furor* for Music and Poetry I find saddening. Poor fellow! Born '42, married '67, died '81. A life of struggle with disease and poverty. The letters are pleasant reading. Note of sincerity throughout—sincerity and affection and humility. Clearly a true soul, but over-strained. "Study of English Literature". I do not feel myself qualified to pronounce on such a work. Modern criticism seems, much of it, to be machine-made. Turned out at so much a vol. at these high-class educational factories.

4th. Very hot weather. Laura's [Mrs. Charles Phillips's] last letter had news of *Anna (Lewis) Mills. Paralysis.* Anna L., Laura McKee, Ella Swain, all children and young girls together at Chapel Hill. Anna married a Wake Forest prof. Laura married Maj. Gulick. Ella married Genl. Atkins (U.S.A.) 1865. Anna sole survivor of the three these many yrs. How many such groups of girls I have known and am surviving today! (Later:) Anna died Feb. 1902.

11th. Wrote to Mr. Albright for Aunt Jenny's benefit. . . . Aunt Jenny tells me she is 87 yrs old. Bro[ther] C[harles]'s cook 35-45 yrs—before and after "freedom came."

13th. Walked with the children to Mrs. Bailey's in morning with club mags. With them in afternoon to Corcoran's store Huron

Ave. to get a pattern. Returning we went into Gray Garden. Cambridge seems to be building as fast as if it was a frontier town and had a boom on hand. Double track laid on Concord Ave. . . .

20th. At the Library and at a 2nd hand bookstore on Brattle St. I am finding that the books I read when a child do not *suit* these days—Miss Edgeworth, Mrs. Sherwood, Washington Irving, and the like.

27th. Letters from L[aura] giving us sad news from old friends. Mrs. *Dr. Mallett* died in Fla. on the 22nd. Mrs. *S. A. Taylor* died on Friday in C.H. 24th. Two old friends—most amiable and lovable women. "Earth breaks up. Time drops away." . . . Mrs. Mallett and Mrs. Taylor. I cannot cease recalling these old neighbors. Both I have known between 30 and 40 years. When I returned to Chapel Hill a widow I found the Mallett family had moved to C[hapel] H[ill] from Fayette[ville] and were established among the prominent families of the place. Mrs. M. was an excellent neighbor, an active and successfully managing woman, useful, practical, intelligent, and a lady every inch of her. I have always liked and respected her. Mrs. Taylor was also "a lady"—refined, agreeable, amiable, cultivated, popular. Always specially kind to young people whose pleasures she did much to promote, a thoroughly good, charitable neighbor, and a perfectly well-bred lady. Chapel Hill will long recall them both. . . .

Sept. 18th (1900). Letter from Laura 13th tells of fire in C.H. burning down two of oldest houses. The one J. B. McDade used long for P. O. in the 50's. The old double-porch one near it where in my childhood *old Mrs. Mitchell* lived, a smaller house between these two used for various purposes. *Harry Sessions* died in it at close of the war in miserable circumstances. Once a restaurant. Once a printing office. . . .

Sept. 30, 1900. Today 105 yrs ago my mother was born in N. Jersey. My father was then a little brown-eyed three-year-old running about his father's house in England. The two were to be brought together 24 yrs later in Harlem, N.Y., where their three children were born. Removed to N.C. 1826, where they now rest.

Sat. (*Oct.*) *20th.* Jane to Boston. Letter from Mary V[erner]. Call from Mrs. McCrady of Charleston, S.C. *Mrs. Cobia's daughter.* It seems wonderful to me that I should, nearly 60 yrs after Mrs. Cobia's marriage to Prof. Roberts—since when I have never seen her—meet with her daughter and grand-daughter! What a volume of history has been written since 1843! The change in myself not least remarkable of all—Everett, Dean of H[arvard] Divinity Sch., died on Tuesday, 23rd. Funeral today. Wrote to bro[ther] Sam.

Tuesday, Jan. 1, 1901. The new century. A memorable date which seems to me the opening one of the *Millennium.* We spent the day quietly; J. and M. paid some calls. Mrs. Gardner came over. Mrs. Schilling in p.m. No one at home but I and the children. Margaret M[itchell] says millennium does not begin till 2,000.

(Mrs. Spencer's last entries in this Journal were made at Cambridge in July and August, 1904, as follows):

9th July, 1904. Nothing is more flattering to the soul than to be interviewed in this way. In the afternoon June and Lee took Prof. and Mrs. Osgood to "Oakley". As I sat alone on the front porch in p.m., our new neighbor, a large black cat belonging to the Dr. (Albert) Hart family lately moved to east of us—walked over deliberately and sat with me, and made acquaintance "cat fashion". I was much pleased. A cat is good company! A well-bred cat and intelligent. What Sir Walter calls "a *conversible cat*". I wrote sitting out there part of a letter to Mary Verner (at Laura's request). Note from Mrs. Winston who rejoices in her *own* very own house, on Fayetteville Street (Raleigh).

10th Sunday. Our days are pleasant now with cool nights. "Crimson ramblers," nasturtiums etc. in full glow....

11th. Wrote to Margaret. June is having painting and papering done in her room. . . .

14th. Been repairing some half-worn underclothings, so as to last thro' the summer. Letter from Mrs. Welling today—written in bed. Brother Sam's first wife's birthday. She would now be about 73-74 yrs. old. Same age with Dr. Battle, I think. I draw a long breath and feel a great sadness when I review life as it appears in myself and others, 50-60 years ago. What mistakes we make—mistakes involving not only our families and friends, but the *unborn!* Are all our steps ordered? *When* are we responsible for our acts?

15th. Letters from Laura, who is now visiting Mrs. Manning. And from Lizzie Maxwell. . . . June to Faneuil Hall today. Laura says the young Negro girls around C.H. have not improved in morals. No better than they should be. . . .

16th. Cornelia and I to Har(vard) Lib. *once more.* A great peaceful pleasure to walk through that campus. I got 2 more vols. of *Duff's Diary* and Farrar's *"Life of Christ."*

17th. Prof. Albert Hart and wife called. He told me Alderman has accepted Uni[versity] of Va. (presidency), and he seemed to *wonder* that he should. I feel that way too. (14th) Prest. Kruger died today, ex-President of the Transvaal. *Born 1825.* Postal from Dr. Battle says that on 14th at early dawn the bones of Dr. and Mrs. Caldwell and old Dr. Wm. Hooper were removed from front of New West Building and placed by the marble Caldwell monument (on University of N.C. campus). A good work too long neglected. *Haywood Purefoy*, respectable col[ored] citizen of C.H., has bequeathed his small property to U.N.C. First donation to Uni. by a colored man. . . . (*19th*) I wrote to Marg[aret] to tell of the unprecedented, unexpected legacy to U.N.C. I feel sure it will interest her as it wd Charles or Sam. Very bright hot days now. . . .

21st. July is going fast. "Time's winged chariot hurrying near". Letter from Mrs. Johnston and from Laura. Trying to make a white lawn for C. Slow work. Laura says Mr. Alderman's lately wedded wife in hosp. in N.Y. . . .

31st. June and the children have taken uncle John Love and gone to spend this lovely day at Norumbega Park—and then she and Lee will take him to dinner at Oakley Club. I am always so pleased to see them all go off on such a pleasant trip. Such pleasures do not come very often in limited lives. J[une] and Co. went first to B[oston] and helped Mr. John to buy a lot of pretty things for gifts to home folks and to *us* also. Kindly generous man! Miss Gardner called in P.M. and we had a good time! Brother Charles' birthday. Dear old Charles! I do feel humbly thankful for my two good brothers—*Charles and Sam.* Both gone leaving me the remembrance of their kindness and affection and manly characters. . . .

Aug. 1, Monday. Another bright day. . . . Dr. Winston writes me a good loving letter from N.H. I have also one from Dr. McIver, Mrs. Welling, Miss McNeir, Fanny Pace, Mrs. Selina T., Mrs. Battle, Mrs. Winston. (Negro man's legacy to Uni. is *denied,* Dr. *Battle writes*). . . .

Aug. 4th. J[une] and her "two" left home at 7 o'clock last evening to take "colonial" [train] for N.C. Will be in Gastonia three wks. Meanwhile Lee and I and Joanna Ahern will hold the fort. We all are well and hearty—thanks to Almighty goodness. I have a good letter from Mrs. Hope Chamberlain who is expecting her fifth child and has nothing to do but put up her feet on a cushion and wait comfortably. [*Author of Old Days in Chapel Hill.*] She writes very well. Letter from Laura who has paid her visit to the old Johnston farm (in Orange County, N.C.) and returned to Dr. Battle's well pleased.

Aug. 8th. Prest. Winston called—staid to lunch. Very pleasant as always. But has grown old—looks it—only 54 yrs old. I sh'd say his constitution is undermined. He made no complaint of ill-health, but we noticed at lunch that he ate a *prescribed* diet. I was *very* glad to see him *once more* [George T. Winston was president of the University of North Carolina, president of the University of Texas, and president of North Carolina State College. He died in 1932.]

13 Aug. Lee left Nora [Phillips] and me tonight, departing for Gastonia to join his family there and bring them home about 26th. Nora and I are comfortable and quiet—with our good maid *Joanna Ahern.*

Aug. 14-15, 1894 [Evidently a mistake for 1904]. Here I close this book, my companion for 22 yrs. A poor record indeed of my reading, etc., etc.—but such as it is some day perhaps my dear granddaughter Cornelia Love may look over its pages and find hints of *her mother's* life for 12 yrs in Chapel Hill and Cambridge wh[ich] will interest her. I lay the book aside with gratitude to the Disposer of my life for the protection He has given me—the blessings and enjoyments, and the time for *preparation.* The end of a long life is now not far off.

NOTES

INDEX

Notes

A Note on Eleanor Swain's Marriage
(See Chapter VI)

Present also in Chapel Hill at this time was W. D. Hamilton, Brevet Brigadier General U.S. Volunteers. In *Sketches of War History* (Ohio Commandery, Loyal Legion, Volume VI, Cincinnati, 1908) he gives a confirmatory picture of the events described by Mrs. Spencer:

In a day or two, Professor Hubbard, of the University, called and invited me and one or two of my officers to dinner. Here we had the pleasure of meeting two very charming ladies, in the persons of his wife and daughter. The husband of the latter was a Confederate officer, at that time a prisoner in Fortress Monroe. The dinner was frugal but well ordered. I took occasion to compliment the white bread, saying that it was something new to us, and certainly very good. Mrs. Hubbard remarked with a smile that it ought to be, as the barrel of flour cost her one thousand dollars, and she had scraped the bottom of the barrel at the last baking, and did not know where the next was to come from.

Two or three days afterward my scouts reported that they had found eighteen barrels of flour in a mill out in the country marked "C.S.A." I sent three teams to bring it in, and did what any gentleman before me would have done under the circumstances: I directed my commissary lieutenant, who was rather an elegant fellow, to black his boots, put on a white collar, if he had

one, and trim himself up, and take a barrel of the flour down to
Mrs. Hubbard with my compliments. This little act of courtesy
brought from the daughter the next morning a beautiful specimen
of the fragrant magnolia in full bloom, and an invitation for me
and the lieutenant, with another officer or two, to meet some friends
at the house of Professor Ritter the next evening. This was appreciated and accepted. . . . On this evening we met a number of
young people of the town, chiefly from the college families. One of
the most attractive was the daughter of a former Governor of the
State and President of the college. She was also a second cousin
to Governor Zeb. Vance, of the State. By the way, the old families
of the Carolinas are very exclusive, and trace a blood relationship
among themselves after the style of the leading families of England. Miss Swain was as brilliant and original as she was elegant
and attractive. I became the especial target of her attack.

"Well," said she, "you Yankees have got here at last. We have
been looking for you for some time, and have a curiosity to know
what you are going to do with us. You have destroyed our country
and our means of support; you have burned our fences and many
of our homes and factories; you have disorganized and robbed
us of our labor; you have killed or disabled our young men, at
least the best of them, but the women are all here; what are you
going to do with us?"

The expression on her strangely bright face as she presented this
formidable indictment almost paralyzed me, but I recovered enough
to venture modestly the suggestion that it might be well for us
to follow the example of the ancient Fabians, who, after they
had overrun the neighboring province and killed the men, began
the reconstruction of the country by marrying the women. She said,
"The North has assumed the responsibility, and we are at your
mercy; but I suppose you will let us have something to say about
that." We passed quite an interesting evening. However, it seemed
to be their wish to learn all they could in regard to the intruders.
It was claimed by Miss Swain that in a social way they were at a
disadvantage. The Northern officers had the means of learning the

character and social standing of the Southern people, while they
themselves could stand upon the temporary prominence their rank
gave them and assume a high position among us, while they might
belong to a very ordinary class at home.

I frankly admitted that this was true in some instances, but said
we had plenty of gentlemen in the army whose standing did not
rest upon appearances, but was the result of their personal energy, high character and ability, and said it would give me pleasure
to present at her convenience a very gallant friend of mine, who
is a good representative of that class, and who, like myself, is a
bachelor, and always expected to remain one; "but, Miss Swain,
I have been thinking, since I have had the pleasure of meeting
you, that if there is a lady in the State of North Carolina that could
make him change his mind on that subject, you could." She bowed
her thanks and inquired his name. I replied that it was General
Smith D. Atkins, of Illinois, commanding the Second Brigade.
She said she would be at home to-morrow evening. The meeting
was arranged accordingly, and one or two other lady friends were
asked to be present.

The next day I called on the General and told him that I had
made an appointment for him in a social way for that evening. He
replied that he did not want to make any social calls, that we were
not here for anything of that kind. I replied that, in my opinion,
he was entirely wrong, that the war was over and it had been decided that we were to remain one people—North and South. That
it was now as much our duty to break down the unfortunate prejudice which existed between us as it had been to break down the
rebellion, and we should devote our best endeavours to bring about
a reconciliation between the sections. He then inquired where I
wanted him to go. I told him that it was to Governor Swain's. He
had already met the Governor, who had been one of the Committee
of Three to meet our forces on our approach to Raleigh, and to
offer the surrender of the city. He consented to make a short call,
and we spent a very pleasant evening at the house of the Governor.
I gave my attention to the ladies of the previous evening, while the

General devoted himself to Miss Swain. About 10 o'clock I suggested that it was time to go to camp. He replied that it was not late. Some time afterward I repeated the suggestion. He responded, "Yes, in a few minutes." After another interval I said if we remained much longer we would have trouble, as I had not the countersign. He replied that he had it. I called at his headquarters the next afternoon, and was told that he had gone down to Governor Swain's on some matter of business. It was the old, old story. A feathered arrow from the ancient bow had pierced the heart the modern bullet had failed to reach. After the war he came back and they were married, and reconstruction in its best form was begun in North Carolina.

A Note on the State Reconstruction Convention
(See Chapter VII)

Letter to Mrs. Spencer from Judge E. G. Reade

One day in 1891 Cornelia was surprised to get a letter from Judge E. G. Reade, who as president of the State Reconstruction Convention had made a famous speech beginning, "We are going home." In explanation he wrote her on January 29:

"I now learn for the first time . . . that my address as the president of the State Reconstruction Convention made you very angry. I beg therefore to say a word as to that.

"I was always a Whig, was passionately fond of the Union, not so much of any party as of the Government. When war threatened, I opposed it. When it came I took our side to the end. When it ended I rejoiced. While it existed I was so much in accord with our people that the Legislature elected me as a judge of the superior court without solicitation. And while I was such, Gov. Vance without solicitation appointed me to the Confederate Senate. When the war closed, my county without solicitation elected me with but 15 votes against me to the State Reconstruction Convention—the ablest body that ever sat in the state. Without my knowing that it was even thought of, and without any preparation for it on my part, I was elected president by acclamation. I had until morning to prepare something to say. What would you have said? I sat down and wrote a finger's length and went to bed, ill at ease. During the night I awoke, got up and lit the gas, and sat down and wrote as follows:

" 'Fellow citizens: We are going home. Let painful reflections on our late separation and pleasant memories of our early union quicken our footsteps towards the old mansion, that we may grasp hard again the hand of friendship that stands at the door, and sheltered by the old homestead, which was built upon a rock and has weathered the storm, enjoy together the long bright future that awaits us.' . . . The convention wept, and it was flashed over the whole country. . . . After the war I was appointed on a committee to investigate the financial affairs of the University. We found that the University owed the North Carolina bank $100,000 for money borrowed to buy stock in the said Bank. The Bank was broke, and its stock was worthless. I made an elaborate argument to show that the University was not bound for that debt, that the transaction was *ultra vires*. The report was approved. And I suppose the debt was saved by the University. . . . We also found a mortgage debt of $24,000 to Miss Mildred Cameron under which I suppose the sale and purchase of which you speak was made by Mr. Cameron. With much admiration for your intelligence, usefulness and goodness, I am, etc."

INDEX

ABBOTT, Rev. Lyman, 217
Adrain, Dr. Robert, 8, 10
Alderman, E. A., 240
Argo, Thomas M., 127
Ashe, Thomas S., 102
Atkins, Brig Gen. Smith D., court-
ship and marriage to Ellie Swain,
62-68; 182
Atkinson, Mrs. Elizabeth Kerr, 244
Aycock, Charles Brantley, 167

BAILEY, W. H., 25
Baldwin, Mary, 176
Barbee, Sam, 2
Battle, Dr. Kemp Plummer, 4, 68,
102, 108, 138; elected president
of University, 157-58
Battle, Laura, 33, 44. *See also* Phil-
lips, Mrs. Charles
Battle, Mrs. Martha, 4, 6
Battle, Judge William Horn, 28, 33,
48, 82, 156, 157
Beck (Mason), Mrs. Spencer's
cook, 205, 206-07, 218, 219, 220
"Billy Barlow," 127, 128
Bingham, Major R. W., 161-62
Brewer, Fisk P., 114
Brokaw, Peter, 180
Bryan, "Brother," 188
Buchanan, James, 40, 41, 72, 81
Burgwyn, W. H. S., 101, 118
Busbee, Fabius H., 101

CALDWELL, Mrs. Helen, 13, 14
Caldwell, Joseph, 10, 13; descrip-
tion of, 14; 22
Cameron, Duncan, 106
Cameron, John D., 155
Cameron, Mildred, 171
Cameron, Paul C., 153-54, 172
Carr, Mrs. John, 3
Centennial Exposition, Philadel-
phia, 1876, 160
Chapel Hill, description of, 12-13
Cheek, Town Commissioner, 172-73
Cheshire, Rev. Joseph B., 4, 5
Church of the Strangers, 90, 91
Cleveland, Grover, inauguration,
192
Columbian Repository, The, 25
Cooper Union, New York, 168
Cornelia Phillips Spencer, The,
ship, 244
Couch, village hermit, 147-48
Craig, Uncle Ben, 101, 140, 189
Craven, Dr., 86
Cushman, Mrs. Charles F., 229

Daily Journal, Wilmington, N. C.,
124
Daily News, Raleigh, N. C., 155
Daily Standard, Raleigh, N. C., 125
Daniels, Josephus, 230
Davis, Jefferson, 53, 86
Davis, Katy, 180

111; needed modernization, 108-
09; "radical faculty," 112-15;
scarcity of students, 123; commencement, 1869, 126; description of, 1870, 133; commencement, 1870, 134; closed, 1870,
140; alumni meeting, 1872, 142;
legislature permits reorganization,
1875, 149; opening, 1875, 154-57;
commencement, 1876, 159; summer normal school, 1877, 162;
economies, 199; centennial, 229

UTLEY, Foster, 224

VANCE, Zebulon B., 20, 48, 53, 73,
78-79, 83, 91, 118, 132-33, 137-38,
145-46, 165, 221
Vanderbilt, Cornelius, 90, 91
van der Meulen, 9
Vermeule, Adrian, 9
Vermeule, Adrian the 18th, 180
Vermeule, Captain Cornelius, 9
Vermeule, Cornelius C., 9, 230
Vermeule, Judith (Julia), 9, 10; de-
scription of, 11

Vermeule, Maria Veghte, 180
Vermeule, Dr. Richard, 9
Verner, Colonel John S., 204

WAITT, University carpenter, 191
Watchman, The, 88, 90, 93
Watchman Publishing Company, 90
Watson, John, 163
Weekly Ledger, Chapel Hill, N. C.,
167
Wetmore, Ichabod, 10
Wheeler, General, guerrilla leader,
55
White and Blue, The, 223
Williams, H. Horace, 215
Williams, Sally, 189-90
Willing, Mrs., 211, 225
Wilson, Dr. Alexander, 84, 119-20
Winston, F. D., 167
Winston, George T., 191, 211, 215,
225
Winston, P. H., 211
Worth, Governor Jonathan, 102

YANCEY, Dr. Charles, 32